REGENTS CRITICS SERIES

General Editor: Paul A. Olson

JOSEPH CONRAD ON FICTION

The first five volumes of the Regents Critic Series, in addition to the present volume, are:

Critical Writings of Ford Madox Ford
   Edited by Frank MacShane

Literary Criticism of George Henry Lewes
   Edited by Alice R. Kaminsky

Literary Criticism of Alexander Pope
   Edited by Bertrand Goldgar

Literary Criticism of Edgar Allan Poe
   Edited by Robert L. Hough

Joseph Conrad

Joseph Conrad on Fiction

Edited by

WALTER F. WRIGHT

UNIVERSITY OF NEBRASKA PRESS · LINCOLN

Thanks are due J. M. Dent & Sons Ltd., Trustees of the Estate of Joseph Conrad, for permission to publish selections from the following copyrighted works: *Conrad's Prefaces to His Works* (London: J. M. Dent, 1937); *A Personal Record*, copyright 1912 (New York: Doubleday & Co., 1924); *The Mirror of the Sea*, copyright 1905 (New York: Doubleday & Co., 1924); *Notes on Life and Letters*, copyright 1921 (New York: Doubleday & Co., 1924); *Last Essays* (London and Toronto: J. M. Dent, 1926); Jean-Aubry, *Joseph Conrad, Life and Letters*, copyright 1927 (New York: Doubleday & Co., 1927); Richard Curle, *Conrad to a Friend* (London: Sampson Low, Marston & Co., 1928); and Edward Garnett, *Letters from Joseph Conrad, 1895–1924* (Indianapolis: Bobbs-Merrill Co., 1928). Thanks also are due Duke University Press for permission to reprint excerpts from *Joseph Conrad, Letters to William Blackwood and David S. Meldrum*, edited by William Blackburn, copyright 1958.

Publishers on the Plains

UNP

Quotations from *Joseph Conrad: Letters to William Blackwood and David S. Meldrum*, edited by William Blackburn, are reprinted by permission of the Duke University Press. All other quotations are by permission of J. M. Dent and Sons.

Regents Critics Series

The Regents Critics Series provides reading texts of significant literary critics in the Western tradition. The series treats criticism as a useful tool: an introduction to the critic's own poetry and prose if he is a poet or novelist, an introduction to other work in his day if he is more judge than creator. Nowhere is criticism regarded as an end in itself but as what it is—a means to the understanding of the language of art as it has existed and been understood in various periods and societies.

Each volume includes a scholarly introduction which describes how the work collected came to be written, and suggests its uses. All texts are edited in the most conservative fashion consonant with the production of a good reading text; and all translated texts observe the dictum that the letter gives life and the spirit kills when a technical or rigorous passage is being put into English. Other types of passages may be more freely treated. Footnoting and other scholarly paraphernalia are restricted to the essential minimum. Such features as a bibliographical checklist or an index are carried where they are appropriate to the work in hand. If a volume is the first collection of the author's critical writing, this is noted in the bibliographical data.

PAUL A. OLSON

University of Nebraska

Contents

Introduction:
Conrad's Critical Perspectives

Whatever Joseph Conrad wrote, whether fiction, criticism, or general observations on life, reveals in its imagery and rhythms the passionate dramatic intensity with which he pursued his art. His tone ranges from the bitterness of revulsion, when he sometimes mocks a story that has been exhausting his nervous energy for weeks, to a nearly ecstatic reminiscence of the adventures of composition. His philosophic commentaries are equally diverse—at times railing at human folly, as in certain letters to Cunninghame Graham, and, at others, stressing the mystic nature of human solidarity. Both extremes—even like those which confront Marlow in *Heart of Darkness*—were for Conrad the very stuff of reality.

It was with reality that the writer of fiction must, of course, begin; and reality was not something that he could find awaiting his factual recording. Quite the contrary. It had to be created by the disciplined imagination. Underlying every sentence in Conrad's literary criticism is a principle stated explicitly in "Books": "In truth every novelist must begin by creating for himself a world, great or little, in which he can honestly believe." Such a world Conrad found in the sea adventures of Cooper's Long Tom and the psychological ordeal of James's Fleda Vetch, in the ingenuous sketches of Daudet and the artful studies of Turgenev and Proust.

Indeed, Conrad's interests in fiction were wide ranging. Though naturally annoyed to find himself called a "spinner of sea-yarns," he could view life as a romance of adventure, a revelation, as in *Typhoon,* of the genius of the human adaptation to the forces of nature, and he could look upon nature itself as "spectacle." If such writers as Cooper or Marryat did not press the symbolism of their incidents, Conrad could still value their writing for its testing of the courage and ingenuity of the human mind. He respected, too, the social novels of Galsworthy and the attempts by Arnold Bennett to catch the tone and color of the five towns and of London. He admitted obliquely to the influence of Maupassant, whose unadorned, unflinching representation of life's tragic hardness he found both honest and artistically meaningful. Two major writers came in for his condemnation. Tolstoi he accused of sentimentality and of using Christianity as a solution to human problems. Though there are incidents in his own novels that are in accord with Christian beliefs, Conrad was distrustful of the Christian perspective for surveying man's relation to the Universe and even to his fellowmen. His strongest censure was for Dostoevski, whom he attacked for "prehistoric mouthings." Ironically, he has sometimes been compared with Dostoevski, since both dealt with inner compulsions, impulses not understood by their heroes, and since the search for atonement in such a story as *Under Western Eyes* recalls that in *Crime and Punishment*. Though he did not expand his violent outbursts against the Russian novelist, Conrad appears to have felt that Dostoevski floundered in sentimentality instead of maintaining artistic restraint. Of his feelings for the Classics and for Shakespeare we have occasional reverential hints. He speaks with pride of his father's translating of Shakespeare, and in *The Mirror of the Sea* he suggests analogy of events with those in the classical epics. Reality was always for Conrad a romance of adventure, potentially of epic proportions; it was most often a tragic one.

For some of the authors whom Conrad admired literary composition was not unduly strenuous; or at least they did not lament its exactions. For Conrad himself it represented nervous fatigue or indeed agony. Yet it was the one great adventure, better even than that offered by ships and the sea because it was all-inclusive. He renounced the life of master mariner, in which he had achieved some competence, because he could not resist the lure of a perilous art at which he was but a novice. Writing of Henry James, who had spent years perfecting his craft, he spoke accurately for both James and himself: "The artist in his calling of interpreter creates . . . because he must. He is so much of a voice that, for him, silence is like death . . . ." Allowing for the nostalgia of the successful practitioner as he looks back on the hazards he has passed, one nevertheless senses in *A Personal Record* the spell under which Conrad performed his toil. Repeatedly in his short stories and novels he demonstrated that the only reward worth having was a "perfect love of the work." Such a love took possession of a sailor—or an author—without his conscious awareness, and yet it blessed only those who deliberately accepted the rigors of their trade and its eternal threat of tragedy. In *A Personal Record* Conrad compared the tribulations of writing to the "westward winter passage round Cape Horn." Each amounted to a "lonely struggle under a sense of over-matched littleness, for no reward that could be adequate, but for the mere winning of a longitude." The nature of the adventure itself was an important subject for criticism.

The task of the novelist being the creation of reality, he had to seek hints of truth in his own experience. His works would always be spiritually autobiographic in that, as author, he could be the "figure behind the veil." In his Author's Note to *Typhoon* Conrad spoke of "a conscientious regard for the truth of my own sensations," and, again, in that to *Within the Tides,* of "the obligation of a more scrupulous fidelity to the truth of my own sensations." Besides the Author's Notes and *A Personal Record,* a number of the letters discuss the transformation that occurred as an event or person from the world of actuality became the touchstone for an incident or a characterization in Conrad's fiction. Most notable, of course, was Almayer. The hero of *Almayer's Folly* is not the man whom the novelist saw in the flesh, and yet Conrad's sensations as he contemplated the tragic derelict gave him his assurance that his novel was not untrue. Indeed, in various Author's Notes and in *A Personal Record* Conrad begins his discussion of a story as a work of art by alluding to its origin in historical fact. Whereas Thomas Hardy, however, sometimes justified inferior poems by saying that their narrated incidents actually happened, Conrad, on the contrary, was always the artist. The incident, for him, had happened, but so had countless others. His point was that he had recognized in it or in a person—even as Henry James did in the "germs" of his stories—an artistic significance. Having made his discovery, he had something valid with which to work. What finally developed was a creation of the artist's imagination.

Inasmuch as the writer of fiction was always present, even though behind the veil, there was inevitably a subjective aspect to his created world. "This world," Conrad remarked in "Books," "cannot be made otherwise than in his own image; it is fated to remain individual and a little mysterious . . . ." Nevertheless, the author could confidently expect to touch cords in the hearts of others; for, even while admitting the individuality of the novelist's world, Conrad continued, ". . . yet it must resemble something already familiar to the experience, the thoughts and the sensations of his readers." And in the Preface to *The Nigger of the "Narcissus"* he had previously written of the author's responsibility to his reader: "My task which I am trying to achieve is, by the power of the written word to make you hear, to make you feel—it is, before all, to make you see."

To make others see, the author himself must first see distinctly and render objectively. Despite the inevitable subjectivity which would give the tone to his art, he must be preoccupied with the concrete substance of his story and search always for the precise, individualizing detail. In several letters Conrad gives instruction in the simple, yet difficult, elements of composition. In each instance he would have his correspondents—Clifford, Galsworthy, Mrs. Sanderson, and others—recast lines that are imprecise and essentially sentimental because they assert rather than exhibit the essence of a scene. He does not correct the passages by applying mechanical rules. Instead, he attacks the problem at its beginning by visualizing the actions which the authors themselves have not adequately seen. In short, with his own sense of life to guide him, he looked always for the concrete, objective images which moved him and which, given the solidarity of mankind, should kindle a sympathetic response in a sensitive reader.

The writer must, of course, employ metaphor and symbol if his fictitious persons and incidents were to have universal implication. In his very first work Conrad struggled, at times tediously, to develop the symbolic importance of his scenes, but by 1900 he had learned how to convey it obliquely; and though his metaphors continued occasionally to be florid, he generally thereafter evoked rather than asserted the implications of his scenes. In *The Mirror of the Sea, A Personal Record,* and the Author's Notes the symbolic nature of art is taken for granted. It is through art as symbol that communication with a reader takes place, for it thus becomes a touchstone for the reader's creative interpretation of his own spiritual experience.

"Give me the right word and the right accent and I will move the world"—in this famous pronouncement Conrad used the morally neutral right word *move,* as the power of rhetoric could be for ill as well as good, though he, of course, hoped that his own words and accent would make for the world's enlightenment. And for his purposes he chose the English language. Although Ford Madox Ford reported that sometimes, in searching for an apt phrase, he and Conrad would come up with a French term, Conrad explicitly stated that there was no accident in his determining to write in English. What he does not say anywhere, but what is implicit in his fiction is that he always had a feeling for the etymology of English words and that common metaphors had for him a freshness stemming from their newness. The language was, in short, vividly concrete.

Often in a single letter or essay we find Conrad talking about the philosophic questions that relate literature to life, his own mental habits as a novelist, and the craft of literary composition. For a moment the focus is on one of the three, but they are finally inseparable. In discussing the genius of other novelists he was usually more detached than when speaking of himself; but he was still engaged in a romance of discovery, and the tone of his critical essays conveys the excitement of exploration. Indeed, he may be said to have defined his own role as critic in the words he quoted from Anatole France: "The good critic is he who relates the adventures of his soul among masterpieces."

Note on the Text

Except as indicated the essays and Author's Notes are not abridged. Only relevant parts of letters have been included; though some of the shorter selections seem fragmentary when read by themselves, they help fill out the pattern of Conrad's thought. A few obvious slips by Conrad, preserved with notation in Professor William Blackburn's edition of *Joseph Conrad: Letters to William Blackwood and David S. Meldrum* have been corrected without comment. All other known pertinent letters appear in *Joseph Conrad, Life and Letters,* edited by G. Jean-Aubry; *Letters from Joseph Conrad, 1895–1924,* edited by Edward Garnett; and *Conrad to a Friend,* edited by Richard Curle.

WALTER F. WRIGHT

University of Nebraska

Significant Dates in Conrad's Life

December 3, 1857: Birth

About October 17, 1874—April 24, 1878: Marseilles sojourn and western voyages

Early June, 1880: Passing of examination for position of third mate

September 21, 1881—March, 1883: Intermittent service on the *Palestine* (the *Judea* of "Youth")

July 4, 1883: Obtaining of certificate as first mate

November 11, 1886: Passing of captain's examination

Early 1888: First command (ship in *The Shadow Line*)

1889: Beginning of *Almayer's Folly*

May 12, 1890—end of 1890: Congo trip

January 14, 1894: Cessation of Voyaging

March 24, 1896: Marriage

August 3, 1924: Death

I.

FROM THE LETTERS (1895–1923)

In the following selections, three asterisks (* * *) indicate that a portion of the original has been omitted.

I.

From the Letters (1895–1923)

To Edward Garnett, September 24, 1895

Nothing now can unmake my mistake. I shall try—but I shall try without faith, because all my work is produced unconsciously (so to speak) and I cannot meddle to any purpose with what is within myself.—I am sure you understand what I mean— It isn't in me to improve what has got itself written.—

Still with your help I may try. All the paragraphs marked by you to that effect shall be cut out. For Willems[1] to want to escape from *both* women *is* the very idea. Only—don't you see—I did not feel it so. Shame! The filiation of feelings in Willems on the evening when Aissa speaks to him arises from my view of that man—of the effect produced upon him by the loss of things precious to him coming (the loss) after his passion is appeased. Consequently—his deliberate effort to recall the passion as a last resort, as the last refuge from his regrets, from the obsession of his longing to return whence he came. It's an impulse of thought not of the senses. The senses are done with. Nothing lasts! So with Aissa. Her passion is burnt out too. There is in her that desire to be something for him—to be in his mind, in his heart— to shelter him in her affection—her woman's affection which is simply the ambition to be an important factor in another's life. They both long to have a significance in the order of nature or of society. To me they are typical of mankind where every individual wishes to assert his power, woman by sentiment, man by achievement of some sort—mostly base. I myself—as you see from this—have been ambitious to make it clear and have failed in that as Willems fails in his effort to throw off the trammels of earth and of heaven.

1. In *The Outcast of the Islands.*

3

So much in defence of my view of the case. For the execution I have no word to say. It is very feeble and all the strokes fall beside the mark. Why?—If I knew that—if I knew the causes of my weakness I would destroy them and then produce nothing but colossal masterpieces—which 'no fellow could understand.' As it is I am too lazy to change my thoughts, my words, my images, and my dreams. Laziness is a sacred thing. It's the sign of our limitations beyond which there is nothing worth having. Nobody is lazy to accomplish things without any effort—and things that can only be attained by effort are not worth having.—

In the treatment of the last scenes I wanted to convey the kind of placidity that is caused by extreme surprise. You must not forget that they are all immensely amazed. That's why they are so quiet.—(At least I wanted them to be quiet and only managed to make them colourless.) That's why I put in the quiet morning—the immobility of surrounding matter emphasized only by the flutter of small birds. Then the sense of their position penetrated the hearts—stirs them. They wake up to the reality. Then comes violence: Joanna's slap in Aissa's face, Aissa's shot—and the end just as he sees the joy of sunshine and of life.—

To Edward Noble, October 28, 1895

You have any amount of stuff in you, but you (I think) have not found your way yet.[2] Remember that death is not the most pathetic,—the most poignant thing,—and you must treat events only as illustrative of human sensation,—as the outward sign of inward feelings,—of live feelings,—which alone are truly pathetic and interesting. You have much imagination: much more than I ever will have if I live to be a hundred years old. That much is clear to me. Well, that imagination (I wish I had it) should be used to create human souls: to disclose human hearts,—and not to create events that are properly speaking *accidents* only. To accomplish it you must cultivate your poetic faculty,—you must give yourself up to emotions (no easy task). You must

2. In reference to a manuscript by Noble which had been rejected by Macmillan.

squeeze out of yourself every sensation, every thought, every image,—mercilessly, without reserve and without remorse: you must search the darkest corners of your heart, the most remote recesses of your brain,—you must search them for the image, for the glamour, for the right expression. And you must do it sincerely, at any cost: you must do it so that at the end of your day's work you should feel exhausted, emptied of every sensation and every thought, with a blank mind and an aching heart, with the notion that there is nothing,—nothing left in you. To me it seems that it is the only way to achieve true distinction—even to go some way towards it.

To Edward Garnett, June 19, 1896

Since I sent you that part 1st[3] (on the eleventh of the month) I have written one page. Just one page. I went about thinking and forgetting—sitting down before the blank page to find that I could not put one sentence together. To be able to think and unable to express is a fine torture. I am undergoing it—without patience. I don't see the end of it. It's very ridiculous and very awful. Now I've got all my people together I don't know what to do with them. The progressive episodes of the story *will* not emerge from the chaos of my sensations. I feel nothing clearly. And I am frightened when I remember that I have to drag it all out of myself. Other writers have some starting point. Something to catch hold of. They start from an anecdote—from a newspaper paragraph (a book may be suggested by a casual sentence in an old almanack). They lean on dialect—or on tradition—or on history—or on the prejudice or fad of the hour; they trade upon some tie or some conviction of their time—or upon the absence of these things—which they can abuse or praise. But at any rate they know something to begin with—while I don't. I have had some impressions, some sensations—in my time:—impressions and sensations of common things. And it's all faded—my very being seems faded and thin like the ghost of a blonde and sentimental woman, haunting romantic ruins per-

3. Of *The Rescuer,* renamed *The Rescue,* finally published in 1920.

vaded by rats. I am exceedingly miserable. My task appears to me as sensible as lifting the world without that fulcrum which even that conceited ass, Archimedes, admitted to be necessary.

To Edward Garnett, August 5, 1896

You see I must justify—give a motive—to my yacht people, the artificial, civilized creatures that are to be brought in contact with the primitive Lingard.[4] I must do that—or have a Clark Russell puppet show which would be worse than starvation.

To Edward Garnett, November 29, 1896

As to lack of incident[5] well—it's life. The incomplete joy, the incomplete sorrow, the incomplete rascality or heroism—the incomplete suffering. Events crowd and push and nothing happens. You know what I mean. The opportunities do not last long enough. Unless in a boy's book of adventures. Mine were never finished. They fizzled out before I had a chance to do more than another man would.

To Miss Helen Watson,[6] January 27, 1897

The story just finished is called *The Nigger: A Tale of Ships and Men*. Candidly, I think it has certain qualities of art that make it a thing apart. I tried to get through the veil of details at the essence of life. But it is a rough story,—dealing with rough men and an immense background. I do not ask myself how much I have succeeded. I only dare to hope that it is not a shameful failure, that perhaps, here and there, may be found a few men and women who will see what I have tried for. It would be triumph enough for me.

To Edward Garnett, February 13, 1897

I had this morning a charming surprise in the shape of the "Spoils of Poynton" sent me by H. James with a very characteristic and friendly inscription on the fly leaf. I need not tell you

4. In *The Rescuer*.
5. In *The Nigger of the "Narcissus."*
6. Later Mrs. E. L. Sanderson.

how pleased I am. I have already read the book. It is as good as anything of his—almost—a story of love and wrongheadedness revolving round a houseful of artistic furniture. It's Henry James and nothing but Henry James. The delicacy and tenuity of the thing are amazing. It is like a great sheet of plate glass—you don't know it's there till you run against it. Of course I do not mean to say it is anything as gross as plate glass. It's only as *pellucid* as clean plate glass. The only fault I find is its length. It's just a trifle too long. Personally I don't complain as you may imagine, but I imagine with pain the man in the street tryng to read it! And my common humanity revolts at the evoked image of his suffering. One could almost see the globular lobes of his brain painfully revolving and crushing mangling the delicate thing. As to his exasperation it is a thing impossible to imagine and too horrid to contemplate. * * *

My wife is this moment reading reverently James' book, and trying honestly to distinguish its head from its tail. Her reverence is not affected. It is a perfectly genuine sentiment inspired by me; but her interest is, I suspect, affected for the purpose of giving me pleasure. And she will read every line! 'Pon my word it's most touching and only women are capable of such delicately penetrating sacrifices. I do nothing but yawn and tear my hair.

To E. L. Sanderson, May, 1897

I am conceited enough about it,[7]—God knows,—but He also knows the spirit in which I approached the undertaking to present faithfully some of His benighted and suffering creatures; the humble, the obscure, the sinful, the erring upon whom rests His Gaze of Ineffable Pity. My conscience is at peace in that matter, and it is with confidence and love that I send the work to you,—to read and to judge.

To R. B. Cunninghame Graham, August 5, 1897

Mr. Kipling has the wisdom of the passing generations,—and holds it in perfect sincerity. Some of his work is of impeccable

7. *The Nigger of the "Narcissus."*

form and because of that *little* thing, he will sojourn in Hell only a very short while. He squints with the rest of his excellent sort. It is a beautiful squint: it is an useful squint. And—after all,—perhaps he sees round the corner? And suppose Truth is just round the corner, like the elusive and useless loafer it is? I can't tell. No one can tell. It is impossible to know. It is impossible to know anything, tho' it is possible to believe a thing or two.

To R. B. Cunninghame Graham, August 9, 1897

You understood perfectly what I tried to say about Mr. Kipling,—but I did not succeed in saying exactly what I wanted to say. I wanted to say, in effect, that in the chaos of printed matter Kipling's *ébauches* appear by contrast finished and impeccable. I judge the man in his time,—and space. It is a small space and as to his time I leave it to your tender mercy. I wouldn't in his defence spoil the small amount of steel that goes to the making of a needle. As to posterity, it won't smile. Not it! Posterity will be busy thieving, lying, selling its little soul for sixpence (from the noblest motives), and will remember no one, except perhaps one or two quite too atrocious mountebanks: and the half-dozen men lost in that *bagarre* are more likely to weep than to smile over those masterpieces of our time.

To William Blackwood, September 4, 1897

I delayed sending you my acknowledgement for the Sep^{er} issue.[8] I beg to do so now. The appreciation of Mrs. Oliphant's work is just in the right note. It is justice—and discriminating justice—rendered to that serene talent. I think she wrote too much (perhaps it's envy; to me it's simply unconceivable) but she was ever faithful to her artistic temperament—she always *expressed* herself. She was a *better artist* than George Eliot; and, at her best *immensely* superior to any living woman novelist

---

8. The September, 1897, number of *Blackwood's Magazine* included "Mrs. Oliphant as a Novelist," 305–319; "During the Armistice: Impressions of the War," by Walter B. Harris, 436–448; *Dariel: A Romance of Surrey*, by R. D. Blackmore, 348–374; and "The Two Tragedies—A Note," by George Saintsbury, 395–401.

I can call to mind. Harris (an old friend of mine—in his work) can write more than a bit. Not to every one is given to be so graphic and so easy at the same time. Besides his point of view is most sympathetic to me. Blackmore is himself—of course. But professor Saintsbury's paper interested me most—a bit of fundamental criticism most cleverly expounded.

To William Blackwood, September 6, 1897

—The situation[9] 'per se' is not new. Consequently all the effect must be produced in the working out—in the manner of telling. This necessity from my point of view is fascinating. I am sure you will understand my feeling though you may differ with me in the view. On the other hand the situation is not prosaic. It is suitable for a romance. The human interest of the tale is in the contact of Lingard the simple, masterful, imaginative adventurer with a type of civilized woman—a complex type. He is a man tenacious of purpose, enthusiastic in undertaking, faithful in friendship. He jeopardises the success of his plans first to assure her safety and then absolutely sacrifices them to what he believes the necessary conditions of her happiness. He is throughout mistrusted by the whites whom he wishes to save; he is unwillingly forced into a contest with his Malay friends. Then when the rescue, for which he had sacrificed all the interests of his life, is accomplished, he has to face his reward—an inevitable separation. This episode of his life lifts him out of himself; I want to convey in the action of the story the stress and exaltation of the man under the influence of a sentiment which he hardly understands and yet which is real enough to make him as he goes on reckless of consequences. It is only at the very last that he is perfectly enlightened when the work of rescue and destruction is ended and nothing is left to him but to try and pick up as best he may the broken thread of his life. Lingard—not the woman— is the principal personage. That's why all the first part is given up to the presentation of his personality. It illustrates the method I intend to follow. I aim at stimulating vision in the reader. If after reading the *part 1st* you don't *see* my man then I've abso-

9. In *The Rescue.*

lutely failed and must begin again—or leave the thing alone. Of course the paraphernalia of the story are hackneyed. The yacht, the shipwreck, the pirates, the coast—all this has been used times out of number; whether it has been done, that's another question. Be it as it may I think rightly or wrongly I can present it in a fresh way. At any rate, as I wish to obtain the effect of reality in my story and also wanted the woman—that kind of woman— there was no other way to bring her there but in the time-honoured yacht. Nothing impossible shall happen. I shall tell of some events I've seen, and also relate things I've heard. One or two men I've known—about others I've been told many interminable tales. The French Brig "Amitié" was in 1866 stranded on the coast and attacked by some vagabonds belonging to a certain Haji Saman. I had the story from the captain of the brig. In 1848 an Englishman called Wyndham had been living for many years with the Sultan of Sulu and was the general purveyor of arms and gunpowder. In 1850 or 51 he financed a very lively row in Celebes. He is mentioned in Dutch official documents as a great nuisance—which he, no doubt, was. I've heard several versions of his end (occurred in the sixties) all very lamentable. In the seventies Lingard had a great if occult influence with the Rajah of Bali. He was a meddler but very disinterested and was greatly respected by the natives. As late as 1888 arms have been landed on the coast of that island—that to my personal knowledge. Thus facts can bear out my story but as I am writing fiction not secret history—facts don't matter.

To Edward Garnett, September 29, 1897

I am hoist with my own petard. My dear fellow what I aimed at was just to produce the effect of cold water in every one of my man's speeches.[10] I swear to you that was my intention. I wanted to produce the effect of insincerity, of artificiality. Yes! I wanted the reader to *see him think* and then to hear him speak— and shudder. The whole point of the joke is there. I wanted the truth to be first dimly seen through the fabulous untruth of that

10. In "The Return."

man's convictions—of his idea of life—and then to make its way
out with a rush at the end. But if I have to explain that to you—
to you!—then I've egregiously failed. I've tried with all my might
to avoid just these trivialities of rage and distraction which you
judge necessary to the truth of the picture. I counted it a virtue,
and lo and behold! You say it is a sin. Well! Never more! It is
evident that my fate is to be descriptive and descriptive only.
There are things I *must* leave alone.

To Edward Garnett, October 11, 1897

You see I wanted to give out the gospel of the beastly
bourgeois—and wasn't clever enough to do it in a more natural
way.[11] Hence the logic which resembles the logic of a melodrama.
The childishness of mind coming to the surface. All this I feel. I
don't see; because if I did see it I would also see the other way
the mature way—the way of art. I would work from conviction to
conviction—through inevitable moments to the final situation.
Instead of which I went on creating the moments for the illustration of the idea. Am I right in that view? If so the story is bad
art. It is built on the same falsehood as a melodrama. * * *

But the book is very delightful in a way. Look at the logic:
He found his mutton-chop very tough *therefore* he arose and
cursed his aunt. And the idea of that battered Gadfly in kid
gloves finding his revenge in scolding, is—well—feminine, or I
have lived all these bitter years in vain.[12]

It is perfectly delightful. I don't remember ever reading a
book I disliked so much.

To Edward Garnett, November 26, 1897

Well, we shall see. Humphry James is good.[13] Is he very
deep or very simple? And by the bye, R. Bridges is a poet. I'm
damned if he ain't! There's more poesy in one page of "Shorter
Poems" than in the whole volume of Tennyson.[14] This is my

11. In "The Return."
12. *The Gadfly*, by Ethel Voynich, 1897, is a theological romance.
13. *Paddy's Woman*, by James, appeared in 1897.
14. Conrad seldom discussed poetry.

deliberate opinion. And what a descriptive power! The man hath wings—sees from on high. It is the real thing—a direct appeal to mankind, not a certain kind of man. It is natural beauty—not would-be beautiful notions. I love him.

To Edward Garnett, December 5, 1897

I had Crane here last Sunday. We talked and smoked half the night. He is strangely hopeless about himself. I like him. The two stories are excellent. Of course *A Man and Some Others* is the best of the two but the boat thing[15] interested me more. His eye is very individual and his expression satisfies me artistically. He certainly is *the* impressionist and his temperament is curiously unique. His thought is concise, connected, never very deep—yet often startling. He is *the only* impressionist and *only* an impressionist. Why is he not immensely popular? With his strength, with his rapidity of action, with that amazing faculty of vision— why is he not? He has outline, he has colour, he has movement, with that he ought to go very far. But—will he? I sometimes think he won't. It is not an opinion—it is a feeling. I could not explain why he disappoints me—why my enthusiasm withers as soon as I close the book. While one reads, of course he is not to be questioned. He is the master of his reader to the very last line—then— apparently for no reason at all—he seems to let go his hold. It is as if he had gripped you with greased fingers. His grip is strong but while you feel the pressure on your flesh you slip out from his hand—much to your own surprise. That is my stupid impression and I give it to you in confidence. It just occurs to me that it is perhaps my own self that is slippery. I don't know. *You* would know. No matter.

To R. B. Cunninghame Graham, December 6, 1897

I heard of the H. and S. play through G. B. S. in the *S. R.* More Algebra. Do you understand? I allude in this luminous way to *Admiral Guinea*.[16] I haven't seen a play for years, but

15. "The Open Boat."

16. *Admiral Guinea*, a romantic play by Henley and Stevenson, could well be labeled "unbelievable." G. B. S. is, of course, Shaw; and *S. R.* is the *Saturday Review*.

I have read this one. And that's all I can say about it. I have
no notion of a play. No play grips me on the stage or off. Each
of them seems to me an amazing freak of folly. They are all
unbelievable and as disillusioning as a bang on the head. I greatly
desire to write a play myself. It is my dark and secret ambition.
And yet I can't conceive how a sane man can sit down deliberately
to write a play and not go mad before he has done. The actors
appear to me like a lot of *wrong-headed* lunatics pretending to
be sane. Their malice is stitched with white threads. They are
disguised and ugly. To look at them breeds in my melancholy
soul thoughts of murder and suicide,—such is my anger and my
loathing of their transparent pretences. There is a taint of subtle
corruption in their blank voices, in their blinking eyes, in the
grimacing faces, in the false light, in the false passion, in the
words that have been learned by heart. But I love a marionette-
show. Marionettes are beautiful,—especially those of the old kind
with wires, thick as my little finger, coming out of the top of the
head. Their impassibility in love, in crime, in mirth, in sorrow,—
is heroic, superhuman, fascinating. Their rigid violence when
they fall upon one another to embrace or to fight is simply a
joy to behold. I never listen to the text mouthed somewhere out
of sight by invisible men who are here to-day and rotten to-morrow. I love the marionettes that are without life, that come so
near to being immortal!

To R. B. Cunninghame Graham, December 14, 1897

   But as I said I have been meditating over your letter. You
say: "Singleton,[17] with an education." Well, yes! Everything is
possible, and most things come to pass (when you don't want
them). However I think Singleton with an education is impossible.
But first of all,—what education? If it is the knowledge of how
to live, my man essentially possessed it. He was in perfect accord
with his life. If by education you mean scientific knowledge then
the question arises,—what knowledge? How much of it,—in what
direction? Is it to stop at plane trigonometry or at conic sections?
Or is he to study Platonism or Pyrrhonism, or the philosophy of

17. In *The Nigger of the "Narcissus."*

the gentle Emerson? Or do you mean the kind of knowledge which would enable him to scheme, and lie, and intrigue his way to the forefront of a crowd no better than himself? Would you seriously, of malice prepense, cultivate in that unconscious man the power to think? Then he would become conscious,—and much smaller,—and very unhappy. Now he is simple and great like an elemental force. Nothing can touch him but the curse of decay,— the eternal decree that will extinguish the sun, the stars, one by one, and in another instant shall spread a frozen darkness over the whole universe. Nothing else can touch him,—he does not think.

Would you seriously wish to tell such a man "Know thyself! Understand that you are nothing, less than a shadow, more insignificant than a drop of water in the ocean, more fleeting than the illusion of a dream?" Would you?

To R. B. Cunninghame Graham, January 7, 1898

Read the *Badge*.[18] It won't hurt you,—or only very little. Crane-ibn-Crane el Yankee is all right. The man sees the outside of many things and the inside of some.

To R. B. Cunninghame Graham, January 31, 1898

What makes mankind tragic is not that they are the victims of nature, it is that they are conscious of it. To be part of the animal kingdom under the conditions of this earth is very well,— but as soon as you know of your slavery, the pain, the anger, the strife,—the tragedy begins. We can't return to nature, since we can't change our place in it. Our refuge is in stupidity, in drunkenness of all kinds, in lies, in beliefs, in murder, thieving, reforming, in negation, in contempt,—each man according to the promptings of his particular devil. There is no morality, no knowledge and no hope: there is only the consciousness of ourselves which drives us about a world that, whether seen in a convex or a concave mirror, is always but a vain and floating appearance. *Ote-toi de là que je m'y mette* is no more of a sound rule than would be the reverse doctrine. It is however much easier to practise.

18. Stephen Crane's *The Red Badge of Courage.*

To R. B. Cunninghame Graham, February, 1898

You are misguided by the desire of the Impossible,—and I envy you. Alas! what you want to reform are not institutions,—it is human nature. Your faith will never move that mountain. Not that I think mankind intrinsically bad. It is only silly and cowardly. Now you know that in cowardice is every evil,— especially, that cruelty so characteristic of our civilization. But, without it, mankind would vanish. No great matter truly. But will you persuade humanity to throw away sword and shield? Can you persuade even me,—who writes these words in the fulness of an irresistible conviction? No, I belong to the wretched gang. We all belong to it. We are born initiated, and succeeding generations clutch the inheritance of fear and brutality without a thought, without a doubt, without compunction, in the name of God.

To Edward Garnett, May, 1898

I've sent you today a copy of the *Children* etc., 3 or 4 of your own books and that amazing masterpiece *Bel-Ami*[19] The technique of that work gives to one acute pleasure. It is simply enchanting to see how it's done.

To David S. Meldrum, August 10, 1898

If America is in the way of the dates I shall not Write any slower for it. I *never mean* to be slow[20] The stuff comes out at its own rate. I am always ready to put it down; nothing would induce me to lay down my pen if I *feel* a sentence—or even a word ready to my hand. The trouble is that too often—alas! —I've to Wait for the sentence—for the word.

What wonder then that during the long blank hours the doubt creeps into the mind and I ask myself whether I am fitted for that work. The worst is that while I am thus powerless to produce

---

19. *The Children of the Sea* was the title of the American edition of *The Nigger of the "Narcissus."* For Conrad's admiration of Maupassant, see also his essay "Guy de Maupassant."

20. Conrad was writing *Lord Jim* and trying to make progress on *The Rescue.*

my imagination is extremely active: whole paragraphs, whole pages, whole chapters pass through my mind. Everything is there: descriptions, dialogue, reflexion—everything—everything but the belief, the conviction, the only thing needed to make me put pen to paper. I've thought out a volume in a day till I felt sick in mind and heart and gone to bed, completely done up, without having written a line. The effort I put out should give birth to Masterpieces as big as Mountains—and it brings forth a ridiculous mouse now and then.

To Mrs. Anna E. Bontine, November 22, 1898

On Henry James's last I share your opinion. The second of the *Two Magics*[21] is unworthy of his talent. The first[22] evades one, but leaves a kind of phosphorescent trail in one's mind.

To William Blackwood, December 13, 1898

I had a treat in the shape of a N° of the *Singapore Free Press* 2½ columns about "Mr. Conrad at home and abroad."[23] Extremely laudatory but in fact telling me I don't know anything about it. Well I never did set up as an authority on Malaysia. I looked for a medium in which to express myself. I am inexact and ignorant no doubt (most of us are) but I don't think I sinned so recklessly. Curiously enough all the details about the little characteristic acts and customs which they hold up as proof I have taken out (to be safe) from undoubted sources—dull, wise books. It is rather staggering to find myself so far astray. In *Karain,* for instance, there's not a single action of my man (and good many of his expressions) that cannot be backed by a traveller's tale—I mean a serious traveller's. And yet this story "can only be called Malay in Mr. Conrad's sense". Sad.

To Mme. Angèle Zagórska, Christmas, 1898 (Original in Polish; translated in G. Jean-Aubry, *The Life and Letters of Joseph Conrad*)

With regard to Grant Allen's *Woman Who Did, c'est un*

21. "Covering End."
22. "The Turn of the Screw."
23. The September 1, 1898, number included "The Trail of the Bookworm: Mr. Joseph Conrad at Home and Abroad," by Hugh Clifford.

livre mort. The *Woman Who Did* had a kind of success, of curiosity mostly and that only amongst the philistines—the sort of people who read Marie Corelli and Hall Caine. All three are very popular with the public—and they are also puffed in the press. There are no lasting qualities in their work. The thought is commonplace and the style (?) without any distinction. They are popular because they express the common thought, and the common man is delighted to find himself in accord with people he supposes distinguished. This is the secret of many popularities. (You can develop this idea as an explanation of the enthusiasm of the public for books which are of no value.) As to Allen, he is considered a man of letters among scholars and a scholar among men of letters. He writes popular scientific manuals equally well. Marie Corelli is *not* noticed critically by the serious reviews. She is simply ignored. Her books sell largely. Hall Caine is a kind of male Marie Corelli.

Among the people in literature who deserve attention the first is Rudyard Kipling (his last book *The Day's Work,* novel), J. M. Barrie—a Scotsman. His last book *Sentimental Tommy* (last year). George Meredith did not bring out anything this year. The last volumes of the charming translation of Turgeniev came out a fortnight ago. The translation is by Mrs. Constance Garnett. George Moore has published the novel *Evelyn Innes—un succès d'estime.* He is supposed to belong to the naturalistic school and Zola is his prophet. *Tout ça c'est très vieux jeu.* A certain Mr. T. Watts-Dunton published the novel *Aylwin,* a curiosity success, as this Watts-Dunton (who is a barrister) is supposed to be the friend of different celebrities in the world of Fine Arts (especially in the pre-Raphaelite School). He has crammed them all into his book. H. G. Wells published this year *The War of the Worlds* and *The Invisible Man.* He is a very original writer with a very individualistic judgment in all things and an astonishing imagination.

To Mrs. Anna E. Bontine, January 12, 1899

I share your opinion of Maupassant.[24] The man is a great artist,

24. In reference to *Des Vers.*

who sees the essential in everything. He is not a great poet,—
perhaps no poet at all, yet I like his verses. I like them immensely.

To John Galsworthy, February 11, 1899

Yes, it is good criticism. Only I think that to say Henry
James does not write from the heart is maybe hasty. He is cosmopolitan, civilized, very much *homme du monde* and the
acquired (educated if you like) side of his temperament,—that
is,—restraints, the instinctive, the nurtured, fostered, cherished
side is always presented to the reader first. To me even the
R. T.[25] seems to flow from the heart because and only because
the work, approaching so near perfection, yet does not strike
cold. Technical perfection, unless there is some real glow to
illumine and warm it from within, must necessarily be cold. I
argue that in H. J. there is such a glow and not a dim one
either, but to us used, absolutely accustomed, to unartistic expression of fine, headlong, honest (or dishonest) sentiments the art
of H. J. does appear heartless. The outlines are so clear, the
figures so finished, chiselled, carved and brought out that we
exclaim,—we, used to the shades of the contemporary fiction, to
the more or less malformed shades,—we exclaim,—stone! Not at
all. I say flesh and blood,—very perfectly presented,—perhaps with
too much perfection of *method*.

The volume of short stories entitled, I think, *The Lesson of
the Master* contains a tale called "The Pupil," if I remember
rightly, where the underlying feeling of the man,—his really wide
sympathy,—is seen nearer the surface. Of course he does not
deal in primitive emotions. I maintain he is the most civilized
of modern writers. He is also an idealizer. His heart shows itself
in the delicacy of his handling. Things like "The Middle Years"
and "The Altar of the Dead" in the vol. entitled *Terminations*
would illustrate my meaning. Moreover, your cousin admits the
element of pathos. Mere technique won't give the elements of
pathos. I admit he is not *forcible*,—or let us say, the only forcible
thing in his work is his technique. Now a literary intelligence
would be naturally struck by the wonderful technique, and that is

25. *The Real Thing and Other Tales.*

so wonderful in its way that it dominates the bare expression. The more so that the expression is only of delicate shades. He is never in deep gloom or in violent sunshine. But he feels deeply and vividly every delicate shade. We cannot ask for more. Not everyone is a Turgeniev. Moreover Turgeniev is not civilized (therein much of his charm for us) in the sense H. J. is civilized.

To William Blackwood, February 14, 1899

Besides I thought of two other stories (more in the 'note' of my 'Maga'[26] work) one of them being called *First Command*[27] and the other (a sketch) entitled *A Seaman*. These are not written. They creep about in my head but [have] got to be caught and tortured into some kind of shape. I think—I think they would turn out as good as (they say) *Youth* is.

To R. B. Cunninghame Graham, February 26, 1899

In a little while came the books. *Vous me gâtez*. I've read *Vathek*[28] at once. *C'est très bien*. What an infernal imagination! The style is cold and I do not see in the work that immense promise as set forth by the introduction. Chaucer I have dipped into, reading aloud as you advised. I am afraid I am not English enough to appreciate fully the father of English literature. Moreover I am in general insensible to verse.

To William Blackwood, August 22, 1899

I am glad you like Jim so far. Your good opinion gives one confidence. From the nature of things treated the story can not be as dramatic (in a certain sense) as the *H of D*. It is certainly more like *Youth*. It is however longer and more varied. The structure of it is a little loose—this however need not detract from its interest—from the "general reader" point of view. The question of *art* is so endless, so involved and so obscure that one is tempted to turn one's face resolutely away from it. I've certainly an idea—apart from the idea and the subject of the story—which guides

26. *Blackwood's Magazine.*
27. Renamed *The Shadow Line.*
28. By William Beckford.

me in my writing, but I would be hard put to it if requested to give it out in the shape of a fixed formula. After all in this as in every other human endeavour one is answerable only to one's conscience.

I have this day sent off another 3000 words to your London office. 2000 more are actually written or rather scrawled and awaiting the domestic typewriter. I devote myself exclusively to *Jim*. I find I can't live with more than one story at a time. It's a kind of literary monogamism. You know how desperately slow I work. Scores of notions present themselves—expressions suggest themselves by the dozen, but the inward voice that decides:—this is well—this is right—is not heard sometimes for days together. And meantime one must live!

To Sir Hugh Clifford, October 9, 1899

Of course, the matter is admirable—the knowledge, the feeling, the sympathy; it is sure to win perfect and full recognition. It is all sterling metal; a thing of absolute value. There can be no question of it, not only for those who know but even for those who approach the book[29] with blank minds on the subject of the race you have, in more than one sense, made your own. And as to the manner—well! I know you are not a seeker after mere expression and I beg leave to offer only one remark.

You do not leave enough to the imagination. I do not mean as to facts—the facts cannot be too explicitly stated; I am alluding simply to the phrasing. True, a man who knows so much (without taking into account the manner in which his knowledge was acquired) may well spare himself the trouble of meditating over the words, only that words, groups of words, words standing alone, are symbols of life, have the power in their sound or their aspect to present the very thing you wish to hold up before the mental vision of your readers. The things "as they are" exist in words; therefore words should be handled with care lest the picture, the image of truth abiding in facts, should become distorted—or blurred.

29. Clifford's *In a Corner of Asia.*

These are the considerations for a mere craftsman—you may say; and you may also conceivably say that I have nothing else to trouble my head about. However, the *whole* of the truth lies in the presentation; therefore the expression should be studied in the interest of veracity. This is the only morality of *art* apart from *subject*.

I have traveled a good way from my original remark—not enough left to the imagination in the phrasing. I beg leave to illustrate my meaning from extracts on p. 261—not that I pose for an accomplished craftsman or fondly think I am free from that very fault and others much worse. No; it is only to explain what I mean.

... "When the whole horror of his position forced itself with an agony of realization upon his frightened mind, Pa' Tûa for a space lost his reason." ... In this sentence the reader is borne down by the full expression. The words: *with an agony of realization* completely destroy the effect—therefore interfere with the truth of the statement. The word *frightened* is fatal. It seems as if it had been written without any thought at all. It takes away all sense of reality—for if you read the sentence *in its place on the page* you will see that the word *"frightened"* (or indeed any word of the sort) is inadequate to express the true state of that man's mind. No word is adequate. The imagination of the reader should be left free to arouse his feeling.

"... When the whole horror of his position forced itself upon his mind, Pa' Tûa for a space lost his reason. ..." This is truth; this it is which, thus stated, carries conviction because it is a *picture* of a mental state. And look how finely it goes on with a perfectly legitimate effect. ... "He screamed aloud, and the hollow of the rocks took up his cries" ... It is magnificent! It is suggestive. It is truth effectively stated. But *"and hurled them back to him mockingly"* is nothing at all. It is a phrase anybody can write to fit any sort of situation; it is the sort of thing that writes itself; it is the sort of thing I write twenty times a day and (with the fear of overtaking fate behind me) spend half my nights in taking out of my work—upon which depends the daily bread of the house (literally—from day to day); not to mention (I dare hardly think of it) the future of my child, of those nearest and dearest to me, between whom and the bleakest want there is only my pen—as long as life lasts. And I can sell all I write—as much as I can write!

This is said to make it manifest that I practise the faith which I take the liberty to preach—if you allow me to say so—in a brotherly spirit. To return.

Please observe how strikingly the effect is carried on.

"When the whole horror of his position forced itself upon his mind Pa' Tûa for a space lost his reason. He screamed aloud, and the hollow of the rocks took up his cries; the bats awoke in thousands and joined the band that rustled and squeaked above the man," etc., etc. In the last two lines the words hurrying—motiveless—already—defenceless—are not essential and therefore not true to the fact. The impression of *hurrying motiveless* has been given already in lines 2, 3, 4, at the top of the page. If they *joined,* it is because the others were *already* flying. *Already* is repetition. *Defenceless* is inadequate for a man held in the merciless grip of a rock.

And pray believe me that if I have selected this passage, it is because I am alive to its qualities and not because I have looked consciously for its defects.

For the same reason I do not apologize for my remarks. They are not an impertinence, they are a tribute to the work, that appeals so strongly to me by its subject, partly—but most by its humanity, its comprehension, by its spirit and by its expression too—which I have made a subject of critical analysis. If I have everlastingly bored you, you must forgive me. I trust you will find no other cause of offence.

To William Blackwood, October 27, 1899

The beginning wobbles a good deal; I did cut up shamefully the proofs without being able to put it firmly on its feet;[30] however my little band of faithfuls professes itself (in various letters) to be immensely pleased.

30. Serialization of *Lord Jim* began in the October, 1899, number of *Blackwood's Magazine.*

To William Blackwood, November 8, 1899

Criticism is poor work, and to expose the weaknesses of humanity as exhibited in literary (?) work is a thankless and futile task. I've always thought that R. Macaulay's smashing of R. Montgomery's poems (!)[31] was a pathetic example of mighty truth powerless before the falsehood of pretences, like the great sea before a very small rock. To point out to the crowd beauties not manifest to the common eye, to flash the light of one's sympathetic perception upon great, if not obvious, qualities, and even upon generous failings that hold the promise of better things this is indeed a toil worthy of a man's pen, a task that would repay for the time given up, for the strength expended for that sadness that comes of thinking over the sincere endeavour of a soul—for ever debarred from attaining perfection. But the blind distribution of praise or blame, done with a light heart and an empty mind, which is of the very essence of 'periodical' criticism seems to me to be a work less useful than skirt-dancing and not quite as honourable as pocket-picking.

There is too a sort of curse upon the critical exercise of human thought. Should one attempt honestly an analysis of another man's production it is ten to one, that one will get the credit for all sorts of motives except for that of sincere conviction; this is the taint of the literary life; and though writing to you I would not expose myself to the risk of being misunderstood I prefer to say nothing critical about John Buchan's story.[32] I am willing to admit it is grammatically written—(I know nothing of grammar myself as he who runs may see)—if anybody desires to make that assertion. I do happen however to know one or two things that might conceivably be found to have a bearing upon the story and on these I shall hold my peace.

There is one thing (though hardly pertaining to criticism proper) which ought to be said of that—production. It is this: its idea, its feeling, its suggestion *and even the most subtly sig-*

31. *Omnipresence of the Deity,* reviewed by Macaulay in the *Edinburgh Review,* April, 1830.

32. "The Far Islands," a short romance of adventure, appeared in *Blackwood's Magazine,* November, 1899, pp. 604–619.

nificant incidents have been wrenched alive out of Kipling's tale *"The finest Story in the World."* What became of the idea, of the feeling, of the suggestion and of the incidents, in the process of that wrenching I leave it for the pronouncement not of posterity but of any contemporary mind that would be brought (for less than ten minutes) to the consideration of Mr. Buchan's story. The thing is patent—it is the only impression that remains after reading the last words—it argues naïveness of an appalling kind or else a most serene impudence. I write strongly—because I feel strongly.

One does not expect style, construction, or even common intelligence in the fabrication of story; but one has the right to demand some sort of sincerity and to expect common honesty. When that fails—what remains?

To William Blackwood, February 20, 1900

Yesterday I got hold of Jim again. When I get into the stride a fortnight will see the end of the story, though I shall not hurry myself since the end of a story is a very important and difficult part; the *most* difficult for me, to execute—that is. It is always *thought out* before the story is begun.

To William Blackwood, July 19, 1900

The end of Lord Jim in accordance with a meditated resolve is presented in a bare almost bald relation of matters of fact. The situation—the problem if you will—of that sensitive nature has been already commented upon, illustrated and contrasted. It is my opinion that in the working out of the catastrophe psychologic disquisition should have no place. The reader ought to know enough by that time. I enlarge a little upon the new character which is introduced (that of Brown the desperate adventurer) so as to preserve the sense of verisimilitude and for the sake of final contrast; but all the rest is nothing but a relation of events—strictly, a narrative.

To William Blackwood, November 7, 1900

Hueffer's talent has been from the first sympathetic to me. Throughout, his feeling is true and its expression genuine with ease and moderation. He does not stand on his head for the purpose of getting a new and striking view of his subject. Such a method of procedure may be in favour nowadays but I prefer the old way, with the feet on the ground. Neither does he tear his hair with enthusiasm and paint his Ports red;[33] but there is—it seems to me—a good deal of force in his quiet phrasing. His facts I believe to be right and his theories have some authority to back them and at any rate are no worse—I believe—than many theories of all sorts that born yesterday jostle us today, and shall fall to pieces to-morrow.

To William Blackwood, July 4, 1901

Meantime I enclose here an epitome of the part stating the events with which it deals. From parts I, II & IV[34] you will be able to judge of the literary qualities and defects of our tale. This tale—which we call a romance—has been grubbed out of the British Museum by Hueffer. All the details of the political feeling in Jamaica (about 1821) are authentic. There was really a perfectly innocent young Englishman who was tried for piracy and escaped the gallows by the merest hair's-breadth. There did exist a nest of pirates about that time on the coast of Cuba. They were a sorry lot—I admit. O'Brien is our own invention, and he is possible enough—I mean historically possible. Good many Irishmen took refuge in Spain, made careers, and founded families. For the rest you'll see we do not go in for analysis of character seeking rather to present a succession of picturesque scenes and personalities. We try to produce a variation from the usual type of romance our point of view being that the feeling of the romantic in life lies principally in the glamour memory throws over the past and arises from contact with a different race and a different temperament; so that the Spanish girl seems romantic to Kemp while that ordinary good young man seems

33. In *The Cinque Ports*, by Ford Madox Hueffer (Ford Madox Ford).
34. Of *Seraphina*, renamed *Romance*. The original source was *The Atrocities of the Pirates*, by Aaron Smith (1824). "Cuban Pirates: A True Narrative," based upon it, appeared in *All the Year Round* (1870), pp. 172–178.

romantic and even heroic not only to Seraphina but to Sanchez and Don Riego too.

To William Blackwood, November 7, 1901

The last *Linesman*[35] was of a really superior excellence. I've ordered the book.[36] As to *Charlotte*[37] the genuineness of its conception the honesty of its feeling make that work as welcome as a breath of fresh air to a breast oppressed by all the fumes and cheap perfumes of fiction that is thrown on the altar of publicity in the hopes of propitiating the god of big sales. It is refreshing indeed. And of course I won't say the display, but the *outlay* of skill, very quiet, very sure skill, is of no mean order. Altogether a delightful piece of work.

To John Galsworthy, November 11, 1901

There is a certain caution of touch which will militate against popularity. After all, to please the public (if one isn't a sugary imbecile or an inflated fraud) one must handle one's subject intimately. Mere intimacy with the subject won't do. And conviction is found for others,—not for the author, only in certain contradictions and irrelevancies to the general conception of character (or characters) and of the subject. Say what you like, man lives in his eccentricities (so called) alone. They give a vigour to his personality which mere consistency can never do. One must explore deep and believe the incredible to find the few particles of truth floating in an ocean of insignificance. And before all one must divest oneself of every particle of respect for one's character. You are really most profound and attain the greatest art in handling the people you do not respect. For instance the minor characters in *V. R.*[38] And in this volume I am

35. "Night," by "Linesman" (M. H. Grant), *Blackwood's Magazine*, November, 1901, pp. 579–590, has for its subject a night attack during the Boer War.

36. *Words of an Eyewitness: The Struggle in Natal*, by M. H. Grant, 1901.

37. *The Conquest of Charlotte* was serialized in *Blackwood's Magazine*, July, 1901—July, 1902.

38. *Villa Rubein*.

bound to recognize that Forsyte is the best. I recognize this with a certain reluctance because indubitably there is more beauty (and more felicity of style too) in the *M. of D.*[39] The story of the mine shows best your strength and your weakness. There is hardly a word I would have changed; there are things in it that I would give a pound of my flesh to have written. Honestly,— there are. And your mine-manager remains unconvincing because he is too confoundedly perfect in his very imperfections. The fact is you want more scepticism at the very foundation of your work. Scepticism, the tonic of minds, the tonic of life, the agent of truth,—the way of art and salvation. In a book you should love the idea and be scrupulously faithful to your conception of life. There lies the honour of the writer, not in the fidelity to his personages. You must never allow them to decoy you out of yourself. As against your people you must preserve an attitude of perfect indifference, the part of creative power. A creator must be indifferent; because directly the "Fiat!" has issued from his lips, there are the creatures made in his image that'll try to drag him down from his eminence,—and belittle him by their worship. Your attitude to them should be purely intellectual, more independent, freer, less rigorous than it is. You seem, for their sake, to hug your conceptions of right and wrong too closely. There is exquisite atmosphere in your tales. What they want now is more air.

To Arnold Bennett, March 10, 1902

The thing[40] as written is undeniable. To read it was to me quite a new experience of the language; and the delight was great enough to make me completely disregard the subject.

This at first; but as you may suppose I've read the book more than once. Unfortunately, I don't know how to criticize; to discuss, however, I am ready. Now the book (as a novel, not as a piece of writing) *is* disputable.

Generally, however, I may say that the die has not been struck hard enough. Here's a piece of pure metal scrupulously

39. *The Man of Devon and Other Stories.*
40. Bennett's *A Man from the North.*

shaped, with a true—and more—a beautiful ring: but the die
has not been struck hard enough. I admit that the outlines of the
design are sharp enough. What it wants is a more emphatic
modelling; more relief. And one could even quarrel with the
design itself.

Nothing would give me greater pleasure than to have it
out with you, the book there on the table, to be thumped and
caressed. I would quarrel not with the truth of your conception
but with the realism thereof. You stop just short of being absolutely real because you are faithful to your dogmas of realism.
Now realism in art will never approach reality. And your art,
your gift, should be put to the service of a larger and freer faith.

To William Blackwood, May 31, 1902

My work shall not be an utter failure because it has the
solid basis of a definite intention—first: and next because it is
not an endless analysis of affected sentiments but in its essence
it is action (strange as this affirmation may sound at the present
time) nothing but action—action observed, felt and interpreted
with an absolute truth to my sensations (which are the basis of
art in literature)—action of human beings that will bleed to a
prick, and are moving in a visible world.[41]

To David S. Meldrum, Autumn, (?) 1902

Yes. Hermann and his wife are the people I wanted to *do*:
the story of Falk being more or less of a foil to the main purpose.
However I thought that I did bring his personality out towards
the end distinctly enough. If I did not—as I fear—it is simply want
of skill in finding the essential trait in an image clear enough
to my own eye. I wanted to make him stand for so much that I
neglected, in a manner, to set him on his feet. This is one of my
weaknesses—one of these things that make me swear at a finished
work so often.

I am heartened greatly by what you say of the wretched
"Tether." The old man does not wobble it seems to me. The

---

41. In reference to Conrad's fiction in general.

Elliot episode has a fundamental significance in so far that it exhibits the first weakening of old Whalley's character before the assault of poverty. As you notice he says nothing of his position but goes off and takes advantage of the information. At the same time it gives me the opportunity to introduce Massy from way back without the formal narrative paragraphs. But the episode is mainly the first sign of that fate we carry within us. A character like Whalley's cannot cease to be frank with impunity. He is not frank with his old friend—such as the old friend is. For, if Elliot had been a genuine sort of man Whalley's secrecy would have been that of an intolerable fool. The pathos for me is in this that the concealment of his extremity is as it were forced upon him. Nevertheless it is weakness—it is deterioration. Next he conveys a sort of false impression to Massy—on justifiable grounds. I indicate the progress of the shaking the character receives and make it possible thus to by and by present the man as concealing the oncoming of blindness—and so on; till at last he conceals the criminal wrecking of his ship by committing suicide. And always there is just that shadow, that ghost of justification which should secure the sympathy of the reader.

To Sir Hugh Clifford, February 26, 1903

The fault I would find is a certain immaturity or rather superficialness in Maurice's character.[42] That sort of romantic and adventurous impulse argues a certain depth of character, a certain firmness of fibre, a resolution that will stand more than a shock or two—whereas that young man seems as nervous as a cat in his disappointment, in his disenchantment, in his horror. He is terribly unscrupulous and too emotional to be quite convincing in his emotion. It looks a little as though he were not quite responsible for his actions and his feelings. When one thinks of a Christian, and presumably a gentleman, already disillusioned (for you do strike that note almost at once) for nothing as it were, for a half-faded whim, carefully shooting at the Dutch officers and then directly afterwards beside himself with horror

42. Maurice is a character in Clifford's *A Free-Lance To-day*.

at the mutilation of the dead bodies, one mistrusts the genuineness of both manifestations. In short, it seems to me that you make him too savage and too squeamish, in particular instances, and too unthinking in general.

To H. G. Wells, November 30, 1903

Is *Men in the Moon* doing well for you—I mean *really* well? After all, my dear boy, for all our faith in our good intentions and even in our achievements, a paper-success (as I call it) is not a strong enough tonic. I say so because for me, writing—*the only possible writing*—is just simply the conversion of nervous force into phrases. With you too, I am sure, tho' in your case it is the disciplined intelligence which gives the signal—the impulse. For me it is a matter of chance, stupid chance. But the fact remains that when the nervous force is exhausted the phrases don't come—and no tension of will can help.

To John Galsworthy, 1908

The social background of the story[43] is too big for the personages in front and perhaps a little too remote. If the story had been the story of the loves of Martin and Thyme, it would have been impossible to make those objections, or at any rate very difficult to make them. As it is, the background is connected with the action, not by the developments of the action itself, but more or less by analysis. That, I think, is a defect. But that observation, I am ready to admit, may spring not from the truth of things but from some defect of my understanding which causes me to be blind to subtler connections existing both in your mind and in your work. I may have missed many delicate indications. A book like this demands many auditions. It is anything but simple. Its suggestions are multiple (in which by the bye it does not resemble the work of Turgeniev, whom the idle paragraphist proclaims your chosen master) and run in and out of each other.

Yes! It is a complicated book. It is possible to view it in

43. *Shadows*, revised and published as *Fraternity*.

innumerable ways for it excites imagination at every step. But before all it is the book of a moralist.

For that is, my dear Jack, what you are—a humanitarian moralist. You are revealing yourself as a moralist in all the greatness of your talent.

This fact which you cannot help and which may lead you yet to become the Idol of the Public—if I may so express myself—arises as the greatest danger in the way of your art. It may prevent the concentration of effort in one single direction—because your art will always be trying to assert itself against the impulse of your moral feelings. This may lead to a certain uncertainty of intention which may conceivably lead further to a vain harrowing of your feelings—tho' I don't believe that it will ever lead you into the gratuitous atrocity, of, say, *Ivan Illyith*[44] or the monstrous stupidity of such a thing as the *Kreutzer Sonata,* for instance; where an obvious degenerate not worth looking at twice, totally unfitted not only for married life but for any sort of life, is presented as a sympathetic victim of some sort of sacred truth that is supposed to live within him.

To Edward Garnett, August 28, 1908

At any rate I think I have always written with dignity, with more dignity than the above-alluded-to butterfly[45] ever could command. And that not certainly from lack of conviction which often takes that outward form. The fact is that I have approached things human in a spirit of piety foreign to those lovers of humanity who would like to make of life a sort of Cook's Personally Conducted Tour—from the cradle to the grave. I have never debased that quasi-religious sentiment by tears and groans and sighs, I have neither grinned nor gnashed my teeth. In a word I have behaved myself decently—which, except in the gross conventional sense, is not so easy as it looks. Therefore there are those who reproach me with the pose of brutality with the lack of all heart delicacy, sympathy—sentiment—idealism. There is

44. "The Death of Ivan Ilyitch." Conrad never spoke favorably of Tolstoi.
45. Conrad had called Carlyle a butterfly.

even one abandoned creature who says I am a neo-platonist?
What on earth is that?

To Arthur Symons, August 29, 1908

One thing that I am certain of is that I have approached
the object of my task, things human, in a spirit of piety. The
earth is a temple where there is going on a mystery play, childish
and poignant, ridiculous and awful enough, in all conscience.
Once in I've tried to behave decently. I have not degraded any
quasi-religious sentiment by tears and groans; and if I have been
amused or indignant, I've neither grinned nor gnashed my teeth.
In other words, I've tried to write with dignity, not out of regard
for myself, but for the sake of the spectacle, the play with an
obscure beginning and an unfathomable *dénouement*.

I don't think that this has been noticed. It is your penitent
beating the floor with his forehead and the ecstatic worshipper
at the rails that are obvious to the public eye. The man standing
quietly in the shadow of the pillar, if noticed at all, runs the
risk of being suspected of sinister designs. Thus I've been called
a heartless wretch, a man without ideals and a *poseur* of brutality. But I will confess to you under seal of secrecy that *I don't
believe* I am such as I appear to mediocre minds.

To Mrs. E. L. Sanderson, September, 1910

Something truly pagan is too vague. That's what I meant
when I said (in the letter) that your expression, tho' direct, was
sometimes not precise enough.[46] In letters suggestiveness itself,—a
great quality—must be obtained by precise expression. I feel with
you that there is "something truly pagan in the mystery, etc.,
etc., etc."—but the sentence in itself means nothing. To awaken
a responsive feeling, something exact must be said. What is pagan-
ism? The pagan piety was an emotion evoked by the wonder,
harm and fear of the visible world. I think that in this instance
you meant the suggestion of fear, dread, "in the mystery of
deserts," etc., etc. I may be wrong. My sentence certainly is not

46. In reference to a passage in one of Mrs. Sanderson's African sketches.

good in itself but as an example it will serve. In writing and especially in descriptive writing one must guard oneself against the *"à peu près,"*—the horrid danger of the "near enough."

To Edward Garnett, August 4, 1911

I have expressed to Pinker my view of his sending to you a story rejected already by the Century. It was not fair either to you or me. As to faking a "sunny" ending to my story[47] I would see all the American Magazines and all the American Editors damned in heaps before lifting my pen for that task. I have never been particularly anxious to rub shoulders with the piffle they print with touching consistency from year's end to year's end.

The story itself, I suppose, is not "done" since it has failed to convince you. It is the story of the *Costa Rica* which was not more than five years old when I was in Singapore. The man's name was Sutton. He died in just that way—but I don't think he died of Slav temperament. He was just about to go home to marry a girl (of whom he used to talk to everybody and anybody) and bring her out there when his ship was run on a reef by the commander of a Dutch gun-boat whom he had managed to offend in some way. He haunted the beach in Macassar for months and lies buried in the fort there.

Only 18 months ago Charles Marris, master and owner of the *Araby Maid* island-trader, came to see me in Aldington. He was in England to see his people who farm in Somersetshire. He said to me: "We are all reading your books out there." We had a long talk about men and things of the Archipelago. He said: "You ought to write the story of the *Costa Rica*. There's a good many of us left yet who remember Sutton." And I said I would, before long.

That's how Freya came to be written. But of course facts are nothing unless they are made credible—and it is there that I have failed.

To Mrs. Edward Garnett, October 20, 1911

You are a good critic. That girl does not move. No excuse

47. "Freya of the Seven Isles."

can be offered for such a defect but there is an explanation. I wanted a pivot for the action to turn on. And I had to be very careful because if I had allowed myself to make more of her she would have killed the artistic purpose of the book: the development of a single mood. It isn't that I was afraid or ignorant of her possibilties. Indeed they were very tempting. But it had to be a performance on one string. It had to be. You may think such self-imposed limitation a very stupid thing. But something of the kind must be done or else novel-writing becomes a mere debauch of the imagination. No doubt if I had taken another line the book would have been richer. But what I aimed at this time was an effect of virtuosity before anything else. Still I need not have made Miss Haldin[48] a mere peg as I am sorry to admit she is. Result of over caution.

Your kind appreciation of the book gives me great pleasure and I am glad you think it is true—as [far as it] goes. I am quite aware it does not go very far. But the fact is that I know extremely little of Russians. Practically nothing. In Poland we have nothing to do with them. One knows they are there. And that's disagreeable enough. In exile the contact is even slighter if possible if more unavoidable. I crossed the Russian frontier at the age of ten. Not having been to school then I never knew Russian. I could not tell a Little Russian from a Great Russian to save my life. In the book as you must have seen I am exclusively concerned with ideas.

To Edward Garnett, May 27, 1912

I do hope you are not too disgusted with me for not thanking you for the "Karamazov" before. It was very good of you to remember me; and of course I was extremely interested. But it's an impossible lump of valuable matter. It's terrifically bad and impressive and exasperating. Moreover, I don't know what D[ostoevski] stands for or reveals, but I do know that he is too Russian for me. It sounds to me like some fierce mouthings from prehistoric ages. I understand the Russians have just 'discovered' him. I wish them joy.

48. In *Under Western Eyes.*

To Edward Garnett, February 23, 1914

Dislike as definition of my attitude to Tols[toi]: is but a rough and approximate term. I judge him not—for this reason. That his anti-sensualism is suspect to me. In that matter (which is not worth the fuss which is made about it) the pros and the antis seem to me tarred with the same brush. Moreover the base from which he starts—Christianity—is distasteful to me. I am not blind to its services but the absurd oriental fable from which it starts irritates me. Great, improving, softening, compassionate it may be but it has lent itself with amazing facility to cruel distortion and is the only religion which, with its impossible standards, has brought an infinity of anguish to innumerable souls—on this earth.

However I don't suppose these views of mine can interest you and I only meant to send you a word of thanks. Why I should fly out like this on Xtianity which has given to mankind the beautiful Xmas pudding I don't know, unless that, like some good dogs, I get snappish as I grow old.

To Ford Madox Hueffer, August 30, 1915

Yes! *mon cher!* our world of 15 years ago is gone to pieces: what will come in its place, God knows, but I imagine doesn't care.

Still what I always said was the only immortal line in *Romance:* "Excellency, a few goats," survives,—esoteric, symbolic, profound and comic,—it survives.

To Sir Sidney Colvin, March 18, 1917

Perhaps you won't find it presumption if, after 22 years of work, I may say that I have not been very well understood. I have been called a writer of the sea, of the tropics, a descriptive writer, a romantic writer—and also a realist. But as a matter of fact all my concern has been with the "ideal" value of things, events, and people. That and nothing else. The humorous, the pathetic, the passionate, the sentimental *aspects* came in of themselves—*mais en vérité c'est les valeurs idéales des faits et gestes humains qui se sont imposés à mon activité artistique.*

Whatever dramatic and narrative gifts I may have are always, instinctively, used with that object—to get at, to bring forth *les valeurs idéales.*

To Edward Garnett, May, 1917

As far as I know you are the only man who had seen T[urgeniev] not only in his relation to mankind but in his relation to Russia. And he is great in both. But to be so great and at the same time so fine is fatal to an artist—as to any other man for that matter. It isn't Dostoievski the grimacing haunted creature who is under a curse; it is Turgeniev. Every gift has been heaped on his cradle. Absolute sanity and the deepest sensibility, the clearest vision and the most exquisite responsiveness, penetrating insight for the significant, for the essential in human life and in the visible world, the clearest mind, the warmest heart, the largest sympathy—and all that in perfect measure! There's enough there to ruin any writer. For you know my dear Edward that if you and I were to catch Antinous and exhibit him in a booth of the world's fair, swearing that his life was as perfect as his form, we wouldn't get one per cent of the crowd struggling next door to catch the sight of the double-headed Nightingale or of some weak-kneed giant grinning through a collar. * * * To be frank I don't want to appear as qualified to speak on things Russian. It wouldn't be true. I admire Turgeniev but in truth Russia was for him no more than the canvas for the painter. If his people had all lived in the moon he would have been just as great an artist. They are very much like Shakespeare's Italians. One doesn't think of it.

To Barrett H. Clark, May 4, 1918

Coming now to the subject of your inquiry, I wish at first to put before you a general proposition: that a work of art is very seldom limited to one exclusive meaning and not necessarily tending to a definite conclusion. And this for the reason that the nearer it approaches art, the more it acquires a symbolic character. This statement may surprise you, who may imagine that I am alluding to the Symbolist School of poets or prose writers. Theirs, however, is only a literary proceeding against which I have nothing to say. I am concerned here with something much larger. But no doubt you have meditated on this and kindred questions yourself.

So I will only call your attention to the fact that the symbolic conception of a work of art has this advantage, that it makes a triple appeal covering the whole field of life. All the great creations of literature have been symbolic, and in that way have gained in complexity, in power, in depth and in beauty.

I don't think you will quarrel with me on the ground of lack of precision; for as to precision of images and analysis my artistic conscience is at rest. I have given there all the truth that is in me; and all that the critics may say can make my honesty neither more nor less. But as to "final effect" my conscience has nothing to do with that. It is the critic's affair to bring to its contemplation his own honesty, his sensibility and intelligence. The matter for his conscience is just his judgment. If his conscience is busy with petty scruples and trammelled by superficial formulas then his judgment will be superficial and petty. But an artist has no right to quarrel with the inspirations, either lofty or base, of another soul.

To Hugh Dent, June 24, 1920

On returning home yesterday I found an absurd wire from the — — — asking me to say whether that forthcoming book of mine[49] had in it "any message for the young." Could anything be more silly than such an inquiry and, especially, to a man like me who had never flapped any "message" in the face of the world? I was sorely tempted to answer that it all depended whether the "young" in question was an ass or not. But I controlled my feelings and wired a reply to the effect that "in a work exclusively artistic in its aim to appeal to emotions there should be something for everybody, young or old, who was at all susceptible to aesthetic impressions."

To Edward Garnett, July 11, 1920

Please tell the writer of the critical note on Mrs. Travers[50]

49. *The Rescue.*
50. The heroine of *The Rescue.*

that speaking in all sincerity I am immensely gratified by her appreciation and very much impressed by the acuteness of her analysis. One or two notice writers felt that there was something wrong. And my answer is *to them* that if I had hung Mrs. Travers for five minutes on Lingard's neck (at the last meeting) they would have been perfectly satisfied. To her I would only advance in palliation that one must take account of facts. The blowing-up of the Emma was a fact. It destroyed suddenly the whole emotional situation not only for them all but also for me. To go on after that was no joke. And yet something had to be done at once! I cared too much for Mrs. Travers to play pranks with her on the line of heroics or tenderness; and being afraid of striking a false note I failed to do her justice—not so much *in action*, I think, as in expression.

To Richard Curle, August 18, 1920

If one is to condescend to that sort of thing well then, all considered, I prefer Cinema to Stage. The Movie is just a silly stunt for silly people—but the theatre is more compromising since it is capable of falsifying the very soul of one's work both on the imaginative and on the intellectual side—besides having some sort of inferior poetics of its own which is bound to play havoc with that imponderable quality of creative literary expression which depends on one's individuality.

To Edward Garnett, March 18, 1921

It may be I failed to understand the Ascending Effort,[51] but I did not mean to treat Bourne disrespectfully. The thesis of this book is vitiated by the fact that poetry and religion having their source in an emotional state may act and react on each other worthily—whereas "Science" at its amplest (and Profoundest) is only the exercise of a certain kind of imagination springing either from facts eminently prosaic or from tentative assumptions of the commonest kind of common-sense. And you will admit that Bourne's writing in its slightly grotesque heaviness made it

51. *The Ascending Effort*, by George Bourne. See Conrad's essay "The Ascending Effort."

very difficult to read the whole book in a spirit of impartiality—
let alone benevolence. I agree with you about Tchehov, absolutely. But that great and wonderful man did not write his stories
in praise of the Medical science. Poetical genius must be nour-
ished on knowledge—it can't have too much of it—but you will
imagine easily what a poem in praise of knowledge would be
like—even if an Archangel came down from Heaven on purpose
to write it for our edification.

To Richard Curle, April 24, 1922

I have this morning received the article[52] for the *Blue Peter*.
I think I have given you already to understand the nature of
my feelings. Indeed, I spoke to you very openly, expressing my
fundamental objection to the character you wished to give to it.
I do not for a moment expect that what I am going to say here
will convince you or influence you in the least. And, indeed, I
have neither the wish nor the right to assert my position. I will
only point out to you that my feelings in that matter are at least
as legitimate as your own. It is a strange fate that everything that
I have, of set artistic purpose, laboured to leave indefinite, suggestive, in the penumbra of initial inspiration, should have that
light turned on to it and its insignificance (as compared with, I
might say without megalomania, the ampleness of my conceptions) exposed for any fool to comment upon or even for average
minds to be disappointed with. Didn't it ever occur to you, my
dear Curle, that I knew what I was doing in leaving the facts
of my life and even of my tales in the background? Explicitness,
my dear fellow, is fatal to the glamour of all artistic work, rob-
bing it of all suggestiveness, destroying all illusion. You seem
to believe in literalness and explicitness, in facts and also in
expression. Yet nothing is more clear than the utter insignificance
of explicit statement and also its power to call attention away
from things that matter in the region of art.

There, however, I am afraid we will never agree. Your praise
of my work, allied to your analysis of its origins (which really are
not its origins at all, as you know perfectly well), sounds exag-

52. "Joseph Conrad in the East," by Curle.

gerated by the mere force of contrast. I wouldn't talk like this if I did not attach a very great value to everything you write about me and did not believe in its wide influence. It isn't a matter of literary criticism at all if I venture to point out to you that the dogmatic, excathedra tone that you have adopted in your article positively frightens me. As you tell me that you have a copy of the article by you I'll venture to make a few alterations, more to let you see what is in my mind than with any hope of convincing you. I will only remark to you, my dear, that it is generally known that you are my intimate friend, that the text carries an air of authority and that a lot of dam-fools will ascribe to me the initiative and the sanction of all the views and facts expressed. And one really could not blame them if they thought and said that I must have wanted all those facts disclosed.

All those are my personal feelings. You won't wonder at them if I call your attention to the fact that in "Youth," in which East or West are of no importance whatever, I kept the name of the Port of landing out of the record of "poeticised" sensations. The paragraph you quote of the East meeting the narrator is all right in itself; whereas directly it's connected with ... it becomes nothing at all ... is a damned hole without any beach and without any glamour and in relation to the parag. is not in tone. Therefore the par., when pinned to a particular spot, must appear diminished—a fake. And yet it is true!

However, those are all private feelings. I think too that the impression of gloom, oppression, and tragedy, is too much emphasized. You know, my dear, I have suffered from such judgements in the early days; but now the point of view, even in America, has swung in another direction; and truly I don't believe myself that my tales are gloomy, or even very tragic, that is, not with a pessimistic intention. Anyway, that reputation, whether justified or not, has deprived me of innumerable readers and I can only regret that you have found it necessary to make it, as it were, the ground-tone of your laudatory article.

To C. K. Scott Moncrieff,[53] December 17, 1922

Now as to Marcel Proust, *créateur,* I don't think he has been

53. The translator of Proust.

written about much in English, and what I have seen of it was rather superficial. I have seen him praised for his "wonderful" pictures of Paris life and provincial life. But that has been done admirably before, for us, either in love, or in hatred, or in mere irony. One critic goes so far as to say that P.'s great art reaches the universal and that in depicting his own past he reproduces for us the general experience of mankind. But I doubt it. I admire him rather for disclosing a past like nobody else's, for enlarging, as it were, the general experience of mankind by bringing to it something that has not been recorded before. However, all that is not of much importance. The important thing is that whereas before we had analysis allied to creative art, great in poetic conception, in observation, or in style, his is a creative art absolutely based on analysis. It is really more than that. He is a writer who has pushed analysis to the point when it became creative. All that crowd of personages in their infinite variety through all the gradations of the social scale are made to stand up, to live, and are rendered visible to us by the force of analysis alone. I don't say P. has got no gift of description or characterization; but to take an example from each end of the scale: Françoise, the devoted servant, and le baron de Charlus—a consummate portrait—how many descriptive lines have they got to themselves in the whole body of that immense work? Perhaps, counting the lines, half a page each. And yet no intelligent person can doubt for a moment their plastic and coloured existence. One would think that method (and P. has no other, because his method is the expression of his temperament) may be pushed too far, but as a matter of fact it is never wearisome. There may be here and there among those thousands of pages a paragraph that one might think over subtle, a bit of analysis pushed so far as to vanish into nothingness. But those are very few, and all minor, instances. The intense interest never flags because one has got the feeling that the last word is being said upon a subject much studied, much written about and of undying interest—the last word of its time. Those that have found beauty in Proust's work are perfectly right. It is there. What amazes one is its inexplicable character. In that prose so full of life there is no reverie, no emotion, no marked irony, no warmth of conviction, not even a marked rhythm to charm our fancy. It appeals to our sense of wonder and gains our assent by its veiled greatness. I don't think there ever has been in the whole of literature such an example of the power of analysis and I feel pretty safe in saying that there will never be another.

To Richard Curle, July 14, 1923

I am returning you the article[54] with two corrections as to matters of fact and one of style.

As it stands I can have nothing against it. As to my feelings that is a different matter; and I think that, looking at the intimate character of our friendship and trusting to the indulgence of your affection, I may disclose them to you without reserve.

My point of view is that this is an opportunity, if not unique then not likely to occur again in my lifetime. I was in hopes that on a general survey it could also be made an opportunity for me to get freed from that infernal tail of ships, and that obsession of my sea life which has about as much bearing on my literary existence, on my quality as a writer, as the enumeration of drawing-rooms which Thackeray frequented could have had on his gift as a great novelist. After all, I may have been a seaman, but I am a writer of prose. Indeed, the nature of my writing runs the risk of being obscured by the nature of my material. I admit it is natural; but only the appreciation of a special personal intelligence can counteract the superficial appreciation of the inferior intelligence of the mass of readers and critics. Even Doubleday was considerably disturbed by that characteristic as evidenced in press notices in America, where such headings as "Spinner of sea-yarns—master-mariner—seaman writer" and so forth predominated. I must admit that the letter-press had less emphasis than the headings; but that was simply because they didn't know the facts. That the connection of my ships with my writings stands, with my concurrence I admit, recorded in your book[55] is, of course, a fact. But that was biographical matter

54. By Curle, for the *Times Literary Supplement,* on the "Uniform Edition of Joseph Conrad's Work," published by J. M. Dent and Sons.
55. *Joseph Conrad: A Study,* (1914).

not literary. And where it stands it can do no harm. Undue prominence has been given to it since, and yet you know yourself very
well that in the body of my work barely one-tenth is what may
be called sea stuff, and even of that, the bulk, that is *Nigger*
and *Mirror*, has a very special purpose, which I emphasise myself
in my Prefaces.

Of course, there are seamen in a good many of my books. That
doesn't make them sea stories, any more than the existence of de
Barral in *Chance* (and he occupies there as much space as Captain
Anthony) makes that novel a story about the financial world.
I do wish that all those ships of mine were given a rest, but I
am afraid that when the Americans get hold of them they will
never, never, never get a rest.

The summarizing of Prefaces, though you do it extremely
well, has got this disadvantage that it doesn't give their atmosphere, and indeed it can not give their atmosphere, simply because
those pages are an intensely personal expression, much more
so than all the rest of my writing, with the exception of the
Personal Record perhaps. A question of policy arises there:
whether it is a good thing to give people the bones, as it were.
It may destroy their curiosity for the dish. I am aware, my dear
Richard, that while talking over with you the forthcoming
article, I used the word historical in connection with my fiction
or with my method, or something of the sort. I expressed myself
badly, for I certainly had not in my mind the history of the
books. What I was thinking at the time was a phrase in a long
article in the *Seccolo*. The critic remarked that there was no
difference in method or character between my fiction and my pro-
fessedly autobiographical matter, as evidenced in the *Personal
Record*. He concluded that my fiction was not historical, of
course, but had an authentic quality of development and style,
which in its ultimate effect resembled historical perspective.

My own impression is that what he really meant was that my
manner of telling, perfectly devoid of familiarity as between
author and reader, aimed essentially at the intimacy of a personal communication, without any thought for other effects. As
a matter of fact, the thought for effects is there all the same

(often at the cost of mere directness of narrative) and can be detected in my unconventional grouping and perspective, which are purely temperamental and wherein almost all my "art" consists. That, I suspect, has been the difficulty the critics felt in classifying it as romantic or realistic. Whereas, as a matter of fact, it is fluid, depending on grouping (sequence) which shifts, and on the changing lights giving varied effects of perspective.

It is in those matters gradually, but never completely, mastered that the history of my books really consists. Of course, the plastic matter of this grouping and of those lights has its importance, since without it the actuality of that grouping and that lighting could not be made evident any more than Marconi's electric waves could be made evident without the sending-out and receiving instruments. In other words, without mankind, my art, an infinitesmal thing, could not exist.

To Edward Garnett, August 8, 1923

Subjects in themselves never appear revelatory to me, if only because subjects are, so to speak, common property, lying about on the ground for one man after another to pick up and handle. That is what makes a subject such an insignificant thing, and also invests it with the potentiality of almost infinite suggestion. It depends really on him who picks it up.

II.

ESSAYS ON DIVERS BOOKS
AND AUTHORS

II.

Essays on Divers Books and Authors

"Tales of the Sea" (1898)

It is by his irresistible power to reach the adventurous side in the character, not only of his own but of all nations, that Marryat is largely human. He is the enslaver of youth, not by the literary artifices of presentation, but by the natural glamour of his own temperament. To his young heroes the beginning of life is a splendid and warlike lark, ending at last in inheritance and marriage. His novels are not the outcome of his art, but of his character, like the deeds that make up his record of naval service. To the artist his work is interesting as a completely successful expression of an unartistic nature. It is absolutely amazing to us, as the disclosure of the spirit animating the stirring time when the nineteenth century was young. There is an air of fable about it. Its loss would be irreparable, like the curtailment of national story or the loss of a historical document. It is the beginning and the embodiment of an inspiring tradition.

To this writer of the sea the sea was not an element. It was a stage, where was displayed an exhibition of valour, and of such achievement as the world had never seen before. The greatness of that achievement cannot be pronounced imaginary, since its reality has affected the destinies of nations; nevertheless, in its grandeur it has all the remoteness of an ideal. History preserves the skeleton of facts and, here and there, a figure or a name; but it is in Marryat's novels that we find the mass of the nameless, that we see them in the flesh, that we obtain a glimpse of the everyday life and an insight into the spirit animating the crowd of obscure men who knew how to build for their country such a shining monument of memories.

47

Marryat is really a writer of the Service. What sets him apart is his fidelity. His pen serves his country as well as did his professional skill and his renowned courage. His figures move about between water and sky, and the water and the sky are there only to frame the deeds of the Service. His novels, like amphibious creatures, live on the sea and frequent the shore, where they flounder deplorably. The loves and the hates of his boys are as primitive as their virtues and their vices. His women, from the beautiful Agnes to the witch-like mother of Lieutenant Vanslyperken, are, with the exception of the sailors' wives, like the shadows of what has never been. His Silvas, his Ribieras, his Shriftens, his Delmars remind us of people we have heard of somewhere, many times, without ever believing in their existence. His morality is honourable and conventional. There is cruelty in his fun and he can invent puns in the midst of carnage. His naïveties are perpetrated in a lurid light. There is an endless variety of types, all surface, with hard edges, with memorable eccentricities of outline, with a childish and heroic effect in the drawing. They do not belong to life; they belong exclusively to the Service. And yet they live; there is a truth in them, the truth of their time; a headlong, reckless audacity, an intimacy with violence, an unthinking fearlessness, and an exuberance of vitality which only years of war and victories can give. His adventures are enthralling; the rapidity of his action fascinates; his method is crude, his sentimentality, obviously incidental, is often factitious. His greatness is undeniable.

It is undeniable. To a multitude of readers the navy of to-day is Marryat's navy still. He has created a priceless legend. If he be not immortal, yet he will last long enough for the highest ambition, because he has dealt manfully with an inspiring phase in the history of that Service on which the life of his country depends. The tradition of the great past he has fixed in his pages will be cherished for ever as the guarantee of the future. He loved his country first, the Service next, the sea perhaps not at all. But the sea loved him without reserve. It gave him his professional distinction and his author's fame—a fame such as not often falls to the lot of a true artist.

At the same time, on the other side of the Atlantic, another man wrote of the sea with true artistic instinct. He is not invincibly young and heroic; he is mature and human, though for him also the stress of adventure and endeavour must end fatally in inheritance and marriage. For James Fenimore Cooper nature was not the framework, it was an essential part of existence. He could hear its voice, he could understand its silence, and he could interpret both for us in his prose with all that felicity and sureness of effect that belong to a poetical conception alone. His fame, as wide but less brilliant than that of his contemporary, rests mostly on a novel which is not of the sea. But he loved the sea and looked at it with consummate understanding. In his sea tales the sea inter-penetrates with life; it is in a subtle way a factor in the problem of existence, and, for all its greatness, it is always in touch with the men, who, bound on errands of war or gain, traverse its immense solitudes. His descriptions have the magistral ampleness of a gesture indicating the sweep of a vast horizon. They embrace the colours of sunset, the peace of starlight, the aspects of calm and storm, the great loneliness of the waters, the stillness of watchful coasts, and the alert readiness which marks men who live face to face with the promise and the menace of the sea.

He knows the men and he knows the sea. His method may be often faulty, but his art is genuine. The truth is within him. The road to legitimate realism is through poetical feeling, and he possesses that—only it is expressed in the leisurely manner of his time. He has the knowledge of simple hearts.[1] Long Tom Coffin is a monumental seaman with the individuality of life and the significance of a type. It is hard to believe that Manual and Borroughcliffe, Mr. Marble of Marble-Head, Captain Tuck of the packet-ship *Montauk,* or Daggett, the tenacious commander of

---

1. Significantly, Conrad liked James Fenimore Cooper's simple romances of adventure and, in contrast, disliked Dostoievski's "mouthings." He also dismissed *Moby Dick* as "a rather strained rhapsody with whaling for a subject and not a single sincere line in the 3 vols of it." (Letter to Humphrey Milford, January 15, 1907, quoted by Frank Macshane, "Conrad on Melville," *American Literature* XXIX, No. 4, 464.)

the *Sea Lion* of Martha's Vineyard, must pass away some day and be utterly forgotten. His sympathy is large, and his humour is as genuine—and as perfectly unaffected—as is his art. In certain passages he reaches, very simply, the heights of inspired vision.

He wrote before the great American language was born, and he wrote as well as any novelist of his time. If he pitches upon episodes redounding to the glory of the young republic, surely England has glory enough to forgive him, for the sake of his excellence, the patriotic bias at her expense. The interest of his tales is convincing and unflagging; and there runs through his work a steady vein of friendliness for the old country which the succeeding generations of his compatriots have replaced by a less definite sentiment.

Perhaps no two authors of fiction influenced so many lives and gave to so many the initial impulse towards a glorious or a useful career. Through the distances of space and time those two men of another race have shaped also the life of the writer of this appreciation. Life is life, and art is art—and truth is hard to find in either. Yet in testimony to the achievement of both these authors it may be said that, in the case of the writer at least, the youthful glamour, the headlong vitality of the one and the profound sympathy, the artistic insight of the other—to which he had surrendered—have withstood the brutal shock of facts and the wear of laborious years. He has never regretted his surrender.

"An Observer in Malaya" (1898)

In his new volume,[2] Mr. Hugh Clifford, at the beginning of the sketch entitled "At the Heels of the White Man," expresses his anxiety as to the state of England's account in the Day-Book of the Recording Angel "for the good and the bad we have done—both with the most excellent intentions." The intentions will, no doubt, count for something, though, of course, every nation's conquests are paved with good intentions; or it may be that the Recording Angel, looking compassionately at the strife of hearts, may disdain to enter into the Eternal Book the facts of a struggle which has the reward of its righteousness even on

2. *Studies in Brown Humanity.*

this earth—in victory and lasting greatness, or in defeat and humiliation.

And, also, love will count for much. If the opinion of a looker-on from afar is worth anything, Mr. Hugh Clifford's anxiety about his country's record is needless. To the Malays whom he governs, instructs, and guides he is the embodiment of the intentions, of the conscience and might of his race. And of all the nations conquering distant territories in the name of the most excellent intentions, England alone sends out men who, with such a transparent sincerity of feeling, can speak, as Mr. Clifford does, of the place of toil and exile as "the land which is very dear to me, where the best years of my life have been spent"—and where (I would stake my right hand on it) his name is pronounced with respect and affection by those brown men about whom he writes.

All these studies are on a high level of interest, though not all on the same level. The descriptive chapters, results of personal observation, seem to me the most interesting. And, indeed, in a book of this kind it is the author's personality which awakens the greatest interest; it shapes itself before one in the ring of sentences, it is seen between the lines—like the progress of a traveller in the jungle that may be traced by the sound of the *parang* chopping the swaying creepers, while the man himself is glimpsed, now and then, indistinct and passing between the trees. Thus in his very vagueness of appearance, the writer seen through the leaves of his book becomes a fascinating companion in a land of fascination.

It is when dealing with the aspects of nature that Mr. Hugh Clifford is most convincing. He looks upon them lovingly, for the land is "very dear to him," and he records his cherished impressions so that the forest, the great flood, the jungle, the rapid river, and the menacing rock dwell in the memory of the reader long after the book is closed. He does not say anything, in so many words, of his affection for those who live amid the scenes he describes so well, but his humanity is large enough to pardon us if we suspect him of such a rare weakness. In his preface he expresses the regret at not having the gifts (whatever they may be) of the kailyard school, or—looking up to a very different plane—the genius of Mr. Barrie. He has, however, gifts of his own, and his genius has served his country and his fortunes in another direction. Yet it is when attempting what he professes himself unable to do, in telling us the simple story of Umat, the punkah-puller with unaffected simplicity and half-concealed tenderness, that he comes nearest to artistic achievement.

Each study in this volume presents some idea, illustrated by a fact told without artifice, but with an effective sureness of knowledge. The story of Tukang Burok's love, related in the old man's own words, conveys the very breath of Malay thought and speech. In "His Little Bill," the coolie, Lim Teng Wah, facing his debtor, stands very distinct before us, an insignificant and tragic victim of fate with whom he had quarrelled to the death over a matter of seven dollars and sixty-eight cents. The story of "The Schooner with a Past" may be heard, from the Straits eastward, with many variations. Out in the Pacific the schooner becomes a cutter, and the pearl-divers are replaced by the Black-birds of the Labour Trade. But Mr. Hugh Clifford's variation is very good. There is a passage in it—a trifle—just the diver as seen coming from the depths, that in its dozen lines or so attains to distinct artistic value. And, scattered through the book, there are many other passages of almost equal descriptive excellence.

Nevertheless, to apply artistic standards to this book would be a fundamental error in appreciation. Like faith, enthusiasm, or heroism, art veils part of the truth of life to make the rest appear more splendid, inspiring, or sinister. And this book is only truth, interesting and futile, truth unadorned, simple and straightforward. The Resident of Pahang has the devoted friendship of Umat, the punkah-puller, he has an individual faculty of vision, a large sympathy, and the scrupulous consciousness of the good and evil in his hands. He may as well rest content with such gifts. One cannot expect to be, at the same time, a ruler of men and an irreproachable player on the flute.

"Alphonse Daudet" (1898)

It is sweet to talk decorously of the dead who are part of

our past, our indisputable possession. One must admit regretfully that to-day is but a scramble, that to-morrow may never come; it is only the precious yesterday that cannot be taken away from us. A gift from the dead, great and little, it makes life supportable, it almost makes one believe in a benevolent scheme of creation. And some kind of belief is very necessary. But the real knowledge of matters infinitely more profound than any conceivable scheme of creation is with the dead alone. That is why our talk about them should be as decorous as their silence. Their generosity and their discretion deserve nothing less at our hands; and they, who belong already to the unchangeable, would probably disdain to claim more than this from a mankind that changes its loves and its hates about every twenty-five years—at the coming of every new and wiser generation.

One of the most generous of the dead is Daudet, who, with a prodigality approaching magnificence, gave himself up to us without reserve in his work, with all his qualities and all his faults. Neither his qualities nor his faults were great, though they were by no means imperceptible. It is only his generosity that is out of the common. What strikes one most in his work is the disinterestedness of the toiler. With more talent than many bigger men, he did not preach about himself, he did not attempt to persuade mankind into a belief of his own greatness. He never posed as a scientist or as a seer, not even as a prophet; and he neglected his interests to the point of never propounding a theory for the purpose of giving a tremendous significance to his art, alone of all things, in a world that, by some strange oversight, has not been supplied with an obvious meaning. Neither did he affect a passive attitude before the spectacle of life, an attitude which in gods—and in a rare mortal here and there—may appear godlike, but assumed by some men, causes one, very unwillingly, to think of the melancholy quietude of an ape. He was not the wearisome expounder of this or that theory, here to-day and spurned to-morrow. He was not a great artist, he was not an artist at all, if you like—but he was Alphonse Daudet, a man as naïvely clear, honest, and vibrating as the sunshine of his native land; that regrettably undiscriminating sunshine which matures grapes and pumpkins alike, and cannot, of course, obtain the commendation of the very select who look at life from under a parasol.

Naturally, being a man from the South, he had a rather outspoken belief in himself, but his small distinction, worth many a greater, was in not being in bondage to some vanishing creed. He was a worker who could not compel the admiration of the few, but who deserved the affection of the many; and he may be spoken of with tenderness and regret, for he is not immortal—he is only dead. During his life, the simple man whose business it ought to have been to climb, in the name of Art, some elevation or other, was content to remain below, on the plain, amongst his creations, and take an eager part in those disasters, weaknesses, and joys which are tragic enough in their droll way, but are by no means so momentous and profound as some writers—probably for the sake of Art—would like to make us believe. There is, when one thinks of it, a considerable want of candour in the august view of life. Without doubt a cautious reticence on the subject, or even a delicately false suggestion thrown out in that direction is, in a way, praiseworthy, since it helps to uphold the dignity of man—a matter of great importance, as any one can see; still one cannot help feeling that a certain amount of sincerity would not be wholly blamable. To state, then, with studied moderation a belief that in unfortunate moments of lucidity is irresistibly borne in upon most of us—the blind agitation caused mostly by hunger and complicated by love and ferocity does not deserve either by its beauty, or its morality, or its possible results, the artistic fuss made over it. It may be consoling—for human folly is very *bizarre*—but it is scarcely honest to shout at those who struggle drowning in an insignificant pool: You are indeed admirable and great to be the victims of such a profound, of such a terrible ocean!

And Daudet was honest; perhaps because he knew no better—but he was very honest. If he saw only the surface of things it is for the reason that most things have nothing but a surface. He did not pretend—perhaps because he did not know how—he did not pretend to see any depths in a life that is only a film of unsteady appearances stretched over regions deep indeed, but which have nothing to do with the half-truths, half-thoughts, and whole illusions of existence. The road to these distant regions does not lie through the domain of Art or the domain of Science where well-known voices quarrel noisily in a misty emptiness; it is a path of toilsome silence upon which travel men simple and unknown, with closed lips, or, may be, whispering their pain softly—only to themselves.

But Daudet did not whisper; he spoke loudly, with animation, with a clear felicity of tone—as a bird sings. He saw life around him with extreme clearness, and he felt it as it is—thinner than air and more elusive than a flash of lightning. He hastened to offer it his compassion, his indignation, his wonder, his sympathy, without giving a moment of thought to the momentous issues that are supposed to lurk in the logic of such sentiments. He tolerated the little foibles, the small ruffianisms, the grave mistakes; the only thing he distinctly would not forgive was hardness of heart. This unpractical attitude would have been fatal to a better man, but his readers have forgiven him. Withal he is chivalrous to exiled queens and deformed sempstresses, he is pityingly tender to broken-down actors, to ruined gentlemen, to stupid Academicians; he is glad of the joys of the commonplace people in a commonplace way—and he never makes a secret of all this. No, the man was not an artist. What if his creations are illumined by the sunshine of his temperament so vividly that they stand before us infinitely more real than the dingy illusions surrounding our everyday existence? The misguided man is forever pottering amongst them, lifting up his voice, dotting his i's in the wrong places. He takes Tartarin by the arm, he does not conceal his interest in the Nabob's cheques, his sympathy for an honest Academician *plus bête que nature,* his hate for an architect *plus mauvais que la gale;* he is in the thick of it all. He feels with the Duc de Mora and with Felicia Ruys—and he lets you see it. He does not sit on a pedestal in the hieratic and imbecile pose of some cheap god whose greatness consists in being too stupid to care. He cares immensely for his Nabobs, his kings, his book-keepers, his Colettes, and his Saphos. He vibrates together with his universe, and with lamentable simplicity follows M. de Montpavon on that last walk along the Boulevards.[3]

"*Monsieur de Montpavon marche à la mort,*"[4] and the creator of that unlucky *gentilhomme* follows with stealthy footsteps, with wide eyes, with an impressively pointing finger. And who wouldn't look? But it is hard; it is sometimes very hard to forgive him the dotted i's, the pointing finger, this making plain of obvious mysteries. "*Monsieur de Montpavon marche à la mort,*" and presently on the crowded pavement, takes off his hat with punctilious courtesy to the doctor's wife, who, elegant and unhappy, is bound on the same pilgrimage. This is too much! We feel we cannot forgive him such meetings, the constant whisper of his presence. We feel we cannot, till suddenly the very *naïveté* of it all touches us with the revealed suggestion of a truth. Then we see that the man is not false; all this is done in transparent good faith. The man is not melodramatic; he is only picturesque. He may not be an artist, but he comes as near the truth as some of the greatest. His creations are *seen*; you can look into their very eyes, and these are as thoughtless as the eyes of any wise generation that has in its hands the fame of writers. Yes, they are seen, and the man who is not an artist is seen also, commiserating, indignant, joyous, human and alive in their very midst. Inevitably they *marchent à la mort*—and they are very near the truth of our common destiny: their fate is poignant, it is intensely interesting, and of not the slightest consequence.

"Guy de Maupassant" (1904)

To introduce Maupassant to English readers with apologetic explanations as though his art were recondite and the tendency of his work immoral would be a gratuitous impertinence.

Maupassant's conception of his art is such as one would expect from a practical and resolute mind; but in the consummate simplicity of his technique it ceases to be perceptible. This

3. Conrad's references were chosen to illustrate the range of Daudet's themes and the diversity of his characters.
4. Near the close of *Le Nabab*.

is one of its greatest qualities, and like all the great virtues it is based primarily on self-denial.

To pronounce a judgment upon the general tendency of an author is a difficult task. One could not depend upon reason alone, nor yet trust solely to one's emotions. Used together, they would in many cases traverse each other, because emotions have their own unanswerable logic. Our capacity for emotion is limited, and the field of our intelligence is restricted. Responsiveness to every feeling, combined with the penetration of every intellectual subterfuge, would end, not in judgment, but in universal absolution. *Tout comprendre c'est tout pardonner*. And in this benevolent neutrality towards the warring errors of human nature all light would go out from art and from life.

We are at liberty then to quarrel with Maupassant's attitude towards our world in which, like the rest of us, he has that share which his senses are able to give him. But we need not quarrel with him violently. If our feelings (which are tender) happen to be hurt because his talent is not exercised for the praise and consolation of mankind, our intelligence (which is great) should let us see that he is a very splendid sinner, like all those who in this valley of compromises err by over-devotion to the truth that is in them. His determinism, barren of praise, blame and consolation, has all the merit of his conscientious art. The worth of every conviction consists precisely in the steadfastness with which it is held.

Except for his philosophy, which in the case of so consummate an artist does not matter (unless to the solemn and naïve mind) Maupassant of all writers of fiction demands least forgiveness from his readers. He does not require forgiveness because he is never dull.

The interest of a reader in a work of imagination is either ethical or that of simple curiosity. Both are perfectly legitimate, since there is both a moral and an excitement to be found in a faithful rendering of life. And in Maupassant's work there is the interest of curiosity and the moral of a point of view consistently preserved and never obtruded for the end of personal gratification. The spectacle of this immense talent served by exceptional faculties and triumphing over the most thankless subjects by an unswerving singleness of purpose is in itself an admirable lesson in the power of artistic honesty, one may say of artistic virtue. The inherent greatness of the man consists in this, that he will let none of the fascinations that beset a writer working in loneliness turn him away from the straight path, from the vouchsafed vision of excellence. He will not be led into perdition by the seductions of sentiment, of eloquence, of humour, of pathos; of all that splendid pageant of faults that pass between the writer and his probity on the blank sheet of paper, like the glittering cortège of deadly sins before the austere anchorite in the desert air of Thebaïde. This is not to say that Maupassant's austerity has never faltered; but the fact remains that no tempting demon has ever succeeded in hurling him down from his high, if narrow, pedestal.

It is the austerity of his talent, of course, that is in question. Let the discriminating reader, who at times may well spare a moment or two to the consideration and enjoyment of artistic excellence, be asked to reflect a little upon the texture of two stories included in this volume: "A Piece of String," and "A Sale." How many openings the last offers for the gratuitous display of the author's wit or clever buffoonery, the first for an unmeasured display of sentiment! And both sentiment and buffoonery could have been made very good too, in a way accessible to the meanest intelligence, at the cost of truth and honesty. Here it is where Maupassant's austerity comes in. He refrains from setting his cleverness against the eloquence of the facts. There is humour and pathos in these stories; but such is the greatness of his talent, the refinement of his artistic conscience. that all his high qualities appear inherent in the very things of which he speaks, as if they had been altogether independent of his presentation. Facts, and again facts are his unique concern. That is why he is not always properly understood. His facts are so perfectly rendered that, like the actualities of life itself, they demand from the reader the faculty of observation which is rare, the power of appreciation which is generally wanting in most of us who are guided mainly by empty phrases requiring no effort, demanding from us no qualities except a vague susceptibility to emotion. Nobody has ever gained the vast applause of a crowd by the simple and clear exposition of vital facts. Words alone strung upon a convention have fascinated us as worthless glass beads strung on a thread have charmed at all times our brothers the unsophisticated savages of the islands. Now, Maupassant, of whom it has been said that he is the master of the *mot juste,* has never been a dealer in words. His wares have been, not glass beads, but polished gems: not the most rare and precious, perhaps, but of the very first water of their kind.

That he took trouble with his gems, taking them up in the rough and polishing each facet patiently, the publication of the two posthumous volumes of short stories proves abundantly. I think it proves also the assertion made here that he was by no means a dealer in words. On looking at the first feeble drafts from which so many perfect stories have been fashioned, one discovers that what has been matured, improved, brought to perfection by unwearied endeavour is not the diction of the tale, but the vision of its true shape and detail. Those first attempts are not faltering or uncertain in expression. It is the conception which is at fault. The subjects have not yet been adequately seen. His proceeding was not to group expressive words, that mean nothing, around misty and mysterious shapes dear to muddled intellects and belonging neither to earth nor to heaven. His vision by a more scrupulous, prolonged and devoted attention to the aspects of the visible world discovered at last the right words as if miraculously impressed for him upon the face of things and events. This was the particular shape taken by his inspiration; it came to him directly, honestly in the light of his day, not on the tortuous, dark roads of meditation. His realities came to him from a genuine source, from this universe of vain appearances wherein we men have found everything to make us proud, sorry, exalted, and humble.

Maupassant's renown is universal, but his popularity is restricted. It is not difficult to perceive why. Maupassant is an intensely national writer. He is so intensely national in his logic, in his clearness, in his aesthetic and moral conceptions, that he has been accepted by his countrymen without having had to pay the tribute of flattery either to the nation as a whole, or to any class, sphere or division of the nation. The truth of his art tells with an irresistible force; and he stands excused from the duty of patriotic posturing. He is a Frenchman of Frenchmen beyond question or cavil, and with that he is simple enough to be universally comprehensible. What is wanting to his universal success is the mediocrity of an obvious and appealing tenderness. He neglects to qualify his truth with the drop of facile sweetness; he forgets to strew paper roses over the tombs. The disregard of these common decencies lays him open to the charges of cruelty, cynicism, hardness. And yet it can be safely affirmed that this man wrote from the fulness of a compassionate heart. He is merciless and yet gentle with his mankind; he does not rail at their prudent fears and their small artifices; he does not despise their labours. It seems to me that he looks with an eye of profound pity upon their troubles, deceptions and misery. But he looks at them all. He sees—and does not turn away his head. As a matter of fact he is courageous.

Courage and justice are not popular virtues. The practice of strict justice is shocking to the multitude who always (perhaps from an obscure sense of guilt) attach to it the meaning of mercy. In the majority of us, who want to be left alone with our illusions, courage inspires a vague alarm. This is what is felt about Maupassant. His qualities, to use the charming and popular phrase, are not lovable. Courage being a force will not masquerade in the robes of affected delicacy and restraint. But if his courage is not of a chivalrous stamp, it cannot be denied that it is never brutal for the sake of effect. The writer of these few reflections, inspired by a long and intimate acquaintance with the work of the man, has been struck by the appreciation of Maupassant manifested by many women gifted with tenderness and intelligence. Their more delicate and audacious souls are good judges of courage. Their finer penetration has discovered his genuine masculinity without display, his virility without a pose. They have discerned in his faithful dealings with the world that enterprising and fearless temperament, poor in ideas but rich in power, which appeals most to the feminine mind.

It cannot be denied that he thinks very little. In him extreme energy of perception achieves great results, as in men of action the energy of force and desire. His view of intellectual problems is perhaps more simple than their nature warrants; still a man who has written "Yvette" cannot be accused of want of subtlety But one cannot insist enough upon this, that his subtlety, his humour, his grimness, though no doubt they are his own, are never presented otherwise but as belonging to our life, as found in nature, whose beauties and cruelties alike breathe the spirit of serene unconsciousness.

Maupassant's philosophy of life is more temperamental than rational. He expects nothing from gods or men. He trusts his senses for information and his instinct for deductions. It may seem that he has made but little use of his mind. But let me be clearly understood. His sensibility is really very great; and it is impossible to be sensible, unless one thinks vividly, unless one thinks correctly, starting from intelligible premises to an unsophisticated conclusion.

This is literary honesty. It may be remarked that it does not differ very greatly from the ideal of honesty of the respectable majority, from the honesty of lawgivers, of warriors, of kings, of bricklayers, of all those who express their fundamental sentiment in the ordinary course of their activities, by the work of their hands.

The work of Maupassant's hands is honest. He thinks sufficiently to concrete his fearless conclusions in illuminative instances. He renders them with that exact knowledge of the means and that absolute devotion to the aim of creating a true effect—which is art. He is the most accomplished of narrators.

It is evident that Maupassant looked upon his mankind in another spirit than those writers who make haste to submerge the difficulties of our holding-place in the universe under a flood of false and sentimental assumptions. Maupassant was a true and dutiful lover of our earth. He says himself in one of his descriptive passages: *"Nous autres que séduit la terre..."* It was true. The earth had for him a compelling charm. He looks upon her august and furrowed face with the fierce insight of real passion. His is the power of detecting the one immutable quality that matters in the changing aspects of nature and under the ever-shifting surface of life. To say that he could not embrace in his glance all its magnificence and all its misery is only to say that he was human. He lays claim to nothing that his match-less vision has not made his own. This creative artist has the true imagination; he never condescends to invent anything; he sets up no empty pretences. And he stoops to no littleness in his art—least of all to the miserable vanity of a catching phrase.

"Anatole France" (1904)

The latest volume[5] of M. Anatole France purports, by the declaration of its title-page, to contain several profitable narra-tives. The story of Crainquebille's encounter with human justice stands at the head of them; a tale of a well-bestowed charity closes the book with the touch of playful irony characteristic of the writer on whom the most distinguished amongst his literary countrymen have conferred the rank of Prince of Prose.

Never has a dignity been better borne. M. Anatole France is a good prince. He knows nothing of tyranny but much of com-passion. The detachment of his mind from common errors and current superstitions befits the exalted rank he holds in the Commonwealth of Literature. It is just to suppose that the clamour of the tribes in the forum had little to do with his elevation. Their elect are of another stamp. They are such as their need of precipitate action requires. He is the Elect of the Senate—the Senate of Letters—whose Conscript Fathers have recognized him as *primus inter pares;* a post of pure honour and of no privilege.

It is a good choice. First, because it is just, and next, because it is safe. The dignity will suffer no diminution in M. Anatole France's hands. He is worthy of a great tradition, learned in the lessons of the past, concerned with the present, and as earnest as to the future as a good prince should be in his public action. It is a Republican dignity. And M. Anatole France, with his

5. *Crainquebille, Putois, Riquet et autres récits profitables.* (1904).

sceptical insight into all forms of government, is a good Republican. He is indulgent to the weaknesses of the people, and perceives that political institutions, whether contrived by the wisdom of the few or the ignorance of the many, are incapable of securing the happiness of mankind. He perceives this truth in the serenity of his soul and in the elevation of his mind. He expresses his convictions with measure, restraint and harmony, which are indeed princely qualities. He is a great analyst of illusions. He searches and probes their innermost recesses as if they were realities made of an eternal substance. And therein consists his humanity; this is the expression of his profound and unalterable compassion. He will flatter no tribe, no section in the forum or in the marketplace. His lucid thought is not beguiled into false pity or into the common weakness of affection. He feels that men born in ignorance as in the house of an enemy, and condemned to struggle with error and passions through endless centuries, should be spared the supreme cruelty of a hope for ever deferred. He knows that our best hopes are irrealisable; that it is the almost incredible misfortune of mankind, but also its highest privilege, to aspire towards the impossible; that men have never failed to defeat their highest aims by the very strength of their humanity which can conceive the most gigantic tasks but leaves them disarmed before their irremediable littleness. He knows this well because he is an artist and a master; but he knows, too, that only in the continuity of effort there is a refuge from despair for minds less clear-seeing and philosophic than his own. Therefore he wishes us to believe and to hope, preserving in our activity the consoling illusion of power and intelligent purpose. He is a good and politic prince.

"The majesty of Justice is contained entire in each sentence pronounced by the judge in the name of the sovereign people. Jérome Crainquebille, hawker of vegetables, became aware of the august aspect of the law as he stood indicted before the tribunal of the higher Police Court on a charge of insulting a constable of the force." With this exposition begins the first tale of M. Anatole France's latest volume.

The bust of the Republic and the image of the Crucified

Christ appear side by side above the bench occupied by the President Bourriche and his two Assessors; all the laws divine and human are suspended over the head of Crainquebille.

From the first visual impression of the accused and of the court the author passes by a characteristic and natural turn to the historical and moral significance of those two emblems of State and Religion whose accord is only possible to the confused reasoning of an average man. But the reasoning of M. Anatole France is never confused. His reasoning is clear and informed by a profound erudition. Such is not the case of Crainquebille, a street-hawker, charged with insulting the constituted power of society in the person of a policeman. The charge is not true, nothing was further from his thoughts; but, amazed by the novelty of his position, he does not reflect that the Cross on the wall perpetuates the memory of a sentence which for nineteen hundred years all the Christian peoples have looked upon as a grave miscarriage of justice. He might well have challenged the President to pronounce any sort of sentence, if it were merely to forty-eight hours of simple imprisonment, in the name of the Crucified Redeemer.

He might have done so. But Crainquebille, who has lived pushing every day for half a century his hand-barrow loaded with vegetables through the streets of Paris, has not a philosophic mind. Truth to say he has nothing. He is one of the disinherited. Properly speaking, he has no existence at all, or, to be strictly truthful, he had no existence till M. Anatole France's philosophic mind and human sympathy have called him up from his nothingness for our pleasure, and, as the title-page of the book has it, no doubt for our profit also.

Therefore we behold him in the dock, a stranger to all historical, political or social considerations which can be brought to bear upon his case. He remains lost in astonishment. Penetrated with respect, overwhelmed with awe, he is ready to trust the judge upon the question of his transgression. In his conscience he does not think himself culpable; but M. Anatole France's philosophical mind discovers for us that he feels all the insignificance of such a thing as the conscience of a mere street-hawker in the face of the symbols of the law and before the ministers of social repression. Crainquebille is innocent; but already the young advocate, his defender, has half persuaded him of his guilt.

On this phrase practically ends the introductory chapter of the story which, as the author's dedication states, has inspired an admirable draughtsman and a skilful dramatist, each in his art, to a vision of tragic grandeur. And this opening chapter without a name—consisting of two and a half pages, some four hundred words at most—is a masterpiece of insight and simplicity, resumed in M. Anatole France's distinction of thought and in his princely command of words.

It is followed by six more short chapters, concise and full, delicate and complete like the petals of a flower, presenting to us the Adventure of Crainquebille—Crainquebille before the Justice—An Apology for the President of the Tribunal—Of the Submission of Crainquebille to the Laws of the Republic—Of his Attitude before the Public Opinion, and so on to the chapter of the Last Consequences. We see, created for us in his outward form and innermost perplexity, the old man degraded from his high estate of a law-abiding street-hawker and driven to insult, really this time, the majesty of the social order in the person of another police-constable. It is not an act of revolt, and still less of revenge. Crainquebille is too old, too resigned, too weary, too guileless to raise the black standard of insurrection. He is cold and homeless and starving. He remembers the warmth and the food of the prison. He perceives the means to get back there. Since he has been locked up, he argues with himself, for uttering words which, as a matter of fact he did not say, he will go forth now, and to the first policeman he meets will say those very words in order to be imprisoned again. Thus reasons Crainquebille with simplicity and confidence. He accepts facts. Nothing surprises him. But all the phenomena of social organisation and of his own life remain for him mysterious to the end. The description of the policeman in his short cape and hood, who stands quite still, under the light of a street lamp at the edge of the pavement shining with the wet of a rainy autumn evening along the whole extent of a long and deserted thoroughfare, is a perfect piece of imaginative precision. From under the edge of the hood his eyes look upon Crainquebille, who has just uttered in an uncertain voice the sacramental, insulting phrase of the popular slang—*Mort aux vaches!* They look upon him shining in the deep shadow of the hood with an expression of sadness, vigilance, and contempt.

He does not move. Crainquebille, in a feeble and hesitating voice, repeats once more the insulting words. But this policeman is full of philosophic superiority, disdain, and indulgence. He refuses to take in charge the old and miserable vagabond who stands before him shivering and ragged in the drizzle. And the ruined Crainquebille, victim of a ridiculous miscarriage of justice, appalled at this magnanimity, passes on hopelessly down the street full of shadows where the lamps gleam each in a ruddy halo of falling mist.

M. Anatole France can speak for the people. This prince of the Senate is invested with the tribunitian power. M. Anatole France is something of a Socialist; and in that respect he seems to depart from his sceptical philosophy. But as an illustrious statesman, now no more, a great prince too, with an ironic mind and a literary gift, has sarcastically remarked in one of his public speeches: "We are all Socialists now." And in the sense in which it may be said that we all in Europe are Christians that is true enough. To many of us Socialism is merely an emotion. An emotion is much and is also less than nothing. It is the initial impulse. The real Socialism of to-day is a religion. It has its dogmas. The value of the dogma does not consist in its truthfulness, and M. Anatole France, who loves truth, does not love dogma. Only, unlike religion, the cohesive strength of Socialism lies not in its dogmas but in its ideal. It is perhaps a too materialistic ideal, and the mind of M. Anatole France may not find in it either comfort or consolation. It is not to be doubted that he suspects this himself; but there is something reposeful in the finality of popular conceptions. M. Anatole France, a good prince and a good Republican, will suceed no doubt in being a good Socialist. He will disregard the stupidity of the dogma and the unlovely form of the ideal. His art will find its own beauty in the imaginative presentation of wrongs, of errors, and miseries that call aloud for redress. M. Anatole France is humane. He is also human. He may be able to discard his philosophy; to forget that the evils are many and the remedies are few, that there is no universal panacea, that fatality is invincible, that there is an implacable menace of death in the triumph of the humanitarian idea. He may forget all that because love is stronger than truth.

Besides Crainquebille this volume contains sixteen other stories and sketches. To define them it is enough to say that they are written in M. Anatole France's prose. One sketch entitled "Riquet" may be found incorporated in the volume of "Monsieur Bergeret à Paris." "Putois" is a remarkable little tale, significant, humorous, amusing, and symbolic. It concerns the career of a man born in the utterance of a hasty and untruthful excuse made by a lady at a loss how to decline without offence a very pressing invitation to dinner from a very tyrannical aunt. This happens in a provincial town, and the lady says in effect "Impossible, my dear aunt. To-morrow I am expecting the gardener." And the garden she glances at is a poor garden; it is a wild garden; its extent is insignificant and its neglect seems beyond remedy. "A gardener! What for?" asks the aunt. "To work in the garden." And the poor lady is abashed at the transparence of her evasion. But the lie is told, it is believed, and she sticks to it. When the masterful old aunt inquires, "What is the man's name, my dear?" she answers brazenly, "His name is Putois." "Where does he live?" "Oh, I don't know; anywhere. He won't give his address. One leaves a message for him here and there." "Oh! I see," says the other; "he is a sort of ne'er do well, an idler, a vagabond. I advise you, my dear, to be careful how you let such a creature into your grounds; but I have a large garden, and when you do not want his services I shall find him some work to do, and see he does it too. Tell your Putois to come and see me." And thereupon Putois is born; he stalks abroad, invisible, upon his career of vagabondage and crime, stealing melons from gardens and teaspoons from pantries, indulging his licentious proclivities; becoming the talk of the town and of the country-

side; seen simultaneously in far-distant places; pursued by gen-
darmes, whose brigadier assures the uneasy householders that he
"knows that scamp very well, and won't be long in laying his
hands upon him." A detailed description of his person collected
from the information furnished by various people appears in the
columns of a local newspaper. Putois lives in his strength and
malevolence. He lives after the manner of legendary heroes, of
the gods of Olympus. He is the creation of the popular mind.
There comes a time when even the innocent originator of that
mysterious and potent evil-doer is induced to believe for a moment that he may have a real and tangible presence. All this is
told with the wit and the art and the philosophy which is
familiar to M. Anatole France's readers and admirers. For it is
difficult to read M. Anatole France without admiring him. He has
the princely gift of arousing a spontaneous loyalty, but with
this difference, that the consent of our reason has its place by the
side of our enthusiasm. He is an artist. As an artist he awakens
emotion. The quality of his art remains, as an inspiration, fascinating and inscrutable; but the proceedings of his thought
compel our intellectual admiration.

In this volume the trifle called "The Military Manoeuvres at
Montil," apart from its far-reaching irony, embodies incidentally
the very spirit of automobilism. Somehow or other, how you
cannot tell, the flight over the country in a motor-car, its sensations, its fatigue, its vast topographical range, its incidents down
to the bursting of a tyre, are brought home to you with all the
force of high imaginative perception. It would be out of place to
analyse here the means by which the true impression is conveyed
so that the absurd rushing about of General Decuir, in a 30-horse-
power car, in search of his cavalry brigade, becomes to you a
more real experience than any day-and-night run you may ever
have taken yourself. Suffice it to say that M. Anatole France had
thought the thing worth doing and that it becomes, in virtue of
his art, a distinct achievement. And there are other sketches in
this book, more or less slight, but all worthy of regard—the childhood's recollections of Professor Bergeret and his sister Zoé; the
dialogue of the two upright judges and the conversation of their
horses; the dream of M. Jean Marteau, aimless, extravagant,

apocalyptic, and of all the dreams one ever dreamt, the most essentially dreamlike. The vision of M. Anatole France, the Prince of Prose, ranges over all the extent of his realm, indulgent, and penetrating, disillusioned and curious, finding treasures of truth and beauty concealed from less gifted magicians. Contemplating the exactness of his images and the justice of his judgment, the freedom of his fancy and the fidelity of his purpose, one becomes aware of the futility of literary watch-words and the vanity of all the schools of fiction. Not that M. Anatole France is a wild and untrammelled genius. He is not that. Issued legitimately from the past, he is mindful of his high descent. He has a critical temperament joined to creative power. He surveys his vast domain in a spirit of princely moderation that knows nothing of excesses but much of restraint.

ii

"L'ILE DES PINGOUINS"

M. Anatole France, historian and adventurer, has given us many profitable histories of saints and sinners, of Roman procurators and of officials of the Third Republic, of *grandes dames* and of dames not so very grand, of ornate Latinists and of inarticulate street-hawkers, of priests and generals—in fact, the history of all humanity as it appears to his penetrating eye, serving a mind marvellously incisive in its scepticism, and a heart that, of all contemporary hearts gifted with a voice, contains the greatest treasure of charitable irony. As to M. Anatole France's adventures, these are well-known. They lie open to this prodigal world in the four volumes of the Vie Littéraire, describing the adventures of a choice amongst masterpieces. For such is the romantic view M. Anatole France takes of the life of a literary critic. History and adventure, then, seem to be the chosen fields for the magnificent evolutions of M. Anatole France's prose; but no material limits can stand in the way of a genius. The latest book from his pen—which may be called golden, as the lips of an eloquent saint once upon a time were acclaimed golden by the faithful—this latest book is, up to a certain point, a book of travel.

I would not mislead a public whose confidence I court. The book is not a record of globe-trotting. I regret it. It would have been a joy to watch M. Anatole France pouring the clear elixir compounded of his Pyrrhonic philosophy, his Benedictine erudition, his gentle wit and most humane irony into such an unpromising and opaque vessel. He would have attempted it in a spirit of benevolence towards his fellow men and of compassion for that life of the earth which is but a vain and transitory illusion. M. Anatole France is a great magician, yet there seem to be tasks which he dare not face. For he is also a sage.

It is a book of ocean travel—not, however, as understood by Herr Ballin of Hamburg, the Machiavel of the Atlantic. It is a book of exploration and discovery—not, however, as conceived by an enterprising journal and a shrewdly philanthropic king of the nineteenth century. It is nothing so recent as that. It dates much further back; long, long before the dark age when Krupp of Essen wrought at his steel plates and a German Emperor condescendingly suggested the last improvements in ships' dining-tables. The best idea of the inconceivable antiquity of that enterprise I can give you is by stating the nature of the explorer's ship. It was a trough of stone, a vessel of hollowed granite.

The explorer was St. Maël, a saint of Armorica. I had never heard of him before, but I believe now in his arduous existence with a faith which is a tribute to M. Anatole France's pious earnestness and delicate irony. St. Maël existed. It is distinctly stated of him that his life was a progress in virtue. Thus it seems that there may be saints that are not progressively virtuous. St. Maël was not of that kind. He was industrious. He evangelised the heathen. He erected two hundred and eighteen chapels and seventy-four abbeys. Indefatigable navigator of the faith, he drifted casually in the miraculous trough of stone from coast to coast and from island to island along the northern seas. At the age of eighty-four his high stature was bowed by his long labours, but his sinewy arms preserved their vigour and his rude eloquence had lost nothing of its force.

A nautical devil tempting him by the worldly suggestion of fitting out his desultory, miraculous trough with mast, sail, and rudder for swifter progression (the idea of haste has sprung from the pride of Satan), the simple old saint lent his ear to the subtle arguments of the progressive enemy of mankind.

The venerable St. Maël fell away from grace by not perceiving at once that a gift of heaven cannot be improved by the contrivances of human ingenuity. His punishment was adequate. A terrific tempest snatched the rigged ship of stone in its whirlwinds, and, to be brief, the dazed St. Maël was stranded violently on the Island of Penguins.

The saint wandered away from the shore. It was a flat, round island whence rose in the centre a conical mountain capped with clouds. The rain was falling incessantly—a gentle, soft rain which caused the simple saint to exclaim in great delight: "This is the island of tears, the island of contrition!"

Meantime the inhabitants had flocked in their tens of thousands to an amphitheatre of rocks; they were penguins; but the holy man, rendered deaf and purblind by his years, mistook excusably the multitude of silly, erect, and self-important birds for a human crowd. At once he began to preach to them the doctrine of salvation. Having finished his discourse he lost no time in administering to his interesting congregation the sacrament of baptism.

If you are at all a theologian you will see that it was no mean adventure to happen to a well-meaning and zealous saint. Pray reflect on the magnitude of the issues! It is easy to believe what M. Anatole France says, that, when the baptism of the penguins became known in Paradise, it caused there neither joy nor sorrow, but a profound sensation.

M. Anatole France is no mean theologian himself. He reports with great casuistical erudition the debates in the saintly council assembled in Heaven for the consideration of an event so disturbing to the economy of religious mysteries. Ultimately the baptized penguins had to be turned into human beings; and together with the privilege of sublime hopes these innocent birds received the curse of original sin, with the labours, the miseries, the passions, and the weaknesses attached to the fallen condition of humanity.

At this point M. Anatole France is again a historian. From being the Hakluyt of a saintly adventurer he turns (but more concisely) into the Gibbon of Imperial Penguins. Tracing the development of their civilization, the absurdity of their desires, the pathos of their folly and the ridiculous littleness of their quarrels, his golden pen lightens by relevant but unpuritanical anecdotes the austerity of a work devoted to a subject so grave as the Polity of Penguins. It is a very admirable treatment, and I hasten to congratulate all men of receptive mind on the feast of wisdom which is theirs for the mere plucking of a book from a shelf.

"A Glance at Two Books" (1904)

The national English novelist seldom regards his work—the exercise of his art—as an achievement of active life by which he will produce certain definite effects upon the emotions of his readers, but simply as an instinctive, often unreasoned outpouring of his own emotions. He does not go about building up his book with a precise intention and a steady mind. It never occurs to him that a book is a deed, that the writing of it is an enterprise as much as the conquest of a colony. He has no such clear conception of his craft. Writing from a full heart, he liberates his soul for the satisfaction of his own sentiment; and when he has finished the scene he is at liberty to strike his forehead and exclaim: "this is genius!"

Thackeray is reported to have done this, and there is no reason why any novelist of his type should not. He is, as a matter of fact, writing lyrically (a lyric is the expression of a mood); he is expressing his own moods: I take what the gods give me, he says in all humility, and when the godhead inspires him with what seems good to his heart, to his imagination, to his tenderness or to his indignation, he may say, and use the words literally, "This is genius!"

It is. And it is probably the reason why the distinctively English novelist is always at his best in denunciations of institutions, of types or of conventionalised Society.

It is comparatively easy for us, when we are really moved by the clearness of our vision, to convince an audience that Messrs. A., B. and C. are callous, ferocious or cowardly. We should have to use much more conscious art to give a permanent impression of those gentlemen as purely altruist.

Thus Mr. Osborne, the hard merchant,[6] father of Captain Osborne, is more definite and flawless than many of Thackeray's so-called good characters: and thus Mr. Pecksniff[7] is, through scorn and dislike, rendered more memorable than the brothers Cherryble.[8] It is not perhaps so much that these distinguished writers were completely incapable of loving their fellow-men simply as men, exposed to suffering, temptation and affliction, as that, neglecting the one indispensable thing, neglecting to use their powers of selection and observation, they emotionally excelled in rendering the disagreeable. And that is easy. To find beauty, grace, charm in the bitterness of truth is a graver task.

Thackeray, we imagine, did not love his gentle heroines. He did not love them. He was in love with the sentiments they represented. He was, in fact, in love with what does not exist—and that is why Amelia Osborne does not exist, either in colour, in shape, in grace, in goodness. Turgeniev probably did not love his Lisa, a most pathetic, pure, charming and profound creation, for what she was, in her creator's mind. He loved her disinterestedly, as it were, out of pure warmth of heart, as a human being in the tumult and hazard of life. And that is why we must feel, suffer and live with that wonderful creation. That is why she is as real to us as her stupid mother, as the men of the story, as the sombre Varvard, and all the others that may be called the unpleasant characters in *The House of Gentlefolk*.

I have been reading two books in English which have attracted a good deal of intelligent attention, but neither seems to have been considered as attentively as they might have been from this point of view. The one, *The Island Pharisees*, by Mr. John Galsworthy, is a very good example of the national novel: the other, *Green Mansions*, by Mr. W. H. Hudson, is a proof that

6. In *Vanity Fair*.
7. The delightful hypocrite in Dickens' *Martin Chuzzlewit*.
8. The benefactors of Nicholas in Dickens' *Nicholas Nickleby*.

love, the pure love of rendering the external aspects of things, can exist side by side with the national novel in English letters.

Mr. Galsworthy's hero in *The Island Pharisees,* during his pilgrimage right across the English social system, asks himself: "Why? Why is not the world better? Why are we all humbugs? Why is the social system so out of order?" And he gets no answer to his questions, for, indeed, in his mood no answer is possible, neither is an answer needed for the absolute value of the book. Shelton is dissatisfied with his own people, who are good people, with artists, whose "at homes" he drops into, with marriage settlements and wedding services, with cosmopolitan vagabonds, with Oxford dons, with policemen—with himself and his love.

The exposition of all the characters in the book is done with an almost unerring touch, with a touch indeed that recalls the sureness and the delicacy of Turgeniev's handling. They all live— and Mr. Galsworthy—or rather his hero, John Shelton, finds them all Pharisaic. It is as if he were championing against all these "good" people some intangible lost cause, some altruism, some higher truth that for ever seems to soar out of his grasp. It is not exactly that Shelton is made to uphold the bitter morality of the cosmopolitan vagabond; for Mr. Galsworthy is too good an artist and too good a philosopher to make his Louis Ferrand impossibly attractive or even possibly cynical.

Shelton upholds, not so much the fact as the ideal of honest revolt; he is the knight-errant of a general idea. Therein he ceases to resemble the other heroes of English fiction who are the champions of particular ideas, tilting sometimes at windmills (for the human power of self-deception is great), but with a particular foe always in their eye. Sheldon distinctly does not couch his lance against a windmill. He is a knight-errant, dis-armed and faithful, riding forlorn to an inevitable defeat; his adversary is a giant of a thousand heads and a thousand arms, a monster at once perfectly human and altogether soulless. Though nobody dies in the book, it is really the record of a long and tragic adventure, whose tragedy is not so much in the event as in the very atmosphere, in the cold moral dusk in which the hero moves as if impelled by some fatal whisper, without a sword, corselet or helmet.

Amadis de Gaul would have struck a head off and counted it a doughty deed; Dickens would have flung himself upon pen and paper and made a caricature of the monster, would have flung at him an enormous joke vibrating with the stress of cheap emotions; Shelton, no legendary knight and being no humorist (but, like many simpler men, impelled by the destiny he carries within his breast), goes forth to be delivered, bound hand and foot, to the monster by his charming and limited Antonia. He is classed as an outsider by the men in the best clubs, and his prospective mother-in-law tells him not to talk about things. He comes to grief socially, because in a world, which everyone is interested to go on calling the best of all possible worlds, he has insisted upon touching in challenge all the shields hung before all the comfortable tents: the immaculate shield of his fiancée, of his mother-in-law, of the best men in the best clubs. He gets himself called and thought of as Unsound; and there in his social world the monster has made an end of him.

This is the end of the book; and with it there comes into the world of letters the beginning of Mr. Galsworthy as a novelist. For, paradoxically, a society that could not stand a Hamlet in the flesh at any price will read about him and welcome him on the stage to the end of its own incorrigible existence. This book, where each page lives with an interest of its own, has for its only serious artistic defect that of not being long enough, and for its greatest quality that of a sincere feeling of compassionate regard for mankind expressed nationally through a fine indignation. Of the promise of its method, of the accomplished felicity of its phrasing, I have left myself no room to speak.

The innermost heart of *Green Mansions,* which are the forests of Mr. Hudson's book, is tender, is tranquil, is steeped in that pure love of the external beauty of things that seems to breathe upon us from the pages of Turgeniev's work. The charming quietness of the style soothes the hard irritation of our daily life in the presence of a fine and sincere, of a deep and pellucid personality. If the other book's gift is lyric, *Green Mansions* comes to us with the tone of the elegy. There are the voices of the birds, the shadows of the forest leaves, the Indians gliding through them armed with their blow-pipes, the monkeys peering sadly from above, the very spiders! The birds search for insects; spiders hunt their prey.

Now as I sat looking down on the leaves and the small dancing shadow, scarcely thinking of what I was looking at, I noticed a small spider with a flat body and short legs creep cautiously out on to the upper surface of a small leaf. Its pale red colour, barred with velvet black, first drew my attention to it; for it was beautiful to the eye ...

"It was beautiful to the eye," so it drew the attention of Mr. Hudson's hero. In that phrase dwells the very soul of the book whose voice is soothing like a soft voice speaking steadily amongst the vivid changes of a dream. Only you must note that the spider had come to hunt its prey, having mistaken the small dancing shadow for a fly, because it is there in the fundamental difference of vision lies the difference between book and book. The other type of novelist might say: "It attracted my attention because it was savage and cruel and beautiful only to the eye. And I have written of it here so that it may be hated and laughed at for ever. For, of course, being greedy and rapacious it was stupid also, mistaking a shadow for substance, like certain evil men, we have heard of, that go about crying up the excellence of the world."

"Books" (1905)

"I have not read this author's books, and if I have read them I have forgotten what they were about."

These words are reported as having been uttered in our midst not a hundred years ago, publicly, from the seat of justice, by a civic magistrate. The words of our municipal rulers have a solemnity and importance far above the words of other mortals, because our municipal rulers more than any other variety of our governors and masters represent the average wisdom, temperament, sense and virtue of the community. This generalisation, it ought to be promptly said in the interests of eternal justice (and recent friendship), does not apply to the United States of America. There, if one may believe the long and helpless indignations of their daily and weekly Press, the majority of municipal rulers appear to be thieves of a particularly irrepressible sort. But this by the way. My concern is with a statement issuing from the average temperament and the average wisdom of a great and wealthy community, and uttered by a civic magistrate obviously without fear and without reproach.

I confess I am pleased with his temper, which is that of prudence. "I have not read the books," he says, and immediately he adds, "and if I have read them I have forgotten." This is excellent caution. And I like his style: it is unartificial and bears the stamp of manly sincerity. As a reported piece of prose this declaration is easy to read and not difficult to believe. Many books have not been read; still more have been forgotten. As a piece of civic oratory this declaration is strikingly effective. Calculated to fall in with the bent of the popular mind, so familiar with all forms of forgetfulness, it has also the power to stir up a subtle emotion while it starts a train of thought—and what great force can be expected from human speech? But it is in naturalness that this declaration is perfectly delightful, for there is nothing more natural than for a grave City Father to forget what the books he has read once—long ago—in his giddy youth may be—were about.

And the books in question are novels, or at any rate, were written as novels. I proceed thus cautiously (following my illustrious example) because being without fear and desiring to remain as far as possible without reproach, I confess at once that I have not read them.

I have not; and of the million persons or more who are said to have read them, I never met one yet with the talent of lucid exposition sufficiently developed to give me a connected account of what they are about. But they are books, part and parcel of humanity, and as such, in their ever-increasing, jostling multitude, they are worthy of regard, admiration, and compassion.

Especially of compassion. It has been said a long time ago that books have their fate. They have, and it is very much like the destiny of man. They share with us the great incertitude of ignominy or glory—of severe justice and senseless persecution—of calumny and misunderstanding—the shame of undeserved success. Of all the inanimate objects, of all men's creations, books are the nearest to us, for they contain our very thought, our ambitions, our indignations, our illusions, our fidelity to truth, and our persistent leaning towards error. But most of all they resemble us in their precarious hold on life. A bridge constructed according to the rules of the art of bridge-building is certain of a long, honourable and useful career. But a book as good in its way as the bridge may perish obscurely on the very day of its birth. The art of their creators is not sufficient to give them more than a moment of life. Of the books born from the restlessness, the inspiration, and the vanity of human minds those that the Muses would love best lie more than all others under the menace of an early death. Sometimes their defects will save them. Sometimes a book fair to see may—to use a lofty expression—have no individual soul. Obviously a book of that sort cannot die. It can only crumble into dust. But the best of books drawing sustenance from the sympathy and memory of men have lived on the brink of destruction, for men's memories are short, and their sympathy is, we must admit, a very fluctuating, unprincipled emotion.

No secret of eternal life for our books can be found amongst the formulas of art, any more than for our bodies in a prescribed combination of drugs. This is not because some books are not worthy of enduring life, but because the formulas of art are dependent on things variable, unstable and untrustworthy; on human sympathies, on prejudices, on likes and dislikes, on the sense of virtue and the sense of propriety, on beliefs and theories that, indestructible in themselves, always change their form—often in the lifetime of one fleeting generation.

ii

Of all books, novels, which the Muses should love, make a serious claim on our compassion. The art of the novelist is simple. At the same time it is the most elusive of all creative arts, the most liable to be obscured by the scruples of its servants and votaries, the one pre-eminently destined to bring trouble to the mind and the heart of the artist. After all, the creation of a world is not a small undertaking except perhaps to the divinely gifted. In truth every novelist must begin by creating for himself a world, great or little, in which he can honestly believe. This world cannot be made otherwise than in his own image: it is fated to remain individual and a little mysterious, and yet it must resemble something already familiar to the experience, the thoughts and the sensations of his readers. At the heart of fiction, even the least worthy of the name, some sort of truth can be found—if only the truth of a childish theatrical ardour in the game of life, as in the novels of Dumas the father. But the fair truth of human delicacy can be found in Mr. Henry James's novels; and the comical, appalling truth of human rapacity let loose amongst the spoils of existence lives in the monstrous world created by Balzac. The pursuit of happiness by means lawful and unlawful, through resignation or revolt, by the clever manipulation of conventions or by solemn hanging on to the skirts of the latest scientific theory, is the only theme that can be legitimately developed by the novelist who is the chronicler of the adventures of mankind amongst the dangers of the kingdom of the earth. And the kingdom of this earth itself, the ground upon which his individualities stand, stumble, or die, must enter into his scheme of faithful record. To encompass all this in one harmonious conception is a great feat; and even to attempt it deliberately with serious intention, not from the senseless prompting of an ignorant heart, is an honourable ambition. For it requires some courage to step in calmly where fools may be eager to rush. As a distinguished and successful French novelist once observed of fiction, "C'est un art *trop* difficile."

It is natural that the novelist should doubt his ability to cope with his task. He imagines it more gigantic than it is. And yet literary creation being only one of the legitimate forms of human activity has no value but on the condition of not excluding the fullest recognition of all the more distinct forms of action. This condition is sometimes forgotten by the man of letters, who often, especially in his youth, is inclined to lay a claim of exclusive superiority for his own amongst all the other tasks of the human mind. The mass of verse and prose may glimmer here and there with the glow of a divine spark, but in the sum of human effort it has no special importance. There is no justificative formula for its existence any more than for any other artistic achievement. With the rest of them it is destined to be forgotten, without, perhaps, leaving the faintest trace. Where a novelist has an advantage over the workers in other fields of thought is in his privilege of freedom—the freedom of expression and the freedom of confessing his innermost beliefs—which should console him for the hard slavery of the pen.

iii

Liberty of imagination should be the most precious possession of a novelist. To try voluntarily to discover the fettering dogmas of some romantic, realistic, or naturalistic creed in the free work of its own inspiration, is a trick worthy of human perverseness which, after inventing an absurdity, endeavours to find for it a pedigree of distinguished ancestors. It is a weakness of inferior minds when it is not the cunning device of those who, uncertain of their talent, would seek to add lustre to it by the authority of a school. Such, for instance, are the high priests who have proclaimed Stendhal for a prophet of Naturalism. But Stendhal himself would have accepted no limitation of his freedom. Stendhal's mind was of the first order. His spirit above must be raging with a peculiarly Stendhalesque scorn and indignation. For the truth is that more than one kind of intellectual cowardice hides behind the literary formulas. And Stendhal was pre-eminently courageous. He wrote his two great novels, which so few people have read, in a spirit of fearless liberty.

It must not be supposed that I claim for the artist in fiction the freedom of moral Nihilism. I would require from him many acts of faith of which the first would be the cherishing of an undying hope; and hope, it will not be contested, implies all the piety of effort and renunciation. It is the God-sent form of trust in the magic force and inspiration belonging to the life of this earth. We are inclined to forget that the way of excellence is in the intellectual, as distinguished from emotional, humility. What one feels so hopelessly barren in declared pessimism is just its arrogance. It seems as if the discovery made by many men at various times that there is much evil in the world were a source of proud and unholy joy unto some of the modern writers. That frame of mind is not the proper one in which to approach seriously the art of fiction. It gives an author—goodness only knows why—an elated sense of his own superiority. And there is nothing more dangerous than such an elation to that absolute loyalty towards his feelings and sensations an author should keep hold of in his most exalted moments of creation.

To be hopeful in an artistic sense it is not necessary to think that the world is good. It is enough to believe that there is no impossibility of its being made so. If the flight of imaginative thought may be allowed to rise superior to many moralities current amongst mankind, a novelist who would think himself of a superior essence to other men would miss the first condition of his calling. To have the gift of words is no such great matter. A man furnished with a long-range weapon does not become a hunter or a warrior by the mere possession of a fire-arm; many other qualities of character and temperament are necessary to make him either one or the other. Of him from whose armoury of phrases one in a hundred thousand may perhaps hit the far-distant and elusive mark of art I would ask that in his dealings with mankind he should be capable of giving a tender recognition to their obscure virtues. I would not have him impatient with their small failings and scornful of their errors. I would not have him expect too much gratitude from that humanity whose fate, as illustrated in individuals, it is open to him to depict as ridiculous or terrible. I would wish him to look with a large forgiveness at men's ideas and prejudices, which are by no means the outcome of malevolence, but depend on their education, their social status, even their professions. The good artist should expect no recognition of his toil and no admiration of his genius, because his toil can with difficulty be appraised and his genius cannot possibly mean anything to the illiterate who, even from the dreadful wisdom of their evoked dead, have, so far, culled nothing but inanities and platitudes. I would wish him to enlarge his sympathies by patient and loving observation while he grows in mental power. It is in the impartial practice of life, if anywhere, that the promise of perfection for his art can be found, rather than in the absurd formulas trying to prescribe this or that particular method of technique or conception. Let him mature the strength of his imagination amongst the things of this earth, which it is his business to cherish and know, and refrain from calling down his inspiration ready-made from some heaven of perfections of which he knows nothing. And I would not grudge him the proud illusion that will come sometimes to a writer: the illusion that his achievement has almost equalled the greatness of his dream. For what else could give him the serenity and the force to hug to his breast as a thing delightful and human, the virtue, the rectitude and sagacity of his own City, declaring with simple eloquence through the mouth of a Conscript Father: "I have not read this author's books, and if I have read them I have forgotten. . . ."

"Henry James: An Appreciation" (1905)

The critical faculty hesitates before the magnitude of Mr. Henry James's work. His books stand on my shelves in a place whose accessibility proclaims the habit of frequent communion. But not all his books. There is no collected edition to date, such as some of "our masters" have been provided with; no neat rows of volumes in buckram or half calf, putting forth a hasty claim to completeness, and conveying to my mind a hint of finality, of a surrender to fate of that field in which all these victories have been won. Nothing of the sort has been done for Mr. Henry James's victories in England.

In a world such as ours, so painful with all sorts of wonders, one would not exhaust oneself in barren marvelling over mere bindings, had not the fact, or rather the absence of the material fact, prominent in the case of other men whose writing counts (for good or evil)—had it not been, I say, expressive of a direct truth spiritual and intellectual; an accident of—I suppose—the publishing business acquiring a symbolic meaning from its negative nature. Because, emphatically, in the body of Mr. Henry James's work there is no suggestion of finality, nowhere a hint of sur-render, or even of probability of surrender, to his own victorious achievement in that field where he is a master. Happily, he will never be able to claim completeness; and, were he to confess to it in a moment of self-ignorance, he would not be believed by the very minds for whom such a confession naturally would be meant. It is impossible to think of Mr. Henry James becoming "com-plete" otherwise than by the brutality of our common fate whose finality is meaningless—in the sense of its logic being of a material order, the logic of a falling stone.

I do not know into what brand of ink Mr. Henry James dips his pen; indeed, I heard that of late he had been dictating; but I know that his mind is steeped in the waters flowing from the fountain of intellectual youth. The thing—a privilege—a miracle—what you will—is not quite hidden from the meanest of us who run as we read. To those who have the grace to stay their feet it is manifest. After some twenty years of attentive acquaintance with Mr. Henry James's work, it grows into absolute conviction which, all personal feeling apart, brings a sense of happiness into one's artistic existence. If gratitude, as someone defined it, is a lively sense of favours to come, it becomes very easy to be grate-ful to the author of "The Ambassadors"—to name the latest of his works. The favours are sure to come; the spring of that benevo-lence will never run dry. The stream of inspiration flows brim-ful in a predetermined direction, unaffected by the periods of drought, untroubled in its clearness by the storms of the land of letters, without languor or violence in its force, never running back upon itself, opening new visions at every turn of its course through that richly inhabited country its fertility has created for our delectation, for our judgment, for our exploring. It is, in fact, a magic spring.

With this phrase the metaphor of the perennial spring, of the inextinguishable youth, of running waters, as applied to Mr. Henry James's inspiration, may be dropped. In its volume and force the body of his work may be compared rather to a majestic river. All creative art is magic, is evocation of the unseen in forms persuasive, enlightening, familiar and surprising, for the edification of mankind, pinned down by the conditions of its existence to the earnest consideration of the most insignificant tides of reality.

Action in its essence, the creative art of a writer of fiction may be compared to rescue work carried out in darkness against cross gusts of wind swaying the action of a great multitude. It is rescue work, this snatching of vanishing phases of turbulence, disguised in fair words, out of the native obscurity into a light where the struggling forms may be seen, seized upon, endowed with the only possible form of permanence in this world of relative values—the permanence of memory. And the multitude feels it obscurely too; since the demand of the individual to the artist is, in effect, the cry "Take me out of myself!" meaning really, out of my perishable activity into the light of imperishable consciousness. But everything is relative, and the light of consciousness is only enduring, merely the most enduring of the things of this earth, imperishable only as against the short-lived work of our industrious hands.

When the last aqueduct shall have crumbled to pieces, the last airship fallen to the ground, the last blade of grass have died upon a dying earth, man, indomitable by his training in resistance to misery and pain, shall set this undiminished light of his eyes against the feeble glow of the sun. The artistic faculty, of which each of us has a minute grain, may find its voice in some individual of that last group, gifted with a power of expression and courageous enough to interpret the ultimate experience of mankind in terms of his temperament, in terms of art. I do not mean to say that he would attempt to beguile the last moments of humanity by an ingenious tale. It would be too much to expect—from humanity. I doubt the heroism of the hearers. As to the heroism of the artist, no doubt is necessary. There would be on his part no heroism. The artist in his calling of interpreter creates (the clearest form of demonstration) because he must. He is so much of a voice that, for him, silence is like death; and the postulate was, that there is a group alive, clustered on his threshold to watch the last flicker of light on a black sky, to hear the last word uttered in the stilled workshop of the earth. It is safe to affirm that, if anybody, it will be the imaginative man who would be moved to speak on the eve of that day without to-morrow—whether in austere exhortation or in a phrase of sardonic comment, who can guess?

For my own part, from a short and cursory acquaintance with my kind, I am inclined to think that the last utterance will formulate, strange as it may appear, some hope now to us utterly inconceivable. For mankind is delightful in its pride, its assurance, and its indomitable tenacity. It will sleep on the battlefield among its own dead, in the manner of an army having won a barren victory. It will not know when it is beaten. And perhaps it is right in that quality. The victories are not, perhaps, so barren as it may appear from a purely strategical, utilitarian point of view. Mr. Henry James seems to hold that belief. Nobody has rendered better, perhaps, the tenacity of temper, or known how to drape the robe of spiritual honour about the drooping form of a victor in a barren strife. And the honour is always well won; for the struggles Mr. Henry James chronicles with such subtle and direct insight are, though only personal contests, desperate in their silence, none the less heroic (in the modern sense) for the absence of shouted watchwords, clash of arms and sound of trumpets. Those are adventures in which only choice souls are ever involved. And Mr. Henry James records them with a fearless and insistent fidelity to the *péripéties* of the contest, and the feeling of the combatants.

The fiercest excitements of a romance *"de cape et d' épée,"* the romance of yard-arm and boarding pike so dear to youth, whose knowledge of action (as of other things) is imperfect and limited, are matched, for the quickening of our maturer years, by the tasks set, by the difficulties presented, to the sense of truth, of necessity— before all, of conduct—of Mr. Henry James's men and women. His mankind is delightful. It is delightful in its tenacity; it refuses to own itself beaten; it will sleep on the battlefield. These warlike images come by themselves under the pen; since from the duality of man's nature and the competition of individuals, the life-history of the earth must in the last instance be a history

of a really very relentless warfare. Neither his fellows, nor his
gods, nor his passions will leave a man alone. In virtue of these
allies and enemies, he holds his precarious dominion, he posssesses
his fleeting significance; and it is this relation in all its manifestations, great and little, superficial or profound, and this relation
alone, that is commented upon, interpreted, demonstrated by
the art of the novelist in the only possible way in which the task
can be performed: by the independent creation of circumstance
and character, achieved against all the difficulties of expression, in
an imaginative effort finding its inspiration from the reality of
forms and sensations. That a sacrifice must be made, that something has to be given up, is the truth engraved in the innermost
recesses of the fair temple built for our edification by the masters
of fiction. There is no other secret behind the curtain. All adventure, all love, every success is resumed in the supreme energy
of an act of renunciation. It is the uttermost limit of our power;
it is the most potent and effective force at our disposal on which
rest the labours of a solitary man in his study, the rock on which
have been built commonwealths whose might casts a dwarfing
shadow upon two oceans. Like a natural force which is obscured
as much as illuminated by the multiplicity of phenomena, the
power of renunciation is obscured by the mass of weaknesses,
vacillations, secondary motives and false steps and compromises
which make up the sum of our activity. But no man or woman
worthy of the name can pretend to anything more, to anything
greater. And Mr. Henry James's men and women are worthy of
the name, within the limits his art, so clear, so sure of itself, has
drawn round their activities. He would be the last to claim for
them Titanic proportions. The earth itself has grown smaller
in the course of ages. But in every sphere of human perplexities
and emotions, there are more greatnesses than one—not counting
here the greatness of the artist himself. Wherever he stands, at
the beginning or the end of things, a man has to sacrifice his
gods to his passions or his passions to his gods. That is the problem, great enough, in all truth, if approached in the spirit of
sincerity and knowledge.

    In one of his critical studies, published some fifteen years ago,

Mr. Henry James claims for the novelist the standing of the historian as the only adequate one, as for himself and before his audience. I think that the claim cannot be contested, and that the position is unassailable. Fiction is history, human history, or it is nothing. But it is also more than that; it stands on firmer ground, being based on the reality of forms and the observation of social phenomena, whereas history is based on documents, and the reading of print and handwriting—on second-hand impression. Thus fiction is nearer truth. But let that pass. A historian may be an artist too, and a novelist is a historian, the preserver, the keeper, the expounder, of human experience. As is meet for a man of his descent and tradition, Mr. Henry James is the historian of fine consciences.

Of course, this is a general statement; but I don't think its truth will be, or can be questioned. Its fault is that it leaves so much out; and, besides, Mr. Henry James is much too considerable to be put into the nutshell of a phrase. The fact remains that he has made his choice, and that his choice is justified up to the hilt by the success of his art. He has taken for himself the greater part. The range of a fine conscience covers more good and evil than the range of conscience which may be called, roughly, not fine; a conscience, less troubled by the nice discrimination of shades of conduct. A fine conscience is more concerned with essentials; its triumphs are more perfect, if less profitable, in a worldly sense. There is, in short, more truth in its working for a historian to detect and to show. It is a thing of infinite complication and suggestion. None of these escapes the art of Mr. Henry James. He has mastered the country, his domain, not wild indeed, but full of romantic glimpses, of deep shadows and sunny places. There are no secrets left within his range. He has disclosed them as they should be disclosed—that is, beautifully. And, indeed, ugliness has but little place in this world of his creation. Yet it is always felt in the truthfulness of his art; it is there, it surrounds the scene, it presses close upon it. It is made visible, tangible, in the struggles, in the contacts of the fine consciences, in their perplexities, in the sophism of their mistakes. For a fine conscience is naturally a virtuous one. What is natural about it is just its fineness, and abiding sense of the intangible, ever-present, right. It is most visible in their ultimate triumph, in their emergence from miracle, through an energetic act of renunciation. Energetic, not violent; the distinction is wide, enormous, like that between substance and shadow.

Through it all Mr. Henry James keeps a firm hold of the substance, of what is worth having, of what is worth holding. The contrary opinion has been, if not absolutely affirmed, then at least implied, with some frequency. To most of us, living willingly in a sort of intellectual moonlight, in the faintly reflected light of truth, the shadows so firmly renounced by Mr. Henry James's men and women, stand out endowed with extraordinary value, with a value so extraordinary that their rejection offends, by its uncalled-for scrupulousness, those business-like instincts which a careful Providence has implanted in our breasts. And, apart from that just cause of discontent, it is obvious that a solution by rejection must always present a certain lack of finality, especially startling when contrasted with the usual methods of solution by rewards and punishments, by crowned love, by fortune, by a broken leg or a sudden death. Why the reading public which, as a body, has never laid upon a story-teller the command to be an artist, should demand from him this sham of Divine Omnipotence, is utterly incomprehensible. But so it is; and these solutions are legitimate inasmuch as they satisfy the desire for finality, for which our hearts yearn with a longing greater than the longing for the loaves and fishes of this earth. Perhaps the only true desire of mankind, coming thus to light in its hours of leisure, is to be set at rest. One is never set at rest by Mr. Henry James's novels. His books end as an episode in life ends. You remain with the sense of the life still going on; and even the subtle presence of the dead is felt in that silence that comes upon the artist-creation when the last word has been read. It is eminently satisfying, but it is not final. Mr. Henry James, great artist and faithful historian, never attempts the impossible.

"John Galsworthy" (1906)

When in the family's assembly at Timothy Forsyte's house

there arose a discussion of Francis Forsyte's verses, Aunt Hester expressed her preference for the poetry of Shelley, Byron and Wordsworth, on the ground that, after reading the works of these poets, "one felt that one had read a book." And the reader of Mr. Galsworthy's latest volume of fiction, whether in accord or in difference with the author's view of his subject, would feel that he had read a book.

Beyond that impression one perceives how difficult it is to get critical hold of Mr. Galsworthy's work. He gives you no opening. Defending no obvious thesis, setting up no theory, offering no cheap panacea, appealing to no naked sentiment, the author of *The Man of Property* disdains also the effective device of attacking insidiously the actors of his own drama, or rather of his dramatic comedy. This is because he does not write for effect, though his writing will be found effective enough for all that. This book is of a disconcerting honesty, backed by a discouraging skill. There is not a single phrase in it written for the sake of its cleverness. Not one. Light of touch, though weighty in feeling, it gives the impression of verbal austerity, of a *willed* moderation of thought. The passages of high literary merit, so uniformly sustained as to escape the notice of the reader, expose the natural and logical development of the story with a purposeful progression which is primarily satisfying to the intelligence, and ends by stirring the emotions. In the essentials of matter and treatment it is a book of to-day. Its critical spirit and its impartial method are meant for a humanity which has outgrown the stage of fairy tales, realistic, romantic or even epic.

For the fairy tale, be it not ungratefully said, has walked the earth in many unchallenged disguises, and lingers amongst us to this day wearing, sometimes, amazingly heavy clothes. It lingers; and even it lingers with some assurance. Mankind has come of age, but the successive generations still demand artlessly to be amazed, moved and amused. Certain forms of innocent fun will never grow old, I suppose. But the secret of the long life of the fairy tale consists mainly in this, I suspect: that it is amusing to the writer thereof. Whatever public wants it supplies, it ministers first of all to his vanity in an intimate and delightful way. The pride of fanciful invention; the pride of that invention which soars (on goose's wings) into the empty blue is like the intoxication of an elixir sent by the gods above. And whether it is that the gods are unduly generous, or simply because the sight of human folly amuses their idle malice, that sort of felicity is easier attained pen in hand than the sober pride, always mingled with misgivings, of a single-minded observer and conscientious interpreter of reality. This is why the fairy tale, in its various disguises of optimism, pessimism, romanticism, naturalism and what not, will always be with us. And, indeed, that is very comprehensible; the seduction of irresponsible freedom is very great; and to be tied to the earth (even as the hewers of wood and drawers of water are tied to the earth) in the exercise of one's imagination, by every scruple of conscience and honour, may be considered a lot hard enough not to be lightly embraced. This is why novelists are comparatively rare. But we must not exaggerate. This world, even if one is tied fast to its earthy foundations by the subtle and tyrannical bonds of artistic conviction, is not such a bad place to write fiction in. At any rate, we can know of no other; an excellent reason for us to try to think as well as possible of the world we do know.

In this world, whose realities are discovered, interpreted, commented on, criticised and exposed in works of fiction, Mr. Galsworthy selects for the subject-matter of his book the Family, an institution which has been with us as long, I should think, as the oldest and the least venerable pattern of fairy tale. As Mr. Galsworthy, however, is no theorist but an observer, it is a definite kind of family that falls under his observation. It is the middle-class family; and even with more precision, as we are warned in the sub-title, an upper middle-class family anywhere at large in space and time, but a family, if not exactly of to-day, then of only last evening, so to say. Thus at the outset we are far removed from the vagueness of the traditional "once upon a time in a far country there was a king" which somehow always manages to peep through the solemn disguises of fairy tales masquerading as novels with and without purpose. The Forsytes walk the pavement of London and own some of London's houses.

They wish to own more; they wish to own them all. And maybe they will. Time is on their side. The Forsytes never die—so Mr. Galsworthy tells us, while we watch them assembling in old Jolyon Forsyte's drawing-room on the occasion of June Forsyte's engagement to Mr. Bosinney, incidentally an architect and an artist, but, by the only definition that matters, a man of no property whatever.

A family is not at first sight an alarming phenomenon. But Mr. Galsworthy looks at the Forsytes with the individual vision of a novelist seeking his inspiration amongst the realities of this earth. He points out to us this family's formidable character as a unit of Society, as a reproduction in miniature of Society itself. It is made formidable, he says, by the cohesion of its members (between whom there need not exist either affection or even sympathy) upon a concrete point—the possession of property.

The solidity of the foundation laid by Mr. Galsworthy for his fine piece of imaginative work becomes at once apparent. For whichever came first, family or property, in the beginnings of social organisation, or whether they came together and were indeed at first scarcely distinguishable from each other, it is clear that in the close alliance of these two institutions Society has found the way of its development and nurses the hope of its security. In their sense of property the Forsytes establish the consciousness of their rights and the promise of their duration. It is an instinct, a primitive instinct. The practical faculty of the Forsytes has erected it into a principle; their idealism has expanded it into a sort of religion which has shaped their notions of happiness and decency, their prejudices, their piety, such thoughts as they happen to have and the very course of their passions. Life as a whole has come to be perceptible to them exclusively in terms of property. Preservation, acquisition— acquisition, preservation. Their laws, their morality, their art and their science appear to them, justifiably enough, consecrated to that double and unique end. It is the formula of their virtue.

In this world of Forsytes (who never die) organised in view of acquiring and preserving property, Mr. Galsworthy (who is no inventor of didactic fairy tales) places with the sure instinct of a novelist a man and a woman who are no Forsytes, it is true, but whom he presents as in no sense the declared adversaries of the great principle of property. They only happen to disregard it. And this is a crime. They are simply two people to whom life speaks imperatively in terms of love. And this is enough to establish their irreconcilable antagonism and to precipitate their unavoidable fate. Deprived naturally and suddenly of the support of laws and morality, of all human countenance, and even, in a manner of speaking, of the consolations of religion, they find themselves miserably crushed, both the woman and the man. And the principle of property is vindicated. The woman being the weaker, it is in her case vindicated with consummate cruelty. For a peculiar cowardice is one of the characteristics of this great and living principle. Strong in the worship of so many thousands and in the possession of so many millions, it starts with affright at the slightest challenge, it trembles before mere indifference, it directs its heaviest blows at the disinherited who should appear weakest in its sight. Irene's fate is made unspeakably atrocious, no less—but nothing more. Mr. Galsworthy's instinct and observation serve him well here. In Soames Forsyte's town house, whose front door stands wide open for half an hour or so on a certain foggy night, there is no room for tragedy. It is one of the temples of property, of a sort of unholy religion whose fundamental dogma, public ceremonies and awful secret rites, forming the subject-matter of this remarkable novel, take no account of human dignity. Irene, as last seen crushed and alive within the hopeless portals, remains for us a poignantly pitiful figure and nothing more.

This then, roughly and summarily, is the book in its general suggestion. Going on to particulars which make up the intrinsic value of a work of art, it rests upon the subtle and interdependent relation of Mr. Galsworthy's intellect and feelings which form his temperament, and reveals Mr. Galsworthy's very considerable talent as a writer—a talent so considerable that it commands at once our respectful attention. The foundation of this talent, it seems to me, lies in a remarkable power of ironic insight combined with an extremely keen and faithful eye for all the pheno-

mena on the surface of the life he observes. These are the pur-
veyors of his imagination, whose servant is a style clear, direct,
sane, illumined by a perfectly unaffected sincerity. It is the
style of a man whose sympathy with mankind is too genuine to
allow him the smallest gratification of his vanity at the cost of
his fellow-creatures. In its moderation it is a style sufficiently
pointed to carry deep his remorseless irony and grave enough to
be the dignified vehicle of his profound compassion. Its sustained
harmony is never interrupted by those bursts of cymbals and fifes
which some deaf people acclaim for brilliance. Before all, it is
a style well under control, and therefore it never betrays this
tender and ironic writer into an odious cynicism of laughter or
tears. For there are two kinds of cynicism, the cynicism of the
hyena and the cynicism of the crocodile, which last, by the way,
commands all sorts of respects from the inhabitants of these Isles.
Mr. Galsworthy remains always a man, whether he is amused
or moved.

I am afraid that my unavowed intention in writing about this
book (of which I have talked so much and said so little) has been
discovered by now. Therefore I confess. Confession—public, I
mean—is good for one's conscience. Such is my intention. And it
would be easier to carry out if I only knew exactly the motives
which prompt people to read novels. But I do not know them all.
Some of us, I understand, take up a novel to gratify a natural
malevolence, the author being supposed to hold the mirror up
to the odiously ridiculous nature of our next-door neighbour.
From laboriously-collected information I am, however, led to
believe that most people read novels for amusement. This is as
it should be. But, whatever be their motives, I entertain towards
all novel-readers (for reasons which must remain concealed from
the readers of this paper) the feelings of warm and respectful
affection. I would not try to deceive them for worlds. Never! This
being understood, I go on to declare, in the peace of my heart
and the serenity of my conscience, that if they want amusement
they will find it between the covers of this book. They will find
plenty of it in this episode in the history of the Forsytes, where
the reconciliation of a father and son, the dramatic and poignant

comedy of Soames Forsyte's marital relations, and the tragedy of Bosinney's failure are exposed to our gaze with the remorseless yet sympathetic irony of Mr. Galsworthy's art, in the light of the unquenchable fire burning on the altar of property. They will find amusement, and perhaps also something more lasting—if they care for it. I say this with all the reserves and qualifications which strict truth requires around every statement of opinion. Mr. Galsworthy may possibly be found disappointing by some, but he will never be found futile by anyone, and never uninteresting by the most exacting. I myself, for instance, am not so sure of Bosinney's tragedy. But this hesitation of my mind, for which the author may not be wholly responsible after all, need only be mentioned and no more, in the face of his considerable achievement.

"The Censor of Plays: An Appreciation" (1907)

A couple of years ago I was moved to write a one-act play— and I lived long enough to accomplish the task. We live and learn. When the play was finished I was informed that it had to be licensed for performance. Thus I learned of the existence of the Censor of Plays. I may say without vanity that I am intelligent enough to have been astonished by that piece of information: for facts must stand in some relation to time and space, and I was aware of being in England—in the twentieth-century England. The fact did not fit the date and the place. That was my first thought. It was, in short, an improper fact. I beg you to believe that I am writing in all seriousness and am weighing my words scrupulously.

Therefore I don't say inappropriate. I say improper—that is: something to be ashamed of. And at first this impression was confirmed by the obscurity in which the figure embodying this after all considerable fact had its being. The Censor of Plays! His name was not in the mouths of all men.[9] Far from it. He

---

9. A cancelled passage continued: "His abode was no more distinguished for the veneration of mankind than the abode of the common hangman who at any rate does not kill *proprio motu* and does not suppress people in the dark." (Edward Garnett, *Letters from Joseph Conrad 1895–1924*, p. 208).

seemed stealthy and remote. There was about that figure the scent of the Far East, like the peculiar atmosphere of a Mandarin's back yard, and the mustiness of the Middle Ages, that epoch when mankind tried to stand still in a monstrous illusion of final certitude attained in morals, intellect and conscience.

It was a disagreeable impression. But I reflected that probably the censorship of plays was an inactive monstrosity; not exactly a survival, since it seemed obviously at variance with the genius of the people, but an heirloom of past ages, a bizarre and imported curiosity preserved because of that weakness one has for one's old possessions apart from any intrinsic value; one more object of exotic *virtù,* an oriental *potiche, a magot chinois* conceived by a childish and extravagant imagination, but allowed to stand in stolid impotence in the twilight of the upper shelf.

Thus, I quieted my uneasy mind. Its uneasiness had nothing to do with the fate of my one-act play. The play was duly produced, and an exceptionally intelligent audience stared it coldly off the boards. It ceased to exist. It was a fair and open execution. But having survived the freezing atmosphere of that auditorium I continued to exist, labouring under no sense of wrong. I was not pleased, but I was content. I was content to accept the verdict of a free and independent public, judging after its conscience the work of its free, independent and conscientious servant—the artist.

Only thus can the dignity of artistic servitude be preserved—not to speak of the bare existence of the artist and the self-respect of the man. I shall say nothing of the self-respect of the public. To the self-respect of the public the present appeal against the censorship is being made and I join in it with all my heart.

For I have lived long enough to learn that the monstrous and outlandish figure, the *magot chinois* whom I believed to be but a memorial of our forefathers' mental aberration, that grotesque *potiche* works! The absurd and hollow creature of clay seems to be alive with a sort of (surely) unconscious life worthy of its traditions. It heaves its stomach, it rolls its eyes, it brandishes a monstrous arm: and with the censorship, like a Bravo of old Venice with a more carnal weapon, stabs its victim from behind in the twilight of its upper shelf. Less picturesque than the Venetian in cloak and mask, less estimable, too, in this, that the assassin plied his moral trade at his own risk deriving no countenance from the powers of the Republic, it stands more malevolent, inasmuch that the Bravo striking in the dusk killed but the body, whereas the grotesque thing nodding its mandarin head may in its absurd unconsciousness strike down at any time the spirit of an honest, of an artistic, perhaps of a sublime creation.

This Chinese monstrosity, disguised in the trousers of the Western Barbarian and provided by the State with the immortal Mr. Stiggin's[10] plug hat and umbrella, is with us. It is an office. An office of trust. And from time to time there is found an official to fill it. He is a public man. The least prominent of public men, the most unobtrusive, the most obscure if not the most modest.

But however obscure, a public man may be told the truth if only once in his life. His office flourishes in the shade; not in the rustic shade beloved of the violet but in the muddled twilight of mind where tyranny of every sort flourishes. Its holder need not have either brain or heart, no sight, no taste, no imagination, not even bowels of compassion. He needs not these things. He has power. He can kill thought, and incidentally truth, and incidentally beauty, providing they seek to live in a dramatic form. He can do it, without seeing, without understanding, without feeling anything; out of mere stupid suspicion, as an irresponsible Roman Caesar could kill a senator.[11] He can do that and there is no one to say him nay. He may call his cook (Molière used to do that) from below and give her five acts to judge every morning as a matter of constant practice and still remain the

10. Stiggins is the parson of Emanuel Chapel in Dickens' *The Pickwick Papers*.

11. A cancelled passage continued: "He can go out in the morning this grotesque magistrate of a free commonwealth, catch a donkey on Hampstead Heath lead him into his study and set him down in his curule chair. Has not Caligula made his horse a consul? He can do that and there is no one to say him nay. Perhaps indeed no one could detect the difference." (Garnett, *op. cit.*, footnote 9.)

unquestioned destroyer of men's honest work. He may have a glass too much. This accident has happened to persons of unimpeachable morality—to gentlemen. He may suffer from spells of imbecility like Clodius. He may ... what might he not do! I tell you he is the Caesar of the dramatic world. There has been since the Roman Principate nothing in the way of irresponsible power to compare with the office of the Censor of Plays.

Looked at in this way it has some grandeur, something colossal in the odious and the absurd. This figure in whose power it is to suppress an intellectual conception—to kill thought (a dream for a mad brain, my masters!)—seems designed in a spirit of bitter comedy to bring out the greatness of a Philistine's conceit and his moral cowardice.

But this is England in the twentieth century, and one wonders that there can be found a man courageous enough to occupy the post. It is a matter for meditation. Having given it a few minutes I come to the conclusion in the serenity of my heart and the peace of my conscience that he must be either an extreme megalomaniac or an utterly unconscious being.

He must be unconscious. It is one of the qualifications for his magistracy. Other qualifications are equally easy. He must have done nothing, expressed nothing, imagined nothing. He must be obscure, insignificant and mediocre—in thought, act, speech and sympathy. He must know nothing of art, of life—and of himself. For if he did he would not dare to be what he is.[12] Like that much questioned and mysterious bird, the phoenix, he sits amongst the cold ashes of his predecessor upon the altar of morality, alone of his kind in the sight of wondering generations.

And I will end with a quotation reproducing not perhaps the exact words but the true spirit of a lofty conscience.

"Often when sitting down to write the notice of a play, especially when I felt it antagonistic to my canons of art, to my

---

12. A cancelled passage continued: "He must not even know that his grotesque existence is a direct insult to forty-five million more or less of souls certainly neither more nor less pure than his own, most of them more intelligent—all of them more worthy. I say deliberately all of them because of course the Censor of Plays is unique." (Garnett, *op. cit.*, footnote 9.)

tastes or my convictions, I hesitated in the fear lest my conscientious blame might check the development of a great talent, my sincere judgment condemn a worthy mind. With the pen poised in my hand I hesitated, whispering to myself 'What if I were perchance doing my part in killing a masterpiece.'"

Such were the lofty scruples of M. Jules Lemaître—dramatist and dramatic critic, a great citizen and a high magistrate in the Republic of Letters; a Censor of Plays exercising his august office openly in the light of day, with the authority of a European reputation. But then M. Jules Lemaître is a man possessed of wisdom, of great fame, of a fine conscience—not an obscure hollow Chinese monstrosity ornamented with Mr. Stiggins's plug hat and cotton umbrella by its anxious grandmother—the State.

Frankly, is it not time to knock the improper object off its shelf? It has stood too long there. Hatched in Pekin (I should say) by some Board of Respectable Rites, the little caravan monster has come to us by way of Moscow—I suppose. It is outlandish. It is not venerable. It does not belong here. Is it not time to knock it off its dark shelf with some implement appropriate to its worth and status? With an old broom handle for instance.

"A Happy Wanderer" (1910)

Converts are interesting people. Most of us, if you will pardon me for betraying the universal secret, have, at some time or other, discovered in ourselves a readiness to stray far, ever so far, on the wrong road. And what did we do in our pride and our cowardice? Casting fearful glances and waiting for a dark moment, we buried our discovery discreetly, and kept on in the old direction, on that old, beaten track we have not had courage enough to leave, and which we perceive now more clearly than before to be but the arid way of the grave.

The convert, the man capable of grace (I am speaking here in a secular sense), is not discreet. His pride is of another kind; he jumps gladly off the track—the touch of grace is mostly sudden—and facing about in a new direction may even attain the illusion of having turned his back on Death itself.

Some converts have, indeed, earned immortality by their

exquisite indiscretion. The most illustrious example of a convert, that Flower of chivalry. Don Quixote de la Mancha, remains for all the world the only genuine immortal hidalgo. The delectable Knight of Spain became converted, as you know, from the ways of a small country squire to an imperative faith in a tender and sublime mission. Forthwith he was beaten with sticks and in due course shut up in a wooden cage by the Barber and the Priest, the fit ministers of a justly shocked social order. I do not know if it has occurred to anybody yet to shut up Mr. Luffmann in a wooden cage.[13] I do not raise the point because I wish him any harm. Quite the contrary. I am a humane person. Let him take it as the highest praise—but I must say that he richly deserves that sort of attention.

On the other hand I would not have him unduly puffed up with the pride of the exalted association. The grave wisdom, the admirable amenity, the serene grace of the secular patron-saint of all mortals converted to noble visions are not his. Mr. Luffmann has no mission. He is no Knight sublimely Errant. But he is an excellent Vagabond. He is full of merit. That peripatetic guide, philosopher and friend of all nations, Mr. Roosevelt, would promptly excommunicate him with a big stick. The truth is that the ex-autocrat of all the States does not like rebels against the sullen order of our universe. Make the best of it or perish— he cries. A sane lineal successor of the Barber and the Priest, and a sagacious political heir of the incomparable Sancho Panza (another great Governor), that distinguished littérateur has no mercy for dreamers. And our author happens to be a man of (you may trace them in his books) some rather fine reveries.

Every convert begins by being a rebel, and I do not see myself how any mercy can possibly be extended to Mr. Luffmann. He is a convert from the creed of strenuous life. For this renegade the body is of little account; to him work appears criminal when it suppresses the demands of the inner life; while he was young he did grind virtuously at the sacred handle, and now, he says, he has fallen into disgrace with some people because he believes

---

13. C. Rogue Luffmann had published *Quiet Days in Spain*.

no longer in toil without end. Certain respectable folk hate him—
so he says—because he dares to think that "poetry, beauty, and the
broad face of the world are the best things to be in love with."
He confesses to loving Spain on the ground that she is "the land
of to-morrow, and holds the gospel of never-mind." The universal
striving to push ahead he considers mere vulgar folly. Didn't I
tell you he was a fit subject for the cage?

It is a relief (we are all humane, are we not?) to discover
that this desperate character is not altogether an outcast. Little
girls seem to like him. One of them, after listening to some of
his tales, remarked to her mother, "Wouldn't it be lovely if what
he says were true!" Here you have Woman! The charming creatures will neither strain at a camel nor swallow a gnat. Not publicly. These operations, without which the world they have such
a large share in could not go on for ten minutes, are left to us—
men. And then we are chided for being coarse. This is a refined
objection but does not seem fair. Another little girl—or perhaps
the same little girl—wrote to him in Cordova "I hope Poste-
Restante is a nice place, and that you are very comfortable."
Woman again! I have in my time told some stories which are (I
hate false modesty) both true and lovely. Yet no little girl ever
wrote to me in kindly terms. And why? Simply because I am not
enough of a Vagabond. The dear despots of the fireside have a
weakness for lawless characters. This is amiable, but does not
seem rational.

Being Quixotic, Mr. Luffmann is no Impressionist. He is far
too earnest in his heart, and not half sufficiently precise in his
style to be that. But he is an excellent narrator. More than any
Vagabond I have ever met, he knows what he is about. There
is not one of his quiet days which is dull. You will find in them
a love-story not made up, the *coup-de-foudre,* the lightning-stroke
of Spanish love; and you will marvel how a spell so sudden
and vehement can be at the same time so tragically delicate. You
will find there landladies devoured with jealousy, astute house-
keepers, delightful boys, wise peasants, touchy shopkeepers, all
the *Cosas de España*—and, in addition, the pale girl Rosario. I
recommend that pathetic and silent victim of fate to your benevo-

lent compassion. You will find in his pages the humours of starving workers of the soil, the vision among the mountains of an exulting mad spirit in a mighty body, and many other visions worthy of attention. And they are exact visions for this idealist is no visionary. He is in sympathy with suffering mankind, and has a grasp on real human affairs. I mean the great and pitiful affairs concerned with bread, love, and the obscure, unexpressed needs which drive great crowds to prayer in the holy places of the earth.

But I like his conception of what a "quiet" life is like! His quiet days require no fewer than forty-two of the forty-nine provinces of Spain to take their ease in. For his unquiet days, I presume, the seven—or is it nine?—crystal spheres of Alexandrian cosmogony would afford but a wretchedly straitened space. A most unconventional thing is his notion of quietness. One would take it as a joke; only that, perchance, to the author of "Quiet Days in Spain" all days may seem quiet, because, a courageous convert, he is now at peace with himself.

How better can we take leave of this interesting Vagabond than with the road salutation of passing wayfarers: "And on you be peace! . . . You have chosen your ideal, and it is a good choice. There's nothing like giving up one's life to an unselfish passion. Let the rich and the powerful of this globe preach their sound gospel of palpable progress. The part of the ideal you embrace is the better one, if only in its illusions. No great passion can be barren. May a world of gracious and poignant images attend the lofty solitude of your renunciation!"

"The Ascending Effort" (1910)

Much good paper has been lamentably wasted to prove that science has destroyed, that it is destroying, or some day, may destroy poetry. Meantime, unblushing, unseen and ofter unheard, the guileless poets have gone on singing in a sweet strain. How they dare do the impossible and virtually forbidden thing is a cause for wonder but not for legislation. Not yet. We are at present too busy reforming the silent burglar and planning concerts to soothe the savage breast of the yelling hooligan. As somebody—perhaps a publisher—said lately: "Poetry is of no account now-a-days."

But it is not totally neglected. Those persons with gold-rimmed spectacles whose usual occupation is to spy upon the obvious have remarked audibly (on several occasions) that poetry has so far not given to science any acknowledgement worthy of its distinguished position in the popular mind. Except that Tennyson looked down the throat of a foxglove, that Erasmus Darwin wrote "The Loves of the Plants" and a scoffer "The Loves of the Triangles," poets have been supposed to be inde-corously blind to the progress of science. What tribute, for instance, has poetry paid to electricity? All I can remember on the spur of the moment is Mr. Arthur Symons' line about arc lamps: "Hung with the globes of some unnatural fruit."

Commerce and Manufacture praise on every hand in their not mute but inarticulate way the glories of science. Poetry does not play its part. Behold John Keats, skilful with the surgeon's knife; but when he writes poetry his inspiration is not from the operating table. Here I am reminded, though, of a modern instance to the contrary in prose. Mr. H. G. Wells, who, as far as I know, has never written a line of verse, was inspired a few years ago to write a short story, "Under the Knife." Out of a clock-dial, a brass rod, and a whiff of chloroform, he has conjured for us a sensation of space and eternity, evoked the face of the Unknowable, and an awesome, august voice, like the voice of the Judgment Day; a great voice, perhaps the voice of science itself, uttering the words: "There shall be no more pain!" I advise you to look up that story, so human and so intimate, because Mr. Wells, the writer of prose whose amazing inventiveness we all know, remains a poet even in his most perverse moments of scorn for things as they are. His poetic imagination is sometimes even greater than his inventiveness, I am not afraid to say. But, indeed, imaginative faculty would make any man a poet—were he born without tongue for speech and without hands to seize his fancy and fasten her down to a wretched piece of paper.

The book[14] which in the course of the last few days I have opened and shut several times is not imaginative. But, on the other hand, it is not a dumb book, as some are. It has even a sort of sober and serious eloquence, reminding us that not poetry alone is at fault in this matter. Mr. Bourne begins his "Ascending Effort" with a remark by Sir Francis Galton upon Eugenics that "if the principles he was advocating were to become effective they must be introduced into the national conscience, like a new religion." "Introduced" suggests compulsory vaccination. Mr. Bourne, who is not a theologian, wishes to league together not science and religion, but science and the arts. "The intoxicating power of art," he thinks, is the very thing needed to give the desired effect to the doctrines of science. In uninspired phrase he points to the arts playing once upon a time a part in "popularizing the Christian tenets." With painstaking fervour as great as the fervour of prophets, but not so persuasive, he foresees the arts some day popularizing science. Until that day dawns, science will continue to be lame and poetry blind. He himself cannot smooth or even point out the way, though he thinks that "a really prudent people would be greedy of beauty," and their public authorities "as careful of the sense of comfort as of sanitation."

As the writer of those admirable rustic note-books "The Bettesworth Book" and "Memoirs of a Surrey Labourer," the author has a claim upon our attention. But his seriousness, his patience, his almost touching sincerity, can only command the respect of his readers and nothing more. He is obsessed by science, haunted and shadowed by it, until he has been bewildered into awe. He knows, indeed, that art owes its triumphs and its subtle influence to the fact that it issues straight from our organic vitality, and is a movement of life-cells with their matchless unintellectual knowledge. But the fact that poetry does not seem obviously in love with science has never made him doubt whether it may not be an argument against his haste to see the marriage ceremony performed amid public rejoicings.

14. *The Ascending Effort,* by George Bourne.

Many a man has heard or read and believes that the earth goes round the sun; one small blob of mud among several others, spinning ridiculously with a waggling motion like a top about to fall. This is the Copernican system, and the man believes in the system without often knowing as much about it as its name. But while watching a sunset he sheds his belief; he sees the sun as a small and useful object, the servant of his needs and the witness of his ascending effort, sinking slowly behind a range of mountains, and then he holds the system of Ptolemy. He holds it without knowing it. In the same way a poet hears, reads, and believes a thousand undeniable truths which have not yet got into his blood, nor will do after reading Mr. Bourne's book; he writes, therefore, as if neither truths nor book existed. Life and the arts follow dark courses, and will not turn aside to the brilliant arc-lights of science. Some day, without a doubt,—and it may be a consolation to Mr. Bourne to know it—fully informed critics will point out that Mr. Davies's poem on a dark woman combing her hair[15] must have been written after the invasion of appendicitis, and that Mr. Yeats's "Had I the heaven's embroidered cloths"[16] came before radium was quite unnecessarily dragged out of its respectable obscurity in pitchblende to upset the venerable (and comparatively naïve) chemistry of our young days.

There are times when the tyranny of science and the cant of science are alarming, but there are other times when they are entertaining—and this is one of them. "Many a man prides himself," says Mr. Bourne, "on his piety or his views of art, whose whole range of ideas, could they be investigated, would be found ordinary, if not base, because they have been adopted in compliance with some external persuasion or to serve some timid purpose instead of proceeding authoritatively from the living selection of his hereditary taste." This extract is a fair sample of the book's thought and of its style. But Mr. Bourne seems to

15. Conrad may be alluding to "A Maiden and Her Hair," by W. H. Davies.
16. "He wishes for the Cloths of Heaven."

forget that "persuasion" is a vain thing. The appreciation of great art comes from within.

It is but the merest justice to say that the transparent honesty of Mr. Bourne's purpose is undeniable. But the whole book is simply an earnest expression of a pious wish; and, like the generality of pious wishes, this one seems of little dynamic value—besides being impracticable.

Yes, indeed. Art has served Religion; artists have found the most exalted inspiration in Christianity; but the light of Transfiguration which has illuminated the profoundest mysteries of our sinful souls is not the light of the generating stations, which exposes the depths of our infatuation where our mere cleverness is permitted for a while to grope for the unessential among invincible shadows.

"Turgenev" (1917)

Dear Edward: I am glad to hear that you are about to publish a study of Turgenev,[17] that fortunate artist who has found so much in life for us and no doubt for himself, with the exception of bare justice. Perhaps that will come to him, too, in time. Your study may help the consummation. For his luck persists after his death. What greater luck an artist like Turgenev could wish for than to find in the English-speaking world a translator who has missed none of the most delicate, most simple beauties of his work,[18] and a critic who has known how to analyse and point out its high qualities with perfect sympathy and insight.

After twenty odd years of friendship (and my first literary friendship too) I may well permit myself to make that statement, while thinking of your wonderful Prefaces as they appeared from time to time in the volumes of Turgenev's complete edition, the last of which came into the light of public indifference in the ninety-ninth year of the ninteenth century.

With that year one may say, with some justice, that the age of Turgenev had come to an end too; yet work so simple and human, so independent of the transitory formulas and theories

17. *Turgenev: A Study*, by Edward Garnett.
18. Constance Garnett had translated Turgenev's works.

of art, belongs as you point out in the Preface to "Smoke" "to all time."

Turgenev's creative activity covers about thirty years. Since it came to an end the social and political events in Russia have moved at an accelerated pace, but the deep origins of them, in the moral and intellectual unrest of the souls, are recorded in the whole body of his work with the unerring lucidity of a great national writer. The first stirrings, the first gleams of the great forces can be seen almost in every page of the novels, of the short stories and of "A Sportsman's Sketches"—those marvellous landscapes peopled by unforgettable figures.

Those will never grow old. Fashions in monsters do change, but the truth of humanity goes on for ever, unchangeable and inexhaustible in the variety of its disclosures. Whether Turgenev's art, which has captured it with such mastery and such gentleness, is for "all time" it is hard to say. Since, as you say yourself, he brings all his problems and characters to the test of love we may hope that it will endure at least till the infinite emotions of love are replaced by the exact simplicity of perfected Eugenics. But even by then, I think, women would not have changed much; and the women of Turgenev who understood them so tenderly, so reverently and so passionately—they, at least, are certainly for all time.

Women are, one may say, the foundation of his art. They are Russian of course. Never was a writer so profoundly, so whole-souledly national. But for non-Russian readers, Turgenev's Russia is but a canvas on which the incomparable artist of humanity lays his colours and his forms in the great light and the free air of the world. Had he invented them all and also every stick and stone, brook and hill and field in which they move, his personages would have been just as true and as poignant in their perplexed lives. They are his own and also universal. Any one can accept them with no more question than one accepts the Italians of Shakespeare.

In the larger, non-Russian view, what should make Turgenev sympathetic and welcome to the English-speaking world, is his essential humanity. All his creations, fortunate and unfortunate, oppressed and oppressors are human beings, not strange beasts in a menagerie or damned souls knocking themselves to pieces in the stuffy darkness of mystical contradictions. They are human beings, fit to live, fit to suffer, fit to struggle, fit to win, fit to lose, in the endless and inspiring game of pursuing from day to day the ever-receding future.

I began by calling him lucky, and he was, in a sense. But one ends by having some doubts. To be so great without the slightest parade and so fine without any tricks of "cleverness" must be fatal to any man's influence with his contemporaries.

Frankly, I don't want to appear as qualified to judge of things Russian. It wouldn't be true. I know nothing of them. But I am aware of a few general truths, such as, for instance, that no man, whatever may be the loftiness of his character, the purity of his motives and the peace of his conscience—no man, I say, likes to be beaten with sticks during the greater part of his existence. From what one knows of his history it appears clearly that in Russia almost any stick was good enough to beat Turgenev with in his latter years. When he died the characteristically chicken-hearted Autocracy hastened to stuff his mortal envelope into the tomb it refused to honour, while the sensitive Revolutionists went on for a time flinging after his shade those jeers and curses from which that impartial lover of *all* his countrymen had suffered so much in his lifetime. For he, too, was sensitive. Every page of his writing bears its testimony to the fatal absence of callousness in the man. And now he suffers a little from other things. In truth it is not the convulsed terror-haunted Dostoevski but the serene Turgenev who is under a curse. For only think! Every gift has been heaped on his cradle: absolute sanity and the deepest sensibility, the clearest vision and the quickest responsiveness, penetrating insight and unfailing generosity of judgment, an exquisite perception of the visible world and an unerring instinct for the significant, for the essential in the life of men and women, the clearest mind, the warmest heart, the largest sympathy—and all that in perfect measure. There's enough there to ruin the prospects of any writer. For you know very well, my dear Edward, that if you had Antinous himself in a booth of the world's fair, and killed yourself in protesting that his soul was as perfect as his body, you wouldn't get one per cent of the crowd struggling next door for a sight of the Double-headed Nightingale or of some weak-kneed giant grinning through a horse collar.

From "Stephen Crane: A Note without Dates" (1919)

He had indeed a wonderful power of vision, which he applied to the things of this earth and of our mortal humanity with a penetrating force that seemed to reach, within life's appearances and forms, the very spirit of life's truth. His ignorance of the world at large—he had seen very little of it—did not stand in the way of his imaginative grasp of facts, events, and picturesque men.

His manner was very quiet, his personality at first sight interesting, and he talked slowly with an intonation which on some people, mainly Americans, had, I believe, a jarring effect. But not on me. Whatever he said had a personal note, and he expressed himself with a graphic simplicity which was extremely engaging. He knew little of literature, either of his own country or of any other, but he was himself a wonderful artist in words whenever he took a pen into his hand. Then his gift came out—and it was seen then to be much more than mere felicity of language. His impressionism of phrase went really deeper than the surface. In his writing he was very sure of his effects. I don't think he was ever in doubt about what he could do. Yet it often seemed to me that he was but half aware of the exceptional quality of his achievement.

From "Stephen Crane"[19] (1923)

It was on the ground of the authorship of that book that Crane wanted to meet me. Nothing could have been more flattering than to discover that the author of *The Red Badge of Courage* appreciated my effort[20] to present a group of men held together by a common loyalty, and a common perplexity in a struggle

19. Written as a preface to *Stephen Crane* by Thomas Beer.
20. In *The Nigger of the "Narcissus."*

not with human enemies, but with the hostile conditions testing their faithfulness to the conditions of their own calling.

Apart from the imaginative analysis of his own temperament tried by the emotions of a battlefield, Stephen Crane dealt in his book with the psychology of the mass—the army; while I—in mine—had been dealing with the same subject on a much smaller scale and in more specialized conditions—the crew of a merchant ship, brought to the test of what I may venture to call the moral problem of conduct. This may be thought a very remote connection between these two works, and the idea may seem too far-fetched to be mentioned here; but that was my undoubted feeling at the time. It is a fact that I considered Crane, by virtue of his creative experience with *The Red Badge of Courage,* as eminently fit to pronounce a judgment on my first consciously-planned attempt to render the truth of a phase of life in the terms of my own temperament with all the sincerity of which I was capable.

I had, of course, my own opinion as to what I had done; but I doubted whether anything of my ambitiously comprehensive aim would be understood. I was wrong there, but my doubt was excusable, since I myself would have been hard put to it if requested to give my complex intentions the form of a concise and definite statement. In that period of misgivings which so often follows an accomplished task I would often ask myself, who in the world could be interested in such a thing? It was after reading *The Red Badge,* which came into my hands directly after its publication in England, that I said to myself: "Here's a man who may understand—if he ever sees the book; though, of course, that would not mean that he would like it." * * *

It[21] opens with a phrase that anybody could have uttered, but which, in relation to what is to follow, acquires the poignancy of a meaning almost universal.

From "His War Book"[22] (1925, posthumous)

It delighted soldiers, men of letters, men in the street; it

21. "The Open Boat."
22. Written as a preface to Stephen Crane's *The Red Badge of Courage.*

was welcomed by all lovers of personal expression as a genuine revelation, satisfying the curiosity of a world in which war and love have been subjects of song and story ever since the beginning of articulate speech.

Here we had an artist, a man not of experience but a man inspired, a seer with a gift for rendering the significant on the surface of things and with an incomparable insight into primitive emotions, who, in order to give us the image of war, had looked profoundly into his own breast. * * *

"Mr. Crane has contrived a masterpiece." [the remark of Mr. George Wyndham]

"Contrived"—that word of disparaging sound is the last word I would have used in connection with any piece of work by Stephen Crane, who in his art (as indeed in his private life) was the least "contriving" of men. But as to "masterpiece," there is no doubt that *The Red Badge of Courage* is that, if only because of the marvellous accord of the vivid impressionistic description of action on that woodland battlefield, and the imagined style of the analysis of the emotions in the inward moral struggle going on in the breast of one individual—the Young Soldier of the book, the protagonist of the monodrama presented to us in an effortless succession of graphic and coloured phrases.

Stephen Crane places his Young Soldier in an untried regiment. And this is well contrived—if any contrivance there be in a spontaneous piece of work which seems to spurt and flow like a tapped stream from the depths of the writer's being. In order that the revelation should be complete, the Young Soldier has to be deprived of the moral support which he would have found in a tried body of men matured in achievement to the consciousness of its worth. His regiment had been tried by nothing but days of waiting for the order to move; so many days that it and the Youth within it have come to think of themselves as merely "a part of a vast blue demonstration." The army had been lying camped near a river, idle and fretting, till the moment when Stephen Crane lays hold of it at dawn with masterly simplicity: "The cold passed reluctantly from the earth . . ." These are the first words of the war book which was to give him his crumb of fame.

The whole of that opening paragraph is wonderful in the homely dignity of the indicated lines of the landscape, and the shivering awakening of the army at the break of the day before the battle. In the next, with a most effective change to racy colloquialism of narrative, the action which motivates, sustains and feeds the inner drama forming the subjects of the book, begins with the Tall Soldier going down to the river to wash his shirt. He returns waving his garment above his head. He had heard at fifth-hand from somebody that the army is going to move to-morrow. The only immediate effect of this piece of news is that a negro teamster, who had been dancing a jig on a wooden box in a ring of laughing soldiers, finds himself suddenly deserted. He sits down mournfully. For the rest, the Tall Soldier's excitement is met by blank disbelief, profane grumbling, an invincible incredulity. But the regiment is somehow sobered. One feels it, though no symptoms can be noticed. It does not know what a battle is; neither does the Young Soldier. He retires from the babbling throng into what seems a rather comfortable dug-out and lies down with his hands over his eyes to think. Thus the drama begins.

He perceives suddenly that he had looked upon wars as historical phenomenons of the past. He had never believed in war in his own country. It had been a sort of play affair. He had been drilled, inspected, marched for months, till he has despaired "of ever seeing a Greek-like struggle. Such were no more. Men were better or more timid. Secular and religious education had effaced the throat-grappling instinct, or else firm finance held in check the passions."

Very modern this touch. We can remember thoughts like these round about the year 1914. That Young Soldier is representative of mankind in more ways than one, and first of all in his ignorance. His regiment had listened to the tales of veterans, "tales of grey bewhiskered hordes chewing tobacco with unspeakable valour and sweeping along like the Huns." Still, he cannot put his faith in veterans' tales. Recruits were their prey. They talked of blood, fire, and sudden death, but much of it might have been lies. They were in nowise to be trusted. And the question arises

before him whether he will or will not "run from a battle"?
He does not know. He cannot know. A little panic fear enters
his mind. He jumps up and asks himself aloud, "Good Lord!
What's the matter with me?" This is the first time his words are
quoted, on this day before the battle. He dreads not danger,
but fear itself. He stands before the unknown. He would like to
prove to himself by some reasoning process that he will not "run
from the battle." And in his unblooded regiment he can find no
help. He is alone with the problem of courage.

In this he stands for the symbol of all untried men.

Some critics have estimated him a morbid case. I cannot agree
to that. The abnormal cases are of the extremes; of those who
crumple up at the first sight of danger, and of those of whom
their fellows say, "He doesn't know what fear is." Neither will I
forget the rare favourites of the gods whose fiery spirit is only
soothed by the fury and clamour of a battle. Of such was General
Picton of Peninsular fame. But the lot of the mass of mankind is
to know fear, the decent fear of disgrace. Of such is the Young
Soldier of *The Red Badge of Courage*. He only seems exceptional
because he has got inside of him Stephen Crane's imagination,
and is presented to us with the insight and the power of expression of an artist whom a just and severe critic, on a review of
all his work, has called the foremost impressionist of his time,
as Sterne was the greatest impressionist, but in a different way,
of his age.

This is a generalized, fundamental judgment. More superficially both Zola's *La Débâcle* and Tolstoi's *War and Peace* were
mentioned by critics in connection with Crane's war book. But
Zola's main concern was with the downfall of the imperial
régime he fancied he was portraying; and in Tolstoi's book the
subtle presentation of Rostov's squadron under fire for the first
time is a mere episode lost in a mass of other matter, like a handful of pebbles in a heap of sand. I could not see the relevancy.
Crane was concerned with elemental truth only; and in any case
I think that as an artist he is non-comparable. He dealt with
what is enduring, and was the most detached of men.

That is why his book is short. Not quite two hundred pages.

Gems are small. This monodrama, which happy inspiration or unerring instinct has led him to put before us in narrative form, is contained between the opening words I have already quoted and a phrase on page 194 of the English edition, which runs: "He had been to touch the great death, and found that, after all, it was but the great death. He was a man."

On these words the action ends. We are only given one glimpse of the victorious army at dusk, under the falling rain, "a procession of weary soldiers become a dedraggled train, despondent and muttering, marching with churning effort in a trough of liquid brown mud under a low wretched sky . . .", while the last ray of the sun falls on the river through a break in the leaden clouds.

This war book, so virile and so full of gentle sympathy, in which not a single declamatory sentiment defaces the genuine verbal felicity, welding analysis and description in a continuous fascination of individual style, had been hailed by the critics as the herald of a brilliant career. Crane himself very seldom alluded to it, and always with a wistful smile. Perhaps he was conscious that, like the mortally wounded Tall Soldier of his book who, snatching at the air, staggers out into a field to meet his appointed death on the first day of battle—while the terrified Youth and the kind Tattered Soldier stand by silent, watching with awe "these ceremonies at the place of meeting"—it was his fate, too, to fall early in the fray.

III.
LITERARY REFLECTIONS AND REMINISCENCES

III.

Literary Reflections and Reminiscences

From "The Fine Art," *The Mirror of the Sea* (1906)

In fact, love is rare—the love of men, of things, of ideas, the love of perfected skill. For love is the enemy of haste; it takes count of passing days, of men who pass away, of a fine art matured slowly in the course of years and doomed in a short time to pass away, too, and be no more. Love and regret go hand in hand in this world of changes swifter than the shifting of the clouds reflected in the mirror of the sea. * * *

And an artist is a man of action, whether he creates a personality, invents an expedient, or finds the issue of a complicated situation.

"A Familiar Preface" (1912)

As a general rule we do not want much encouragement to talk about ourselves; yet this little book[1] is the result of a friendly suggestion, and even of a little friendly pressure. I defended myself with some spirit; but, with characteristic tenacity, the friendly voice insisted, 'You know, you really must.'

It was not an argument, but I submitted at once. If one must! . . .

You perceive the force of a word. He who wants to persuade should put his trust not in the right argument, but in the right word. The power of sound has always been greater than the power of sense. I don't say this by way of disparagement. It is better for mankind to be impressionable than reflective. Nothing humanly great—great, I mean, as affecting a whole mass of lives—has come from reflection. On the other hand, you cannot fail

---

1. *Some Reminiscences,* renamed *A Personal Record.*

to see the power of mere words; such words as Glory, for instance, or Pity. I won't mention any more. They are not far to seek. Shouted with perseverence, with ardour, with conviction, these two by their sound alone have set whole nations in motion and upheaved the dry, hard ground on which rests our whole social fabric. There's 'virtue' for you if you like! . . . Of course the accent must be attended to. The right accent. That's very important. The capacious lung, the thundering or the tender vocal chords. Don't talk to me of your Archimedes' lever. He was an absent-minded person with a mathematical imagination. Mathematics command all my respect, but I have no use for engines. Give me the right word and the right accent and I will move the world.

What a dream for a writer! Because written words have their accent, too. Yes! Let me only find the right word! Surely it must be lying somewhere among the wreckage of all the plaints and all the exultations poured out aloud since the first day when hope, the undying, came down on earth. It may be there, close by, disregarded, invisible, quite at hand. But it's no good. I believe there are men who can lay hold of a needle in a pottle of hay at the first try. For myself, I have never had such luck.

And then there is that accent. Another difficulty. For who is going to tell whether the accent is right or wrong till the word is shouted, and fails to be heard, perhaps, and goes down-wind, leaving the world unmoved? Once upon a time there lived an emperor who was a sage and something of a literary man. He jotted down on ivory tablets thoughts, maxims, reflections which chance has preserved for the edification of posterity. Among other sayings—I am quoting from memory—I remember this solemn admonition: 'Let all thy words have the accent of heroic truth.' The accent of heroic truth! This is very fine, but I am thinking that it is an easy matter for an austere emperor to jot down grandiose advice. Most of the working truths on this earth are humble, not heroic; and there have been times in the history of mankind when the accents of heroic truth have moved it to nothing but derision.

Nobody will expect to find between the covers of this little book words of extraordinary potency or accents of irresistible heroism. However humiliating for my self-esteem, I must confess that the counsels of Marcus Aurelius are not for me. They are more fit for a moralist than for an artist. Truth of a modest sort I can promise you, and also sincerity. That complete, praiseworthy sincerity which, while it delivers one into the hands of one's enemies, is as likely as not to embroil one with one's friends.

'Embroil' is perhaps too strong an expression. I can't imagine among either my enemies or my friends a being so hard up for something to do as to quarrel with me. 'To disappoint one's friends' would be nearer the mark. Most, almost all, friendships of the writing period of my life have come to me through my books; and I know that a novelist lives in his work. He stands there, the only reality in an invented world, among imaginary things, happenings, and people. Writing about them, he is only writing about himself. But the disclosure is not complete. He remains, to a certain extent, a figure behind the veil; a suspected rather than a seen presence—a movement and a voice behind the draperies of fiction. In these personal notes there is no such veil. And I cannot help thinking of a passage in the *Imitation of Christ* where the ascetic author, who knew life so profoundly, says that 'there are persons esteemed on their reputation who by showing themselves destroy the opinion one had of them.' This is the danger incurred by an author of fiction who sets out to talk about himself without disguise.

While these reminiscent pages were appearing serially I was remonstrated with for bad economy; as if such writing were a form of self-indulgence wasting the substance of future volumes. It seems that I am not sufficiently literary. Indeed, a man who never wrote a line for print till he was thirty-six cannot bring himself to look upon his existence and his experience, upon the sum of his thoughts, sensations, and emotions, upon his memories and his regrets and the whole possession of his past, as only so much material for his hands. Once before, some three years ago, when I published *The Mirror of the Sea*, a volume of impressions and memories, the same remarks were made to me. Practical remarks. But, truth to say, I have never understood the kind of thrift they recommend. I wanted to pay my tribute to the sea, its ships and its men, to whom I remain indebted for so much which has gone to make me what I am. That seemed to me the only shape in which I could offer it to their shades. There could not be a question in my mind of anything else. It is quite possible that I am a bad economist; but it is certain that I am incorrigible.

Having matured in the surroundings and under the special conditions of sea life, I have a special piety toward that form of my past; for its impressions were vivid, its appeal direct, its demands such as could be responded to with the natural elation of youth and strength equal to the call. There was nothing in them to perplex a young conscience. Having broken away from my origins under a storm of blame from every quarter which had the merest shadow of right to voice an opinion, removed by great distances from such natural affections as were still left to me, and even estranged, in a measure, from them by the totally unintelligible character of the life which had seduced me so mysteriously from my allegiance, I may safely say that through the blind force of circumstances the sea was to be all my world and the merchant service my only home for a long succession of years. No wonder, then, that in my two exclusively sea books—*The Nigger of the 'Narcissus'* and *The Mirror of the Sea* (and in the few short sea stories like *Youth* and *Typhoon*)—I have tried with an almost filial regard to render the vibration of life in the great world of waters, in the hearts of the simple men who have for ages traversed its solitudes, and also that something sentient which seems to dwell in ships—the creatures of their hands and the objects of their care.

One's literary life must turn frequently for sustenance to memories and seek discourse with the shades, unless one has made up one's mind to write only in order to reprove mankind for what it is, or praise it for what it is not, or—generally—to teach it how to behave. Being neither quarrelsome, nor a flatterer, nor a sage, I have done none of these things, and I am prepared to put up serenely with the insignificance which attaches to persons who are not meddlesome in some way or other. But resignation is not indifference. I would not like to be left standing as a mere spectator on the bank of the great stream carrying onward so many lives. I would fain claim for myself the faculty of so much insight as can be expressed in a voice of sympathy and compassion.

It seems to me that in one, at least, authoritative quarter of criticism I am suspected of a certain unemotional, grim acceptance of facts—of what the French would call *sécheresse du coeur*. Fifteen years of unbroken silence before praise or blame testify sufficiently to my respect for criticism, that fine flower of personal expression in the garden of letters. But this is more of a personal matter, reaching the man behind the work, and therefore it may be alluded to in a volume which is a personal note in the margin of the public page. Not that I feel hurt in the least. The charge— if it amounted to a charge at all—was made in the most considerate terms; in a tone of regret.

My answer is that if it be true that every novel contains an element of autobiography—and this can hardly be denied, since the creator can only express himself in his creation—then there are some of us to whom an open display of sentiment is repugnant. I would not unduly praise the virtue of restraint. It is often merely temperamental. But it is not always a sign of coldness. It may be pride. There can be nothing more humiliating than to see the shaft of one's emotion miss the mark of either laughter or tears. Nothing more humiliating! And this for the reason that should the mark be missed, should the open display of emotion fail to move, then it must perish unavoidably in disgust or contempt. No artist can be reproached for shrinking from a risk which only fools run to meet and only genius dare confront with impunity. In a task which mainly consists in laying one's soul more or less bare to the world, a regard for decency, even at the cost of success, is but the regard for one's own dignity which is inseparably united with the dignity of one's work.

And then—it is very difficult to be wholly joyous or wholly sad on this earth. The comic, when it is human, soon takes upon itself a face of pain; and some of our griefs (some only, not all, for it is the capacity for suffering which makes man august in the eyes of men) have their source in weaknesses which must be recognized with smiling compassion as the common inheritance of us all. Joy and sorrow in this world pass into each other, mingling their forms and their murmurs in the twilight of life as mysterious as an overshadowed ocean, while the dazzling brightness of supreme hopes lies far off, fascinating and still, on the distant edge of the horizon.

Yes! I, too, would like to hold the magic wand giving that command over laughter and tears which is declared to be the highest achievement of imaginative literature. Only, to be a great magician one must surrender oneself to occult and irresponsible powers, either outside or within one's breast. We have all heard of simple men selling their souls for love or power to some grotesque devil. The most ordinary intelligence can perceive without much reflection that anything of the sort is bound to be a fool's bargain. I don't lay claim to particular wisdom because of my dislike and distrust of such transactions. It may be my sea training acting upon a natural disposition to keep good hold on the one thing really mine, but the fact is that I have a positive horror of losing even for one moving moment that full possession of myself which is the first condition of good service. And I have carried my notion of good service from my earlier into my later existence. I, who have never sought in the written word anything else but a form of the Beautiful—I have carried over that article of creed from the decks of ships to the more circumscribed space of my desk, and by that act, I suppose, I have become permanently imperfect in the eyes of the ineffable company of pure aesthetes.

As in political so in literary action a man wins friends for himself mostly by the passion of his prejudices and by the consistent narrowness of his outlook. But I have never been able to love what was not lovable or hate what was not hateful out of deference for some general principle. Whether there be any courage in making this admission I know not. After the middle turn of life's way we consider dangers and joys with a tranquil mind. So I proceed in peace to declare that I have always suspected in the effort to bring into play the extremities of emotions the debasing touch of insincerity. In order to move others deeply we must deliberately allow ourselves to be carried away beyond the bounds of our normal sensibility—innocently enough, perhaps, and of necessity, like an actor who raises his voice on the stage above the pitch of natural conversation—but still we have to do that. And surely this is no great sin. But the danger lies in the writer becoming the victim of his own exaggeration, losing the exact notion of sincerity, and in the end coming to despise truth itself as something too cold, too blunt for his purpose—as, in fact, not good enough for his insistent emotion. From laughter and tears the descent is easy to snivelling and giggles.

These may seem selfish considerations; but you can't, in sound morals, condemn a man for taking care of his own integrity. It is his clear duty. And least of all can you condemn an artist pursuing, however humbly and imperfectly, a creative aim. In that interior world where his thought and his emotions go seeking for the experience of imagined adventures, there are no policemen, no law, no pressure of circumstance or dread of opinion to keep him within bounds. Who then is going to say Nay to his temptations if not his conscience?

And besides—this, remember, is the place and the moment of perfectly open talk—I think that all ambitions are lawful except those which climb upward on the miseries or credulities of mankind. All intellectual and artistic ambitions are permissible, up to and even beyond the limit of prudent sanity. They can hurt no one. If they are mad, then so much the worse for the artist. Indeed, as virtue is said to be, such ambitions are their own reward. Is it such a very mad presumption to believe in the sovereign power of one's art, to try for other means, for other ways of affirming this belief in the deeper appeal of one's work? To try to go deeper is not to be insensible. An historian of hearts is not an historian of emotions, yet he penetrates further, restrained as he may be, since his aim is to reach the very fount of laughter and tears. The sight of human affairs deserves admiration and pity. They are worthy of respect, too. And he is not insensible who pays them the undemonstrative tribute of a sigh which is not a sob, and of a smile which is not a grin. Resignation, not mystic, not detached, but resignation open-eyed, conscious, and informed by love, is the only one of our feelings for which it is impossible to become a sham.

Not that I think resignation the last word of wisdom. I am

too much the creature of my time for that. But I think that the proper wisdom is to will what the gods will without, perhaps, being certain what their will is—or even if they have a will of their own. And in this matter of life and art it is not the Why that matters so much to our happiness as the How. As the Frenchman said: 'Il y a toujours la manière.' Very true. Yes. There is the manner. The manner in laughter, in tears, in irony, indignations and enthusiasms, in judgments—and even in love. The manner in which, as in the features and character of a human face, the inner truth is foreshadowed for those who know how to look at their kind.

Those who read me know my conviction that the world, the temporal world, rests on a few very simple ideas; so simple that they must be as old as the hills. It rests notably, among others, on the idea of Fidelity. At a time when nothing which is not revolutionary in some way or other can expect to attract much attention I have not been revolutionary in my writings. The revolutionary spirit is mighty convenient in this, that it frees one from all scruples as regards ideas. Its hard, absolute optimism is repulsive to my mind by the menace of fanaticism and intolerance it contains. No doubt one should smile at these things; but, imperfect Aesthete, I am no better Philosopher. All claim to special righteousness awakens in me that scorn and anger from which a philosophical mind should be free . . .

I fear that trying to be conversational I have only managed to be unduly discursive. I have never been very well acquainted with the art of conversation—that art which, I understand, is supposed to be lost now. My young days, the days when one's habits and character are formed, have been rather familiar with long silences. Such voices as broke into them were anything but conversational. No. I haven't got the habit. Yet this discursiveness is not so irrelevant to the handful of pages which follow. They, too, have been charged with discursiveness, with disregard of chronological order (which is in itself a crime), with unconventionality of form (which is an impropriety). I was told severely that the public would view with displeasure the informal character of my recollections. 'Alas!' I protested, mildly. 'Could I begin with the sacramental words, "I was born on such a date in such a place"? The remoteness of the locality would have robbed the statement of all interest. I haven't lived through wonderful adventures to be related *seriatim*. I haven't known distinguished men on whom I could pass fatuous remarks. I haven't been mixed up with great or scandalous affairs. This is but a bit of psychological document, and even so, I haven't written it with a view to put forward any conclusion of my own.'

But my objector was not placated. These were good reasons for not writing at all—not a defence of what stood written already, he said.

I admit that almost anything, anything in the world, would serve as a good reason for not writing at all. But since I have written them, all I want to say in their defence is that these memories put down without any regard for established conventions have not been thrown off without system and purpose. They have their hope and their aim. The hope that from the reading of these pages there may emerge at last the vision of a personality; the man behind the books so fundamentally dissimilar as, for instance, *Almayer's Folly* and *The Secret Agent*, and yet a coherent, justifiable personality both in its origin and in its action. This is the hope. The immediate aim, closely associated with the hope, is to give the record of personal memories by presenting faithfully the feelings and sensations connected with the writing of my first book and with my first contact with the sea.

In the purposely mingled resonance of this double strain a friend here and there will perhaps detect a subtle accord.

From *A Personal Record*[2] (1912)

Books may be written in all sorts of places. Verbal inspiration may enter the berth of a mariner on board a ship frozen fast in a river in the middle of a town; and since saints are supposed to look benignantly on humble believers, I indulge in the pleasant fancy that the shade of old Flaubert—who imagined himself to be (amongst other things) a descendant of Vikings—might

2. Begun in 1908, *A Personal Record* was published in 1912.

have hovered with amused interest over the decks of a 2,000-ton steamer called the *Adowa*, on board of which, gripped by the inclement winter alongside a quay in Rouen, the tenth chapter of "Almayer's Folly" was begun. With interest, I say, for was not the kind Norman giant with enormous moustaches and a thundering voice the last of the Romantics? Was he not, in his unworldly, almost ascetic, devotion to his art a sort of literary, saint-like hermit?

" 'It has set at last,' said Nina to her mother, pointing to the hills behind which the sun had sunk." ... These words of Almayer's romantic daughter I remember tracing on the grey paper of a pad which rested on the blanket of my bed-place. They referred to a sunset in Malayan Isles, and shaped themselves in my mind, in a hallucinated vision of forests and rivers and seas, far removed from a commercial and yet romantic town of the northern hemisphere. But at that moment the mood of visions and words was cut short by the third officer, a cheerful and casual youth, coming in with a bang of the door and the exclamation: "You've made it jolly warm in here."

It was warm. I had turned on the steam-heater after placing a tin under the leaky water-cock—for perhaps you do not know that water will leak where steam will not. I am not aware of what my young friend had been doing on deck all that morning, but the hands he rubbed together vigorously were very red and imparted to me a chilly feeling by their mere aspect. He has remained the only banjoist of my acquaintance, and being also a younger son of a retired colonel, the poem of Mr. Kipling, by a strange aberration of associated ideas, always seems to me to have been written with an exclusive view to his person. When he did not play the banjo he loved to sit and look at it. He proceeded to this sentimental inspection, and after meditating a while over the strings under my silent scrutiny, inquired airily:

"What are you always scribbling there, if it's fair to ask?"

It was a fair enough question, but I did not answer him, and simply turned the pad over with a movement of instinctive secrecy: I could not have told him he had put to flight the psychology of Nina Almayer, her opening speech of the tenth chapter and the words of Mrs. Almayer's wisdom which were to follow in the ominous oncoming of a tropical night. I could not have told him that Nina had said: "It has set at last." He would have been extremely surprised and perhaps have dropped his precious banjo. Neither could I have told him that the sun of my sea-going was setting too, even as I wrote the words expressing the impatience of passionate youth bent on its desire. * * *

I had given myself up to the idleness of a haunted man who looks for nothing but words wherein to capture his visions. But I admit that outwardly I resembled sufficiently a man who could make a second officer for a steamer chartered by a French company. I showed no sign of being haunted by the fate of Nina and by the mumurs of tropical forests; and even my intimate intercourse with Almayer (a person of weak character) had not put a visible mark upon my features. For many years he and the world of his story had been the companions of my imagination without, I hope, impairing my ability to deal with the realities of sea life. I had had the man and his surroundings with me ever since my return from the eastern waters, some four years before the day of which I speak.[3]

It was in the front sitting-room of furnished apartments in a Pimlico square that they first began to live again with a vividness and poignancy quite foreign to our former real intercourse. I had been treating myself to a long stay on shore, and in the necessity of occupying my mornings, Almayer (that old acquaintance) came nobly to the rescue. Before long, as was only proper, his wife and daughter joined him round my table, and then the rest of that Pantai band came full of words and gestures. Unknown to my respectable landlady, it was my practice directly after my breakfast to hold animated receptions of Malays, Arabs and half-castes. They did not clamour aloud for my attention. They came with a silent and irresistible appeal—and the appeal, I affirm here, was not to my self-love or my vanity. It seems now to have had a moral character, for why should the memory of these beings, seen in their obscure sun-bathed existence, demand

3. Begun in 1889, *Almayer's Folly* was published in 1895.

to express itself in the shape of a novel, except on the ground of that mysterious fellowship which unites in a community of hopes and fears all the dwellers on this earth?

I did not receive my visitors with boisterous rapture as the bearers of any gifts of profit or fame. There was no vision of a printed book before me as I sat writing at that table, situated in a decayed part of Belgravia. After all these years, each leaving its evidence of slowly blackened pages, I can honestly say that it is a sentiment akin to piety which prompted me to render in words assembled with conscientious care the memory of things far distant and of men who had lived. * * *

You may think that this state of forced idleness favoured some advance in the fortunes of Almayer and his daughter. Yet it was not so. As if it were some sort of evil spell, my banjoist cabin-mate's interruption, as related above, had arrested them short at the point of that fateful sunset for many weeks together. It was always thus with this book, begun in '89 and finished in '94—with that shortest of all the novels which it was to be my lot to write. Between its opening exclamation calling Almayer to his dinner in his wife's voice and Abdullah's (his enemy) mental reference to the God of Islam—"The Merciful, the Compassion-ate"—which closes the book, there were to come several long sea passages, a visit (to use the elevated phraseology suitable to the occasion) to the scenes (some of them) of my childhood and the realization of childhood's vain words, expressing a light-hearted and romantic whim.

It was in 1868, when nine years old or thereabouts, that while looking at a map of Africa of the time and putting my finger on the blank space then representing the unsolved mystery of that continent, I said to myself with absolute assurance and an amaz-ing audacity which are no longer in my character now:

"When I grow up I shall go *there.*"

And of course I thought no more about it till after a quarter of a century or so an opportunity offered to go there—as if the sin of childish audacity was to be visited on my mature head. Yes. I did go there: *there* being the region of Stanley Falls which in '68 was the blankest of blank spaces on the earth's figured surface. And the MS. of "Almayer's Folly," carried about me as if it were a talisman or a treasure, went *there* too. That it ever came out of *there* seems a special dispensation of Providence; because a good many of my other properties, infinitely more valuable and useful to me, remained behind through unfortunate accidents of transportation. I call to mind, for instance, a specially awkward turn of the Congo between Kinchassa and Leopoldsville —more particularly when one had to take it at night in a big canoe with only half the proper number of paddlers. I failed in being the second white man on record drowned at that interesting spot through the upsetting of a canoe. The first was a young Belgian officer, but the accident happened some months before my time, and he, too, I believe, was going home; not perhaps quite so ill as myself—but still he was going home. I got around the turn more or less alive, thought I was too sick to care whether I did or not, and, always with "Almayer's Folly" amongst my diminishing baggage, I arrived at the delectable capital Boma, where before the departure of the steamer which was to take me home I had the time to wish myself dead over and over again with perfect sincerity. At that date there were in existence only seven chapters of "Almayer's Folly," but the chapter in my history which followed was that of a long, long illness and very dismal convalescence. Geneva, or more precisely the hydropathic establishment of Champel, is rendered for ever famous by the termination of the eighth chapter in the history of Almayer's decline and fall. The events of the ninth are inextricably mixed up with the details of the proper management of a waterside warehouse owned by a certain city firm whose name does not matter. But that work, undertaken to accustom myself again to the activities of a healthy existence, soon came to an end. The earth had nothing to hold me with for very long. And then that memorable story, like a cask of choice Madeira, got carried for three years to and fro upon the sea. Whether this treatment improved its flavour or not, of course I would not like to say. As far as appearance is concerned, it certainly did nothing of the kind. The whole MS. acquired a faded look and an ancient, yellowish complexion. It became at last unreasonable to suppose that anything in the world would ever happen to Almayer and Nina. And yet something most unlikely to happen on the high seas was to wake them up from their state of suspended animation. What is it that Novalis says? "It is certain my conviction gains infinitely the moment another soul will believe in it." And what is a novel if not a conviction of our fellow-men's existence strong enough to take upon itself a form of imagined life clearer than reality and whose accumulated verisimilitude of selected episodes puts to shame the pride of documentary history? Providence which saved my MS. from the Congo rapids brought it to the knowledge of a helpful soul far out on the open sea. It would be on my part the greatest ingratitude ever to forget the sallow, sunken face and the deep-set, dark eyes of the young Cambridge man (he was a "passenger for his health" on board the good ship *Torrens* outward bound to Australia) who was the first reader of "Almayer's Folly"—the very first reader I ever had. "Would it bore you very much reading a MS. in a handwriting like mine?" I asked him one evening on a sudden impulse at the end of a longish conversation whose subject was Gibbon's History. Jacques (that was his name) was sitting in my cabin one stormy dog-watch below, after bringing me a book to read from his own travelling store.

"Not at all," he answered with his courteous intonation and a faint smile. As I pulled a drawer open his suddenly aroused curiosity gave him a watchful expression. I wonder what he expected to see. A poem, maybe. All that's beyond guessing now. He was not a cold, but a calm man, still more subdued by disease— a man of few words and of an unassuming modesty in general intercourse, but with something uncommon in the whole of his person which set him apart from the undistinguished lot of our sixty passengers. His eyes had a thoughtful introspective look. In his attractive, reserved manner, and in a veiled, sympathetic voice, he asked:

"What is this?" "It is a sort of tale," I answered with an effort. "It is not even finished yet. Nevertheless, I would like to know what you think of it." He put the MS. in the breast-pocket of his jacket; I remember perfectly his thin brown fingers folding it lengthwise. "I will read it to-morrow," he remarked, seizing the door-handle, and then, watching the roll of the ship for a propitious moment, he opened the door and was gone. In the moment of his exit I heard the sustained booming of the wind, the swish of the water on the decks of the *Torrens,* and the subdued, as if distant, roar of the rising sea. I noted the growing disquiet in the great restlessness of the ocean, and responded professionally to it with the thought that at eight o'clock, in another half-hour or so at the furthest, the top-gallant sails would have to come off the ship.

Next day, but this time in the first dog-watch, Jacques entered my cabin. He had a thick, woollen muffler round his throat and the MS. was in his hand. He tendered it to me with a steady look but without a word. I took it in silence. He sat down on the couch and still said nothing. I opened and shut a drawer under my desk, on which a filled-up log-slate lay wide open in its wooden frame waiting to be copied neatly into the sort of book I was accustomed to write with care, the ship's log-book. I turned my back squarely on the desk. And even then Jacques never offered a word. "Well, what do you say?" I asked at last. "Is it worth finishing?" This question expressed exactly the whole of my thoughts.

"Distinctly," he answered in his sedate veiled voice, and then coughed a little.

"Were you interested?" I inquired further, almost in a whisper.

"Very much!"

In a pause I went on meeting instinctively the heavy rolling of the ship, and Jacques put his feet upon the couch. The curtain of my bed-place swung to and fro as it were a punkah, the bulkhead lamp circled in its gimbals, and now and then the cabin door rattled slightly in the gusts of wind. It was in latitude 40° south, and nearly in the longitude of Greenwich, as far as I can remember, that these quiet rites of Almayer's and Nina's resurrection were taking place. In the prolonged silence it occurred to me that there was a good deal of retrospective writing in the story as far as it went. Was it intelligible in its action, I asked myself, as if already the story-teller were being born into the body of a seaman. But I heard on deck the whistle of the officer of the watch and remained on the alert to catch the order that was to follow this call to attention. It reached me as a faint, fierce shout to "Square the yards." "Aha!" I thought to myself, "a westerly blow coming on." Then I turned to my very first reader, who, alas! was not to live long enough to know the end of the tale.

"Now let me ask you one more thing: Is the story quite clear to you as it stands?"

He raised his dark, gentle eyes to my face and seemed surprised.

"Yes! Perfectly."

This was all I was to hear from his lips concerning the merits of "Almayer's Folly." We never spoke together of the book again. A long period of bad weather set in and I had no thoughts left but for my duties, whilst poor Jacques caught a fatal cold and had to keep close in his cabin. When we arrived at Adelaide the first reader of my prose went at once up-country, and died rather suddenly in the end, either in Australia or it may be on the passage while going home through the Suez Canal. I am not sure which it was now, and I do not think I ever heard precisely; though I made inquires about him from some of our return passengers who, wandering about to "see the country" during the ship's stay in port, had come upon him here and there. At last we sailed, homeward bound, and still not one line was added to the careless scrawl of the many pages which poor Jacques had had the patience to read with the very shadows of Eternity gathering already in the hollows of his kind, steadfast eyes.

The purpose instilled into me by his simple and final "Distinctly" remained dormant, yet alive to await its opportunity. I dare say I am compelled, unconsciously compelled, now to write volume after volume, as in past years I was compelled to go to sea, voyage after voyage. Leaves must follow upon each other as leagues used to follow in the days gone by, on and on to the appointed end, which, being Truth itself, is One—one for all men and for all occupations.

I do not know which of the two impulses has appeared more mysterious and more wonderful to me. Still, in writing, as in going to sea, I had to wait my opportunity. Let me confess here that I was never one of those wonderful fellows that would go afloat in a wash-tub for the sake of the fun, and if I may pride myself upon my consistency it was ever just the same with my writing. Some men, I have heard, write in railway carriages, and could do it, perhaps, sitting cross-legged on a clothes-line; but I must confess that my sybaritic disposition will not consent to write without something at least resembling a chair. Line by line, rather than page by page, was the growth of "Almayer's Folly."

And so it happened that I very nearly lost the MS., advanced now to the first words of the ninth chapter, in the Friedrichstrasse railway station (that's in Berlin, you know) on my way to Poland, or more precisely Ukraine. On an early, sleepy morning, changing trains in a hurry, I left my gladstone bag in a refreshment room. A worthy and intelligent *Kofferträger* rescued it. Yet in my anxiety I was not thinking of the MS. but of all the other things that were packed in the bag.

In Warsaw, where I spent two days, those wandering pages were never exposed to the light, except once, to candle-light, while the bag lay open on a chair. I was dressing hurriedly to dine at a sporting club. A friend of my childhood (he had been in the Diplomatic Service, but had turned to growing wheat on paternal acres, and we had not seen each other for over twenty years) was sitting on the hotel sofa waiting to carry me off there.

"You might tell me something of your life while you are dressing," he suggested kindly.

I do not think I told him much of my life-story either then or later. The talk of the select little party with which he made me dine was extremely animated and embraced most subjects under heaven, from big-game shooting in Africa to the last poem published in a very modernist review, edited by the very young and patronized by the highest society. But it never touched upon "Almayer's Folly," and next morning, in uninterrupted obscurity, this inseparable companion went on rolling with me in the south-east direction towards the Government of Kiev. * * *

This is a far cry back from the MS. of "Almayer's Folly," but the public record of these formative impressions is not the whim of an uneasy egotism. These, too, are things human, already distant in their appeal. It is meet that something more should be left for the novelist's children than the colours and figures of his own hard-won creation. That which in their grown-up years may appear to the world about them as the most enigmatic side of their natures and perhaps must remain for ever obscure even to themselves, will be their unconscious response to the still voice of that inexorable past from which his work of fiction and their personalities are remotely derived.

Only in men's imagination does every truth find an effective and undeniable existence. Imagination, not invention, is the supreme master of art as of life. An imaginative and exact rendering of authentic memories may serve worthily that spirit of piety towards all things human which sanctions the conceptions of a writer of tales, and the emotions of the man reviewing his own experience. * * *

It must not be supposed that in setting forth the memories of this half-hour between the moment my uncle left my room till we met again at dinner, I am losing sight of "Almayer's Folly." Having confessed that my first novel was begun in idleness—a holiday task—I think I have also given the impression that it was a much-delayed book. It was never dismissed from my mind, even when the hope of ever finishing it was very faint. Many things came in its way: daily duties, new impressions, old memories. It was not the outcome of a need—the famous need of self-expression which artists find in their search for motives. The necessity which impelled me was a hidden, obscure necessity, a completely masked and unaccountable phenomenon. Or perhaps some idle and frivolous magician (there must be magicians in London) had cast a spell over me through his parlour window as I explored the maze of streets east and west in solitary leisurely walks without chart and compass. Till I began to write that novel I had written nothing but letters, and not very many of these. I never made a note of a fact, of an impression or of an anecdote in my life. The conception of a planned book was entirely outside my mental range when I sat down to write; the ambition of being an author had never turned up amongst these gracious imaginary existences one creates fondly for oneself at times in the stillness and immobility of a day-dream: yet it stands clear as the sun at noonday that from the moment I had done blackening over the first manuscript page of "Almayer's Folly" (it contained about two hundred words and this proportion of words to a page has remained with me through the fifteen years of my writing life), from the moment I had, in the simplicity of my heart and the amazing ignorance of my mind, written that page the die was cast. Never had Rubicon been more blindly forded, without invocation to the gods, without fear of men.

That morning I got up from my breakfast, pushing the chair back, and rang the bell violently, or perhaps I should say resolutely, or perhaps I should say eagerly, I do not know. But manifestly it must have been a special ring of the bell, a common sound made impressive, like the ringing of a bell for the raising of the curtain upon a new scene. It was an unusual thing for me to do. Generally, I dawdled over my breakfast and I seldom took the trouble to ring the bell for the table to be cleared away; but on that morning for some reason hidden in the general mysteriousness of the event I did not dawdle. And yet I was not in a hurry. I pulled the cord casually, and while the faint tinkling somewhere down in the basement went on, I charged my pipe in the usual way and I looked for the matchbox with glances distraught indeed but exhibiting, I am ready to swear, no signs of a fine frenzy. I was composed enough to perceive after some considerable time the matchbox lying there on the mantelpiece right under my nose. And all this was beautifully and safely usual. Before I had thrown down the match my landlady's daughter appeared with her calm, pale face and an inquisitive look, in the doorway. * * *

"Will you please clear away all this at once?" I addressed her in convulsive accents, being at the same time engaged in getting my pipe to draw. This, I admit, was an unusual request. Generally on getting up from breakfast I would sit down in the window with a book and let them clear the table when they liked; but if you think that on that morning I was in the least impatient, you are mistaken. I remember that I was perfectly calm. As a matter of fact I was not at all certain that I wanted to write, or that I meant to write, or that I had anything to write about. No, I was not impatient. I lounged between the mantelpiece and the window, not even consciously waiting for the table to be cleared. It was ten to one that before my landlady's daughter was done I would pick up a book and sit down with it all the morning in a spirit of enjoyable indolence. I affirm it with assurance, and I don't even know now what were the books then lying about the room. Whatever they were they were not the works of great masters, where the secret of clear thought and exact expression can be found. Since the age of five I have been a great reader, as is not perhaps wonderful in a child who was never aware of learning to read. At ten years of age I had read much of Victor Hugo and other romantics. I had read in Polish and in French, history, voyages, novels; I knew "Gil Blas" and "Don Quixote" in abridged editions; I had read in early boyhood Polish poets and some French poets, but I cannot say what I read on the evening before I began to write myself. I believe it was a novel, and it is quite possible that it was one of Anthony Trollope's novels. It is very likely. My acquaintance with him was then very recent. He is one of the English novelists whose works I read for the first time in English. With men of European reputation, with Dickens and Walter Scott and Thackeray, it was otherwise. My first introduction to English imaginative literature was "Nicholas Nickleby." It is extraordinary how well Mrs. Nickleby could chatter disconnectedly in Polish and the sinister Ralph rage in that language. As to the Crummles family and the family of the learned Squeers, it seemed as natural to them as their native speech. It was, I have no doubt, an excellent translation. This must have been in the year '70. But I really believe that I am wrong. That book was not my first introduction to English literature. My first acquaintance was (or were) the "Two Gentlemen of Verona," and that in the very MS. of my father's translation. It was during our exile in Russia, and it must have been less than a year after my mother's death, because I remember

myself in the black blouse with a white border of my heavy mourn-
ing. We were living together, quite alone, in a small house on
the outskirts of the town of T——. That afternoon, instead of
going out to play in the large yard which we shared with our
landlord, I had lingered in the room in which my father generally
wrote. What emboldened me to clamber into his chair I am sure
I don't know, but a couple of hours afterwards he discovered me
kneeling in it with my elbows on the table and my head held in
both hands over the MS. of loose pages. I was greatly confused,
expecting to get into trouble. He stood in the doorway looking
at me with some surprise, but the only thing he said after a
moment of silence was:

"Read the page aloud."

Luckily the page lying before me was not over blotted with
erasures and corrections, and my father's handwriting was otherwise extremely legible. When I got to the end he nodded and I
flew out of doors thinking myself lucky to have escaped reproof
for that piece of impulsive audacity. I have tried to discover
since the reason of this mildness, and I imagine that all unknown
to myself I had earned, in my father's mind, the right to some
latitude in my relations with his writing-table. It was only a
month before, or perhaps it was only a week before that I had
read to him aloud from beginning to end, and to his perfect satisfaction, as he lay on his bed, not being very well at the time,
the proofs of his translation of Victor Hugo's "Toilers of the
Sea." Such was my title to consideration, I believe, and also my
first introduction to the sea in literature. If I do not remember
where, how and when I learned to read, I am not likely to forget
the process of being trained in the art of reading aloud. My
poor father, an admirable reader himself, was the most exacting
of masters. I reflect proudly that I must have read that page of
"Two Gentlemen of Verona" tolerably well at the age of eight.
The next time I met them was in a five shilling one-volume edition of the dramatic works of William Shakespeare, read in
Falmouth, at odd moments of the day, to the noisy accompani-
ment of caulkers' mallets driving oakum into the deck-seams of
a ship in dry dock. We had run in, in a sinking condition and

with the crew refusing duty after a month of weary battling with the gales of the North Atlantic. Books are an integral part of one's life and my Shakespearean associations are with that first year of our bereavement, the last I spent with my father in exile (he sent me away to Poland to my mother's brother directly he could brace himself up for the separation), and with the year of hard gales, the year in which I came nearest to death at sea, first by water and then by fire.

Those things I remember, but what I was reading the day before my writing life began I have forgotten. I have only a vague notion that it might have been one of Trollope's political novels. And I remember, too, the character of the day. It was an autumn day with an opaline atmosphere, a veiled, semi-opaque, lustrous day, with fiery points and flashes of red sunlight on the roofs and windows opposite, while the trees of the square with all their leaves gone were like tracings of indian ink on a sheet of tissue paper. It was one of those London days that have the charm of mysterious amenity, of fascinating softness. The effect of opaline mist was often repeated at Bessborough Gardens on account of the nearness to the river.

There is no reason why I should remember that effect more on that day than on any other day, except that I stood for a long time looking out of the window after the landlady's daughter was gone with her spoil of cups and saucers. I heard her put the tray down in the passage and finally shut the door; and still I remained smoking with my back to the room. It is very clear that I was in no haste to take the plunge into my writing life, if as plunge this first attempt may be described. My whole being was steeped deep in the indolence of a sailor away from the sea, the scene of never-ending labour and of unceasing duty. For utter surrender to indolence you cannot beat a sailor ashore when that mood is on him, the mood of absolute irresponsibility tasted to the full. It seems to me that I thought of nothing whatever, but this is an impression which is hardly to be believed at this distance of years. What I am certain of is, that I was very far from thinking of writing a story, though it is possible and even likely that I was thinking of the man Almayer.

I had seen him for the first time some four years before from the bridge of a steamer moored to a rickety little wharf forty miles up, more or less, a Bornean river. It was very early morning, and a slight mist, an opaline mist as in Bessborough Gardens only without the fiery flicks on roof and chimney-pot from the rays of the red London sun, promised to turn presently into a woolly fog. Barring a small dug-out canoe on the river, there was nothing moving within sight. I had just come up yawning from my cabin. The serang and the Malay crew were overhauling the cargo chains and trying the winches; their voices sounded subdued on the deck below and their movements were languid. That tropical daybreak was chilly. The Malay quartermaster, coming up to get something from the lockers on the bridge, shivered visibly. The forests above and below and on the opposite bank looked black and dank; wet dripped from the rigging upon the tightly stretched deck awnings, and it was in the middle of a shuddering yawn that I caught sight of Almayer. He was moving across a patch of burnt grass, a blurred, shadowy shape with the blurred bulk of a house behind him, a low house of mats, bamboos and palm-leaves with a high-pitched roof of grass.

He stepped upon the jetty. He was clad simply in flapping pyjamas of cretonne pattern (enormous flowers with yellow petals on a disagreeable blue ground) and a thin cotton singlet with short sleeves. His arms, bare to the elbow, were crossed on his chest. His black hair looked as if it had not been cut for a very long time and a curly wisp of it strayed across his forehead. I had heard of him at Singapore; I had heard of him on board; I had heard of him early in the morning and late at night; I had heard of him at tiffin and at dinner; I had heard of him in a place called Pulo Laut from a half-caste gentleman there, who described himself as the manager of a coal-mine; which sounded civilised and progressive till you heard that the mine could not be worked at present because it was haunted by some particularly atrocious ghosts. I had heard of him in a place called Dongola, in the Island of Celebes, when the Rajah of that little-known sea-port (you can get no anchorage there in less than fifteen fathom, which is extremely inconvenient) came on board in a friendly way with only two attendants, and drank bottle after bottle of soda-water on the after-skylight with my good friend and commander Captain C——. At least I heard his name distinctly pronounced several times in a lot of talk in Malay language. Oh, yes, I heard it quite distinctly—Almayer, Almayer—and saw Captain C—— smile while the fat, dingy Rajah laughed audibly. To hear a Malay Rajah laugh outright is a rare experience, I can assure you. And I overheard more of Almayer's name amongst our deck passengers (mostly wandering traders of good repute) as they sat all over the ship—each man fenced round with bundles and boxes—on mats, on pillows, on quilts, on billets of wood, conversing of Island affairs. Upon my word, I heard the mutter of Almayer's name faintly at midnight, while making my way aft from the bridge to look at the patent taffrail-log tinkling its quarter-miles in the great silence of the sea. I don't mean to say that our passengers dreamed aloud of Almayer, but it is indubitable that two of them at least, who could not sleep apparently and were trying to charm away the trouble of insomnia by a little whispered talk at that ghostly hour were referring in some way or other to Almayer. It was really impossible on board that ship to get away definitely from Almayer; and a very small pony tied up forward and whisking its tail inside the galley, to the great embarrassment of our Chinaman cook, was destined for Almayer. What he wanted with a pony goodness only knows, since I am perfectly certain he could not ride it; but here you have the man, ambitious, aiming at the grandiose, importing a pony, whereas in the whole settlement at which he used to shake daily his impotent fist, there was only one path that was practicable for a pony: a quarter of a mile at most, hedged in by hundreds of square leagues of virgin forest. But who knows? The importation of that Bali pony might have been part of some deep scheme, of some diplomatic plan, of some hopeful intrigue. With Almayer one could never tell. He governed his conduct by considerations removed from the obvious, by incredible assumptions, which rendered his logic impenetrable to any reasonable person. I learned all this later. That morning, seeing the figure in pyjamas moving in the mist, I said to myself: "That's the man."

He came quite close to the ship's side and raised a harassed countenance, round and flat, with that curl of black hair over the forehead and a heavy, pained glance.

"Good morning."

"Good morning." * * *

But if I had not got to know Almayer pretty well it is almost certain there would never have been a line of mine in print.

I accepted then—and I am paying yet the price of my sanity. The possessor of the only flock of geese on the East Coast is responsible for the existence of some fourteen volumes, so far. The number of geese he had called into being under adverse climatic conditions was considerably more than fourteen. The tale of volumes will never overtake the counting of heads, I am safe to say; but my ambitions point not exactly that way, and whatever the pangs the toil of writing has cost me I have always thought kindly of Almayer.

I wonder, had he known anything of it, what his attitude would have been? This is something not to be discovered in this world. But if we ever meet in the Elysian Fields—where I cannot depict him to myself otherwise than attended in the distance by his flock of geese (birds sacred to Jupiter)— and he addresses me in the stillness of that passionless region, neither light nor darkness, neither sound nor silence, and heaving endlessly with billowy mists from the impalpable multitudes of the swarming dead, I think I know what answer to make.

I would say, after listening courteously to the unvibrating tone of his measured remonstrances, which should not disturb, of course, the solemn eternity of stillness in the least—I would say something like this:

"It is true, Almayer, that in the world below I have converted your name to my own uses. But that is a very small larceny. What's in a name, O Shade? If so much of your old mortal weakness clings to you yet as to make you feel aggrieved (it was the note of your earthly voice, Almayer), then, I entreat you, seek speech without delay with our sublime fellow-Shade—with him who, in his transient existence as a poet, commented upon the smell of the rose. He will comfort you. You came to me stripped of all prestige by men's queer smiles and the disrespectful chatter of every vagrant trader in the Islands. Your name was the common property of the winds: it, as it were, floated naked over the waters about the Equator. I wrapped round its unhonoured form the royal mantle of the tropics and have essayed to put into the hollow sound the very anguish of paternity—feats which you did not demand from me—but remember that all the toil and all the pain were mine. In your earthly life you haunted me, Almayer. Consider that this was taking a great liberty. Since you were always complaining of being lost to the world, you should remember that if I had not believed enough in your existence to let you haunt my rooms in Bessborough Gardens you would have been much more lost. You affirm that had I been capable of looking at you with a more perfect detachment and a greater simplicity, I might have perceived better the inward marvellousness which, you insist, attended your career upon that tiny pin-point of light, hardly visible, far, far below us, where both our graves lie. No doubt! But reflect, O complaining Shade! that this was not so much my fault as your crowning misfortune. I believed in you in the only way it was possible for me to believe. It was not worthy of your merits? So be it. But you were always an unlucky man, Almayer. Nothing was ever quite worthy of you. What made you so real to me was that you held this lofty theory with some force of conviction and with an admirable consistency."

It is with some such words translated into the proper shadowy expressions that I am prepared to placate Almayer in the Elysian Abode of Shades, since it has come to pass that having parted many years ago, we are never to meet again in this world. * * *

The ethical view of the universe involves us at last in so many cruel and absurd contradictions, where the last vestiges of faith, hope, charity, and even of reason itself, seem ready to perish, that I have come to suspect that the aim of creation cannot be ethical at all. I would fondly believe that its object is purely spectacular: a spectacle for awe, love, adoration, or hate, if you like, but in this view—and in this view alone—never for despair! Those visions, delicious or poignant, are a moral end in themselves. The rest is our affair—the laughter, the tears, the tenderness, the indignation, the high tranquillity of a steeled heart, the detached curiosity of a subtle mind—that's our affair! And the unwearied self-forgetful attention to every phase of the living universe reflected in our consciousness may be our appointed task on this earth. A task in which fate has perhaps engaged nothing of us except our conscience, gifted with a voice in order to bear true testimony to the visible wonder, the haunting terror, the infinite passion and the illimitable serenity; to the supreme law and the abiding mystery of the sublime spectacle.

Chi lo sà? It may be true. In this view there is room for every religion except for the inverted creed of impiety, the mask and cloak of arid despair; for every joy and every sorrow, for every fair dream, for every charitable hope. The great aim is to remain true to the emotions called out of the deep encircled by the firmament of stars, whose infinite numbers and awful distance may move us to laughter or tears (was it the Walrus or the Carpenter, in the poem, who "wept to see such quantities of sand"?), or again, to a properly steeled heart, may matter nothing at all.

The casual quotation, which had suggested itself out of a poem full of merit, leads me to remark that in the conception of a purely spectacular universe, where inspiration of every sort has a rational existence, the artist of every kind finds a natural place; and amongst them the poet as the seer *par excellence*. Even the writer of prose, who in his less noble and more toilsome task should be a man with the steeled heart, is worthy of a place, providing he looks on with undimmed eyes and keeps laughter out of his voice, let who will laugh or cry. Yes! Even he, the prose artist of fiction, which after all is but truth often dragged out of a well and clothed in the painted robe of imaged phrases—even he has his place amongst kings, demagogues, priests, charlatans, dukes, giraffes, Cabinet Ministers, Fabians, bricklayers, apostles, ants, scientists, Kaffirs, soldiers, sailors, elephants, lawyers, dandies, microbes and constellations of a universe whose amazing spectacle is a moral end in itself.

Here I perceive (speaking without offence) the reader assuming a subtle expression, as if the cat were out of the bag. I take the novelist's freedom to observe the reader's mind formulating the exclamation, "That's it! The fellow talks *pro domo.*"

Indeed it was not the intention! When I shouldered the bag I was not aware of the cat inside. But, after all, why not? The fair courtyards of the House of Art are thronged by many humble retainers. And there is no retainer so devoted as he who is allowed to sit on the doorstep. The fellows who have got inside are apt to think too much of themselves. This last remark, I beg to state, is not malicious within the definition of the law of libel. It's fair comment on a matter of public interest. But never mind. *Pro domo.* So be it. For his house *tant que vous voudrez.* And yet in truth I was by no means anxious to justify my existence. The attempt would have been not only needless and absurd but almost inconceivable, in a purely spectacular universe, where no such disagreeable necessity can possibly arise. It is sufficient for me to say (and I am saying it at some length in these pages): *J'ai vécu.* I have existed, obscure amongst the wonders and terrors of my time, as the Abbé Sieyès, the original utterer of the quoted words, had managed to exist through the violences, the crimes, and the enthusiasms of the French Revolution. *J'ai vécu,* as I apprehend most of us manage to exist, missing all along the varied forms of destruction by a hair's-breadth, saving my body, that's clear, and perhaps my soul also, but not without some damage here and there to the fine edge of my conscience, that heirloom of the ages, of the race, of the group, of the family, colourable and plastic, fashioned by the words, the looks, the acts, and even by the silences and abstentions surrounding one's childhood; tinged in a complete scheme of delicate shades and crude colours by the inherited traditions, beliefs, or prejudices—unaccountable, despotic, persuasive, and often, in its texture, romantic.

And often romantic! . . . The matter in hand, however, is to keep these reminiscences from turning into confessions, a form of literary activity discredited by Jean Jacques Rousseau on account of the extreme thoroughness he brought to the work of justifying his own existence; for that such was his purpose is palpably, even grossly, visible to an unprejudiced eye. But then, you see, the man was not a writer of fiction. He was an artless moralist, as is clearly demonstrated by his anniversaries being celebrated with marked emphasis by the heirs of the French Revolution, which was not a

political movement at all, but a great outburst of morality. He
had no imagination, as the most casual perusal of "Émile" will
prove. He was no novelist, whose first virtue is the exact understanding of the limits traced by the reality of his time to the play
of his invention. Inspiration comes from the earth, which has a
past, a history, a future, not from the cold and immutable heaven.
A writer of imaginative prose (even more than any other sort of
artist) stands confessed in his works. His conscience, his deeper
sense of things, lawful and unlawful, gives him his attitude before
the world. Indeed, everyone who puts pen to paper for the reading
of strangers (unless a moralist, who, generally speaking, has no
conscience except the one he is at pains to produce for the use of
others) can speak of nothing else. It is M. Anatole France, the
most eloquent and just of French prose writers, who says that we
must recognise at last that, "failing the resolution to hold our
peace, we can only talk of ourselves."

This remark, if I remember rightly, was made in the course of
a sparring match with the late Ferdinand Brunetière over the
principles and rules of literary criticism. As was fitting for a man
to whom we owe the memorable saying, "The good critic is he
who relates the adventures of his soul amongst masterpieces," M.
Anatole France maintained that there were no rules and no principles. And that may be very true. Rules, principles and standards
die and vanish every day. Perhaps they are all dead and vanished
by this time. These, if ever, are the brave free days of destroyed
landmarks, while the ingenious minds are busy inventing the
forms of the new beacons which, it is consoling to think, will be
set up presently in the old places. But what is interesting to a
writer is the possession of an inward certitude that literary criticism will never die, for man (so variously defined) is, before
everything else, a critical animal. And, as long as distinguished
minds are ready to treat it in the spirit of high adventure, literary
criticism shall appeal to us with all the charm and wisdom of a
well-told tale of personal experience.

For Englishmen especially, of all the races of the earth, a task,
any task, undertaken in an adventurous spirit acquires the merit
of romance. But the critics as a rule exhibit but little of an ad-

venturous spirit. They take risks, of course—one can hardly live without that. The daily bread is served out to us (however sparingly) with a pinch of salt. Otherwise one would get sick of the diet one prays for, and that would be not only improper, but impious. From impiety of that or any other kind—save us! An ideal of reserved manner, adhered to from a sense of proprieties, from shyness, perhaps, or caution, or simply from weariness, induces, I suspect, some writers of criticism to conceal the adventurous side of their calling, and then the criticism becomes a mere "notice," as it were the relation of a journey where nothing but the distances and the geology of a new country should be set down; the glimpses of strange beasts, the dangers of flood and field, the hair's-breadth escapes, and the sufferings (oh, the sufferings too! I have no doubt of the sufferings) of the traveller being carefully kept out; no shady spot, no fruitful plant being ever mentioned either; so that the whole performance looks like a mere feat of agility on the part of a trained pen running in a desert. A cruel spectacle—a most deplorable adventure. "Life," in the words of an immortal thinker of, I should say, bucolic origin, but whose perishable name is lost to the worship of posterity—"life is not all beer and skittles." Neither is the writing of novels. It isn't really. *Je vous donne ma parole d'honneur* that it—is—not. Not *all.* I am thus emphatic because some years ago, I remember, the daughter of a general...

Sudden revelations of the profane world must have come now and then to hermits in their cells, to the cloistered monks of Middle Ages, to lonely sages, men of science, reformers; the revelations of the world's superficial judgment, shocking to the souls concentrated upon their own bitter labour in the cause of sanctity, or of knowledge, or of temperance, let us say, or of art, if only the art of cracking jokes or playing the flute. And thus this general's daughter came to me—I should say one of the general's daughters did. There were three of these bachelor ladies, of nicely graduated ages, who held a neighbouring farmhouse in a united and more or less military occupation. The eldest warred against the decay of manners in the village children, and executed frontal attacks upon the village mothers for the conquest of curtseys. It sounds futile, but it was really a war for an idea. The second skirmished and scouted all over the country; and it was that one who pushed a reconnaissance right to my very table—I mean the one who wore stand-up collars. She was really calling upon my wife in the soft spirit of afternoon friendliness, but with her usual martial determination. She marched into my room swinging her stick ... but no—I musn't exaggerate. It is not my speciality. I am not a humoristic writer. In all soberness, then, all I am certain of is that she had a stick to swing.

No ditch or wall encompassed my abode. The window was open; the door too stood open to that best friend of my work, the warm, still sunshine of the wide fields. They lay around me infinitely helpful, but truth to say I had not known for weeks whether the sun shone upon the earth and whether the stars above still moved on their appointed courses. I was just then giving up some days of my allotted span to the last chapters of the novel "Nostromo,"[4] a tale of an imaginary (but true) seaboard, which is still mentioned now and again, and indeed kindly, sometimes in connection with the word "failure" and sometimes in conjunction with the word "astonishing." I have no opinion on this discrepancy. It's the sort of difference that can never be settled. All I know, is that, for twenty months, neglecting the common joys of life that fall to the lot of the humblest on this earth, I had, like the prophet of old, "wrestled with the Lord" for my creation, for the headlands of the coast, for the darkness of the Placid Gulf, the light on the snows, the clouds on the sky, and for the breath of life that had to be blown into the shapes of men and women, of Latin and Saxon, of Jew and Gentile. These are, perhaps, strong words, but it is difficult to characterise otherwise the intimacy and the strain of a creative effort in which mind and will and conscience are engaged to the full, hour after hour, day after day, away from the world, and to the exclusion of all that makes life really lovable and gentle—something for which a material parallel can only be found in the everlasting sombre stress of the westward winter passage round Cape Horn. For that too is the wrestling of men

4. *Nostromo* was published in 1904.

with the might of their Creator, in a great isolation from the
world, without the amenities and consolations of life, a lonely
struggle under a sense of over-matched littleness, for no reward
that could be adequate, but for the mere winning of a longitude.
Yet a certain longitude, once won, cannot be disputed. The sun
and the stars and the shape of your earth are the witnesses of
your gain; whereas a handful of pages, no matter how much you
have made them your own, are at best but an obscure and ques-
tionable spoil. Here they are. "Failure"—"Astonishing": take your
choice; or perhaps both, or neither—a mere rustle and flutter of
pieces of paper settling down in the night, and undistinguishable,
like the snowflakes of a great drift destined to melt away in sunshine.

"How do you do?"

It was the greeting of the general's daughter. I had heard
nothing—no rustle, no footsteps. I had felt only a moment before
a sort of premonition of evil; I had the sense of an inauspicious
presence—just that much warning and no more; and then came
the sound of the voice and jar as of a terrible fall from a great
height—a fall, let us say, from the highest of the clouds floating
in gentle procession over the fields in the faint westerly air of that
July afternoon. I picked myself up quickly, of course; in other
words, I jumped up from my chair stunned and dazed, every
nerve quivering with the pain of being uprooted out of one world
and flung down into another—perfectly civil.

"Oh! How do you do? Won't you sit down?"

That's what I said. This horrible but, I assure you, perfectly
true reminiscence tells you more than a whole volume of confessions à la Jean Jacques Rousseau would do. Observe! I didn't
howl at her, or start upsetting furniture, or throw myself on the
floor and kick, or allow myself to hint in any other way at the
appalling magnitude of the disaster. The whole world of Costaguana (the country, you may remember, of my seaboard tale),
men, women, headlands, houses, mountains, town, campo (there
was not a single brick, stone, or grain of sand of its soil I had not
placed in position with my own hands); all the history, geography,
politics, finance; the wealth of Charles Gould's silver-mine, and

the splendour of the magnificent Capataz de Cargadores, whose name, cried out in the night (Dr. Monygham heard it pass over his head—in Linda Viola's voice), dominated even after death the dark gulf containing his conquests of treasure and love—all that had come down crashing about my ears. I felt I could never pick up the pieces—and in that very moment I was saying, "Won't you sit down?"

The sea is strong medicine. Behold what the quarter-deck training even in a merchant ship will do! This episode should give you a new view of the English and Scots seamen (a much-caricatured folk) who had the last say in the formation of my character. One is nothing if not modest, but in this disaster I think I have done some honour to their simple teaching. "Won't you sit down?" Very fair; very fair indeed. She sat down. Her amused glance strayed all over the room. There were pages of MS. on the table and under the table, a batch of typed copy on a chair, single leaves had fluttered away into distant corners; there were there living pages, pages scored and wounded, dead pages that would be burnt at the end of the day—the litter of a cruel battlefield, of a long, long and desperate fray. Long! I suppose I went to bed sometimes, and got up the same number of times. Yes, I suppose I slept, and ate the food put before me, and talked connectedly to my household on suitable occasions. But I had never been aware of the even flow of daily life, made easy and noiseless for me by a silent, watchful, tireless affection. Indeed, it seemed to me that I had been sitting at that table surrounded by the litter of a desperate fray for days and nights on end. It seemed so, because of the intense weariness of which that interruption had made me aware— the awful disenchantment of a mind realising suddenly the futility of an enormous task, joined to a bodily fatigue such as no ordinary amount of fairly heavy physical labour could ever account for. I have carried bags of wheat on my back, bent almost double under a ship's deck-beams, from six in the morning till six in the evening (with an hour and a half off for meals), so I ought to know.

And I love letters. I am jealous of their honour and concerned for the dignity and comeliness of their service. I was, most likely, the only writer that neat lady had ever caught in the exercise of his craft, and it distressed me not to be able to remember when it was that I dressed myself last, and how. No doubt that would be all right in essentials. The fortune of the house included a pair of grey-blue watchful eyes that would see to that. But I felt somehow as grimy as a Costaguana lépero after a day's fighting in the streets, rumpled all over and dishevelled down to my very heels. And I am afraid I blinked stupidly. All this was bad for the honour of letters and the dignity of their service. Seen indistinctly through the dust of my collapsed universe, the good lady glanced about the room with a slightly amused serenity. And she was smiling. What on earth was she smiling at? She remarked casually:

"I am afraid I interrupted you."

"Not at all."

She accepted the denial in perfect good faith. And it was strictly true. Interrupted—indeed! She had robbed me of at least twenty lives, each infinitely more poignant and real than her own, because informed with passion, possessed of convictions, involved in great affairs created out of my own substance for an anxiously meditated end.

She remained silent for a while, then said with a last glance all round at the litter of the fray:

"And you sit like this here writing your—your . . ."

"I—what? Oh, yes! I sit here all day."

"It must be perfectly delightful."

I suppose that, being no longer very young, I might have been on the verge of having a stroke; but she had left her dog in the porch, and my boy's dog, patrolling the field in front, had espied him from afar. He came on straight and swift like a cannon-ball, and the noise of the fight, which burst suddenly upon our ears, was more than enough to scare away a fit of apoplexy. We went out hastily and separated the gallant animals. Afterwards I told the lady where she would find my wife—just round the corner, under the trees. She nodded and went off with her dog, leaving me appalled before the death and devastation she had lightly made—and with the awfully instructive sound of the word "delightful" lingering in my ears.

Nevertheless, later on, I duly escorted her to the field gate. I wanted to be civil, of course (what are twenty lives in a mere novel that one should be rude to a lady on their account?), but mainly, to adopt the good sound Ollendorffian style,[5] because I did not want the dog of the general's daughter to fight again (*encore*) with the faithful dog of my infant son (*mon petit garçon*). —Was I afraid that the dog of the general's daughter would be able to overcome (*vaincre*) the dog of my child? —No, I was not afraid . . . But away with the Ollendorff method. However appropriate and seemingly unavoidable when I touch upon anything appertaining to the lady, it is most unsuitable to the origin, character and history of the dog; for the dog was the gift to the child from a man for whom words had anything but an Ollendorffian value, a man almost childlike in the impulsive movements of his untutored genius, the most singleminded of verbal impressionists, using his great gifts of straight feeling and right expression with a fine sincerity and a strong, if, perhaps, not fully conscious conviction. His art did not obtain, I fear, all the credit its unsophisticated inspiration deserved. I am alluding to the late Stephen Crane, the author of "The Red Badge of Courage," a work of imagination which found its short moment of celebrity in the last decade of the departed century. Other books followed. Not many. He had not the time. It was an individual and complete talent, which obtained but a grudging, somewhat supercilious recognition from the world at large. For himself one hestitates to regret his early death. Like one of the men in his "Open Boat," one felt that he was of those whom fate seldom allows to make a safe landing after much toil and bitterness at the oar. I confess to an abiding affection for that energetic, slight, fragile, intensely living and transient figure. He liked me even before we met on the strength of a page or two of my writing, and after we had met I am glad to think he liked me still. He used to point out to me with great earnestness, and even with some severity, that "a boy *ought* to have a dog." I suspect that he was shocked at my neglect of parental duties. Ultimately it was he who provided the dog.

5. A playful reference to H. G. Ollendorff's books for teaching foreign languages.

Shortly afterwards, one day, after playing with the child on the rug for an hour or so with the most intense absorption, he raised his head and declared firmly: "I shall teach your boy to ride." That was not to be. He was not given the time.

But here is the dog—an old dog now. Broad and low on his bandy paws, with a black head on a white body, and a ridiculous black spot at the other end of him, he provokes, when he walks abroad, smiles not altogether unkind. Grotesque and engaging in the whole of his appearance, his usual attitudes are meek, but his temperament discloses itself unexpectedly pugnacious in the presence of his kind. As he lies in the firelight, his head well up, and a fixed, far-away gaze directed at the shadows of the room, he achieves a striking nobility of pose in the calm consciousness of an unstained life. He has brought up one baby, and now, after seeing his first charge off to school, he is bringing up another with the same conscientious devotion but with a more deliberate gravity of manner, the sign of greater wisdom and riper experience, but also of rheumatism, I fear. From the morning bath to the evening ceremonies of the cot you attend, old friend, the little two-legged creature of your adoption, being yourself treated in the exercise of your duties with every possible regard, with infinite consideration, by every person in the house—even as I myself am treated; only you deserve it more. The general's daughter would tell you that it must be "perfectly delightful."

Aha! old dog. She never heard you yelp with acute pain (it's that poor left ear) the while, with incredible self-command, you preserve a rigid immobility for fear of overturning the little two-legged creature. She has never seen your resigned smile when the little two-legged creature, interrogated sternly, "What are you doing to the good dog?" answers with a wide, innocent stare: "Nothing. Only loving him, mamma dear!"

The general's daughter does not know the secret terms of self-imposed tasks, good dog, the pain that may lurk in the very rewards of rigid self-command. But we have lived together many years. We have grown older, too; and though our work is not quite done yet we may indulge now and then in a little introspection before the fire—meditate on the art of bringing up babies and on the perfect delight of writing tales where so many lives come and go at the cost of one which slips imperceptibly away. * * *

I only love letters; but the love of letters does not make a literary man, any more than the love of the sea makes a seaman. And it is very possible too, that I love the letters in the same way a literary man may love the sea he looks at from the shore—a scene of great endeavour and of great achievements changing the face of the world, the great open way to all sorts of undiscovered countries. No, perhaps I had better say that the life at sea—and I don't mean a mere taste of it, but a good broad span of years, something that really counts as real service—is not, upon the whole, a good equipment for a writing life. God forbid, though, that I should be thought of as denying my masters of the quarter-deck. I am not capable of that sort of apostasy. I have confessed my attitude of piety towards their shades in three or four tales, and if any man on earth more than another needs to be true to himself as he hopes to be saved, it is certainly the writer of fiction.

What I meant to say, simply, is that the quarter-deck training does not prepare one sufficiently for the reception of literary criticism. Only that, and no more. But this defect is not without gravity. If it be permissible to twist, invert, adapt (and spoil) M. Anatole France's definition of a good critic, then let us say that the good author is he who contemplates without marked joy or excessive sorrow the adventures of his soul amongst criticisms. Far be from me the intention to mislead an attentive public into the belief that there is no criticism at sea. That would be dishonest, and even impolite. Everything can be found at sea, according to the spirit of your quest—strife, peace, romance, naturalism of the most pronounced kind, ideals, boredom, disgust, inspiration—and every conceivable opportunity, including the opportunity to make a fool of yourself—exactly as in the pursuit of literature. But the quarter-deck criticism is somewhat different from literary criticism. This much they have in common, that before the one and the other the answering back, as a general rule, does not pay.

Yes, you find criticism at sea, and even appreciation—I tell you everything is to be found on salt water—criticism generally impromptu, and always *viva voce*, which is the outward, obvious difference from the literary operation of that kind, with consequent freshness and vigour which may be lacking in the printed word. With appreciation, which comes at the end, when the critic and the criticised are about to part, it is otherwise. The sea appreciation of one's humble talents has the permanency of the written word, seldom the charm of variety, is formal in its phrasing. There the literary master has the superiority, though he, too, can in effect but say—and often says it in the very phrase—"I can highly recommend." Only usually he uses the word "We," there being some occult virtue in the first person plural, which makes it specially fit for critical and royal declarations. I have a small handful of these sea appreciations, signed by various masters, yellowing slowly in my writing-table's left-hand drawer, rustling under my reverent touch, like a handful of dry leaves plucked for a tender memento from the tree of knowledge. Strange! It seems that it is for these few bits of paper, headed by the names of a few ships and signed by the names of a few Scots and English shipmasters, that I have faced the astonished indignations, the mockeries and the reproaches of a sort hard to bear for a boy of fifteen; that I have been charged with the want of patriotism, the want of sense, and the want of heart too; that I went through agonies of self-conflict and shed secret tears not a few, and had the beauties of the Furca Pass spoiled for me, and have been called an "incorrigible Don Quixote," in allusion to the book-born madness of the knight. For that spoil! They rustle, those bits of paper —some dozen of them in all. In that faint, ghostly sound there live the memories of twenty years, the voices of rough men now no more, the strong voice of the everlasting winds, and the whisper of a mysterious spell, the murmur of the great sea, which must have somehow reached my inland cradle and entered my unconscious ear, like that formula of Mohammedan faith the Mussulman father whispers into the ear of his new-born infant, making him one of the faithful almost with his first breath. I do not know whether I have been a good seaman, but I know I have been a very faithful one. And after all there is that handful of "characters" from various ships to prove that all these years have not been altogether a dream. There they are, brief, and monotonous in tone, but as suggestive bits of writing to me as any inspired page to be found in literature. But then, you see, I have been called romantic. Well, that can't be helped. But stay. I seem to remember that I have been called a realist also. And as that charge too can be made out, let us try to live up to it, at whatever cost, for a change. With this end in view, I will confide to you coyly, and only because there is no one about to see my blushes by the light of the midnight lamp, that these suggestive bits of quarter-deck appreciation one and all contain the words "strictly sober."

Did I overhear a civil mumur, "That's very gratifying to be sure"? Well, yes, it is gratifying—thank you. It is at least as gratifying to be certified sober as to be certified romantic, though such certificates would not qualify one for the secretaryship of a temperance association or for the post of official troubadour to some lordly democratic institution such as the London County Council, for instance. The above prosaic reflection is put down here only in order to prove the general sobriety of my judgment in mundane affairs. I make a point of it because a couple of years ago, a certain short story of mine being published in a French translation, a Parisian critic—I am almost certain it was M. Gustave Kahn, in the *Gil-Blas*—giving me a short notice, summed up his rapid impression of the writer's quality in the words *un puissant rêveur*. So be it! Who would cavil at the words of a friendly reader? Yet perhaps not such an uncondi-tional dreamer as all that. I will make bold to say that neither at sea nor ashore have I ever lost the sense of responsibility. There is more than one sort of intoxication. Even before the most seductive reveries I have remained mindful of the sobriety of interior life, that asceticism of sentiment, in which alone the naked form of truth, such as one conceives it, such as one feels it, can be rendered without shame. It is but a maudlin and indecent verity that comes out through the strength of wine. I have tried to be a sober worker all my life—all my two lives. I did so from taste, no doubt, having an instinctive horror of losing my sense of full self-possession, but also from artistic conviction. Yet there are so many pitfalls on each side of the true path that, having gone some way, and feeling a little battered and weary, as a middle-aged traveller will from the mere daily difficulties of the march, I ask myself whether I have kept always calm, always faithful to that sobriety wherein there is power, and truth, and peace.

IV.
AUTHOR'S NOTES AND PREFACES

IV.

Author's Notes and Prefaces

Almayer's Folly (1895)

I am informed that in criticizing that literature which preys on strange people and prowls in far-off countries, under the shade of palms, in the unsheltered glare of sunbeaten beaches, amongst honest cannibals and the more sophisticated pioneers of our glorious virtues, a lady—distinguished in the world of letters—summed up her disapproval of it by saying that the tales it produced were 'decivilized.' And in that sentence not only the tales but, I apprehend, the strange people and the far-off countries also, are finally condemned in a verdict of contemptuous dislike.

A woman's judgment: intuitive, clever, expressed with felicitous charm—infallible. A judgment that has nothing to do with justice. The critic and the judge seems to think that in those distant lands all joy is a yell and a war dance, all pathos is a howl and a ghastly grin of filed teeth, and that the solution of all problems is found in the barrel of a revolver or on the point of an assegai. And yet it is not so. But the erring magistrate may plead in excuse the misleading nature of the evidence.

The picture of life, there as here, is drawn with the same elaboration of detail, coloured with the same tints. Only in the cruel serenity of the sky, under the merciless brilliance of the sun, the dazzled eye misses the delicate detail, sees only the strong outlines, while the colours, in the steady light, seem crude and without shadow. Nevertheless it is the same picture.

And there is a bond between us and that humanity so far away. I am speaking here of men and women—not of the charming and grateful phantoms that move about in our mud and smoke and are softly luminous with the radiance of all our

159

virtues; that are posssessed of all refinements, of all sensibilities, of all wisdom—but, being only phantoms, possess no heart.

The sympathies of those are (probably) with the immortals: with the angels above or the devils below. I am content to sympathize with common mortals, no matter where they live; in houses or in tents, in the streets under a fog, or in the forests behind the dark line of dismal mangroves that fringe the vast solitude of the sea. For, their land—like ours—lies under the inscrutable eyes of the Most High. Their hearts—like ours—must endure the load of the gifts from Heaven: the curse of facts and the blessing of illusions, the bitterness of our wisdom and the deceptive consolation of our folly.

The Nigger of the "Narcissus" (1897)

A work that aspires, however humbly, to the condition of art should carry its justification in every line. And art itself may be defined as a single-minded attempt to render the highest kind of justice to the visible universe, by bringing to light the truth, manifold and one, underlying its every aspect. It is an attempt to find in its forms, in its colours, in its light, in its shadows, in the aspects of matter, and in the facts of life what of each is fundamental, what is enduring and essential—their one illuminating and convincing quality—the very truth of their existence. The artist, then, like the thinker or the scientist, seeks the truth and makes his appeal. Impressed by the aspect of the world the thinker plunges into ideas, the scientist into facts—whence, presently, emerging they make their appeal to those qualities of our being that fit us best for the hazardous enterprise of living. They speak authoritatively to our common sense, to our intelligence, to our desire of peace, or to our desire of unrest; not seldom to our prejudices, sometimes to our fears, often to our egoism—but always to our credulity. And their words are heard with reverence, for their concern is with weighty matters: with the cultivation of our minds and the proper care of our bodies, with the attainment of our ambitions, with the perfection of the means and the glorification of our precious aims.

It is otherwise with the artist.

Confronted by the same enigmatical spectacle the artist des-
cends within himself, and in that lonely region of stress and strife,
if he be deserving and fortunate, he finds the terms of his appeal.
His appeal is made to our less obvious capacities: to that part of
our nature which, because of the warlike conditions of existence,
is necessarily kept out of sight within the more resisting and
hard qualities—like the vulnerable body within a steel armour.
His appeal is less loud, more profound, less distinct, more stirring—and sooner forgotten. Yet its effect endures for ever. The
changing wisdom of successive generations discards ideas, questions facts, demolishes theories. But the artist appeals to that
part of our being which is not dependent on wisdom; to that
in us which is a gift and not an acquisition—and, therefore, more
permanently enduring. He speaks to our capacity for delight and
wonder, to the sense of mystery surrounding our lives; to our
sense of pity, and beauty, and pain; to the latent feeling of fellowship with all creation—and to the subtle but invincible conviction of solidarity that knits together the loneliness of innumerable hearts, to the solidarity in dreams, in joy, in sorrow, in
aspirations, in illusions, in hope, in fear, which binds men to
each other, which binds together all humanity—the dead to the
living and the living to the unborn.

It is only some such train of thought, or rather of feeling,
that can in a measure explain the aim of the attempt, made in the
tale which follows, to present an unrestful episode in the obscure
lives of a few individuals out of all the disregarded multitude of
the bewildered, the simple, and the voiceless. For, if any part of
truth dwells in the belief confessed above, it becomes evident that
there is not a place of splendour or a dark corner of the earth
that does not deserve, if only a passing glance of wonder and
pity. The motive, then, may be held to justify the matter of the
work; but this preface, which is simply an avowal of endeavour,
cannot end here—for the avowal is not yet complete.

Fiction—if it at all aspires to be art—appeals to temperament.
And in truth it must be, like painting, like music, like all art,
the appeal of one temperament to all the other innumerable
temperaments whose subtle and resistless power endows passing

events with their true meaning, and creates the moral, the emotional atmosphere of the place and time. Such an appeal to be effective must be an impression conveyed through the senses; and, in fact, it cannot be made in any other way, because temperament, whether individual or collective, is not amenable to persuasion. All art, therefore, appeals primarily to the senses, and the artistic aim when expressing itself in written words must also make its appeal through the senses, if its high desire is to reach the secret spring of responsive emotions. It must strenuously aspire to the plasticity of sculpture, to the colour of painting, and to the magic suggestiveness of music—which is the art of arts. And it is only through complete, unswerving devotion to the perfect blending of form and substance; it is only through an unremitting never-discouraged care for the shape and ring of sentences that an approach can be made to plasticity, to colour, and that the light of magic suggestiveness may be brought to play for an evanescent instant over the commonplace surface of words: of the old, old words, worn thin, defaced by ages of careless usage.

The sincere endeavour to accomplish that creative task, to go as far on that road as his strength will carry him, to go undeterred by faltering, weariness, or reproach, is the only valid justification for the worker in prose. And if his conscience is clear, his answer to those who, in the fullness of a wisdom which looks for immediate profit, demand specifically to be edified, consoled, amused; who demand to be promptly improved, or encouraged, or frightened, or shocked, or charmed, must run thus: My task which I am trying to achieve is, by the power of the written word to make you hear, to make you feel—it is, before all, to make you see. That—and no more, and it is everything. If I succeed, you shall find there according to your deserts: encouragement, consolation, fear, charm—all you demand—and, perhaps, also that glimpse of truth for which you have forgotten to ask.

To snatch in a moment of courage, from the remorseless rush of time, a passing phase of life, is only the beginning of the task. The task approached in tenderness and faith is to hold up unquestioningly, without choice and without fear, the rescued fragment before all eyes in the light of a sincere mood. It is to show its vibration, its colour, its form; and through its movement, its form, and its colour, reveal the substance of its truth—disclose its inspiring secret: the stress and passion within the core of each convincing moment. In a single-minded attempt of that kind, if one be deserving and fortunate, one may perchance attain to such clearness of sincerity that at last the presented vision of regret or pity, of terror or mirth, shall awaken in the hearts of the beholders that feeling of unavoidable solidarity; of the solidarity in mysterious origin, in toil, in joy, in hope, in uncertain fate, which binds men to each other and all mankind to the visible world.

It is evident that he who, rightly or wrongly, holds by the convictions expressed above cannot be faithful to any one of the temporary formulas of his craft. The enduring part of them— the truth which each only imperfectly veils—should abide with him as the most precious of his possessions, but they all: Realism, Romanticism, Naturalism, even the unofficial sentimentalism (which, like the poor, is exceedingly difficult to get rid of), all these gods must, after a short period of fellowship, abandon him— even on the very threshold of the temple—to the stammerings of his conscience and to the outspoken consciousness of the difficulties of his work. In that uneasy solitude the supreme cry of Art for Art itself, loses the exciting ring of its apparent immorality. It sounds far off. It has ceased to be a cry, and is heard only as a whisper, often incomprehensible, but at times and faintly encouraging.

Sometimes, stretched at ease in the shade of a roadside tree, we watch the motions of a labourer in a distant field, and after a time, begin to wonder languidly as to what the fellow may be at. We watch the movements of his body, the waving of his arms, we see him bend down, stand up, hesitate, begin again. It may add to the charm of an idle hour to be told the purpose of his exertions. If we know he is trying to lift a stone, to dig a ditch, to uproot a stump, we look with a more real interest at his efforts; we are disposed to condone the jar of his agitation upon the restfulness of the landscape; and even, if in a brotherly frame of mind, we may bring ourselves to forgive his failure. We understood his object, and, after all, the fellow has tried, and perhaps he had not the strength—and perhaps he had not the knowledge. We forgive, go on our way—and forget.

And so it is with the workman of art. Art is long and life is short, and success is very far off. And thus, doubtful of strength to travel so far, we talk a little about the aim—the aim of art, which, like life itself, is inspiring, difficult—obscured by mists. It is not in the clear logic of a triumphant conclusion; it is not in the unveiling of one of those heartless secrets which are called the Laws of Nature. It is not less great, but only more difficult.

To arrest, for the space of a breath, the hands busy about the work of the earth, and compel men entranced by the sight of distant goals to glance for a moment at the surrounding vision of form and colour, of sunshine and shadows; to make them pause for a look, for a sigh, for a smile—such is the aim, difficult and evanescent, and reserved only for a very few to achieve. But sometimes, by the deserving and the fortunate, even that task is accomplished. And when it is accomplished—behold!—all the truth of life is there: a moment of vision, a sigh, a smile—and the return to an eternal rest.

Lord Jim (1917)

When this novel first appeared in book form a notion got about that I had been bolted away with. Some reviewers maintained that the work starting as a short story had got beyond the writer's control. One or two discovered internal evidence of the fact, which seemed to amuse them. They pointed out the limitations of the narrative form. They argued that no man could have been expected to talk all that time, and other men to listen so long. It was not, they said, very credible.

After thinking it over for something like sixteen years I am not so sure about that. Men have been known, both in the tropics and in the temperate zone, to sit up half the night 'swapping yarns.' This, however, is but one yarn, yet with interruptions affording some measure of relief; and in regard to the listeners' endurance, the postulate must be accepted that the story *was* interesting. It is the necessary preliminary assumption. If I hadn't believed that it *was* interesting I could never have begun to write it. As to the mere physical possibility we all know that some speeches in Parliament have taken nearer six than three hours in delivery; whereas all that part of the book which is Marlow's narrative can be read through aloud, I should say, in less than three hours. Besides—though I have kept strictly all such insignificant details out of the tale—we may presume that there must have been refreshments on that night, a glass of mineral water of some sort to help the narrator on.

But, seriously, the truth of the matter is, that my first thought was of a short story, concerned only with the pilgrim ship episode; nothing more. And that was a legitimate conception. After writing a few pages, however, I became for some reason discontented and I laid them aside for a time. I didn't take them out of the drawer till the late Mr. William Blackwood suggested I should give something again to his magazine.

It was only then that I perceived that the pilgrim ship episode was a good starting-point for a free and wandering tale; that it was an event, too, which could conceivably colour the whole 'sentiment of existence' in a simple and sensitive character. But all these preliminary moods and stirrings of spirit were rather obscure at the time, and they do not appear clearer to me now after the lapse of so many years.

The few pages I had laid aside were not without their weight in the choice of subject. But the whole was rewritten deliberately. When I sat down to it I knew it would be a long book, though I didn't foresee that it would spread itself over thirteen numbers of *Maga*.

I have been asked at times whether this was not the book of mine I liked best. I am a great foe to favouritism in public life, in private life, and even in the delicate relationship of an author to his works. As a matter of principle I will have no favourites; but I don't go so far as to feel grieved and annoyed by the preference some people give to my Lord Jim. I won't even say that I 'fail to understand . . .' No! But once I had occasion to be puzzled and surprised.

A friend of mine returning from Italy had talked with a lady there who did not like the book. I regretted that, of course, but what surprised me was the ground of her dislike. 'You know,' she said, 'it is all so morbid.'

The pronouncement gave me food for an hour's anxious thought. Finally I arrived at the conclusion that, making due allowances for the subject itself being rather foreign to women's normal sensibilities, the lady could not have been an Italian. I wonder whether she was European at all? In any case, no Latin temperament would have perceived anything morbid in the acute consciousness of lost honour. Such a consciousness may be wrong, or it may be right, or it may be condemned as artificial; and, perhaps, my Jim is not a type of wide commonness. But I can safely assure my readers that he is not the product of coldly perverted thinking. He's not a figure of northern mists either. One sunny morning in the commonplace surroundings of an eastern roadstead, I saw his form pass by—appealing—significant—under a cloud—perfectly silent. Which is as it should be. It was for me, with all the sympathy of which I was capable, to seek fit words for his meaning. He was 'one of us.'

Youth (1917)

The three stories in this volume lay no claim to unity of artistic purpose. The only bond between them is that of the time in which they were written. They belong to the period immediately following the publication of *The Nigger of the 'Narcissus,'* and preceding the first conception of *Nostromo,* two books which, it seems to me, stand apart and by themselves in the body of my work. It is also the period during which I contributed to *Maga;* a period dominated by *Lord Jim* and associated in my grateful memory with the late Mr. William Blackwood's encouraging and helpful kindness.

Youth was not my first contribution to *Maga.* It was the second. But that story marks the first appearance in the world of the man Marlow, with whom my relations have grown very intimate in the course of years. The origins of that gentleman (nobody as far I know had ever hinted that he was anything but

that)—his origins have been the subject of some literary speculation of, I am glad to say, a friendly nature.

One would think that I am the proper person to throw a light
on the matter; but in truth I find that it isn't so easy. It is pleasant
to remember that nobody had charged him with fradulent purposes or looked down on him as a charlatan; but apart from that
he was supposed to be all sorts of things: a clever screen, a mere
device, a 'personator,' a familiar spirit, a whispering 'daemon.'
I myself have been suspected of a meditated plan for his capture.

That is not so. I made no plans. The man Marlow and I
came together in the casual manner of those health-resort acquain-
tances which sometimes ripen into friendships. This one has
ripened. For all his assertiveness in matters of opinion he is not
an intrusive person. He haunts my hours of solitude, when, in
silence, we lay our heads together in great comfort and harmony; but as we part at the end of a tale I am never sure that
it may not be for the last time. Yet I don't think that either
of us would care much to survive the other. In his case, at any
rate, his occupation would be gone and he would suffer from
that extinction, because I suspect him of some vanity. I don't
mean vanity in the Solomonian sense. Of all my people he's the
one that has never been a vexation to my spirit. A most discreet,
understanding man . . .

Even before appearing in book-form *Youth* was very well
received. It lies on me to confess at last, and this is as good a
place for it as another, that I have been all my life—all my two
lives—the spoiled adopted child of Great Britain and even of the
Empire; for it was Australia that gave me my first command. I
break out into this declaration not because of a lurking tendency
to megalomania, but, on the contrary, as a man who has no very
notable illusions about himself. I follow the instincts of vain-
glory and humility natural to all mankind. For it can hardly
be denied that it is not their own deserts that men are most proud
of, but rather of their prodigious luck, of their marvellous fortune: of that in their lives for which thanks and sacrifices must
be offered on the altars of the inscrutable gods.

Heart of Darkness also received a certain amount of notice from the first; and of its origins this much may be said: it is well known that curious men go prying into all sorts of places (where they have no business) and come out of them with all kinds of spoil. This story, and one other, not in this volume, are all the spoil I brought out from the centre of Africa, where, really, I had no sort of business. More ambitious in its scope and longer in the telling, *Heart of Darkness* is quite as authentic in fundamentals as *Youth*. It is, obviously, written in another mood, I won't characterize the mood precisely, but anybody can see that it is anything but the mood of wistful regret, of reminiscent tenderness.

One more remark may be added. *Youth* is a feat of memory. It is a record of experience; but that experience, in its facts, in its inwardness and in its outward colouring, begins and ends in myself. *Heart of Darkness* is experience, too; but it is experience pushed a little (and only very little) beyond the actual facts of the case for the perfectly legitimate, I believe, purpose of bringing it home to the minds and bosoms of the readers. There it was no longer a matter of sincere colouring. It was like another art altogether. That sombre theme had to be given a sinister resonance, a tonality of its own, a continued vibration that, I hoped, would hang in the air and dwell on the ear after the last note had been struck.

After saying so much there remains the last tale of the book, still untouched. *The End of the Tether* is a story of sea-life in a rather special way; and the most intimate thing I can say of it is this: that having lived that life fully, amongst its men, its thoughts and sensations, I have found it possible, without the slightest misgiving, in all sincerity of heart and peace of conscience, to conceive the existence of Captain Whalley's personality and to relate the manner of his end. This statement acquires some force from the circumstance that the pages of that story—a fair half of the book—are also the product of experience. That experience belongs (like *Youth's*) to the time before I ever thought of putting pen to paper. As to its 'reality,' that is for the readers to determine. One had to pick up one's facts here and there. More skill would have made them more real and the whole composition more interesting. But here we are approaching the veiled region of artistic values which it would be improper and indeed dangerous for me to enter. I have looked over the proofs, have corrected a misprint or two, have changed a word or two—and that's all. It is not very likely that I shall ever read *The End of the Tether* again. No more need be said. It accords best with my feelings to part from Captain Whalley in affectionate silence.

Nostromo (1917)

Nostromo is the most anxiously meditated of the longer novels which belong to the period following upon the publication of the *Typhoon* volume of short stories.

I don't mean to say that I became then conscious of any impending change in my mentality and in my attitude towards the tasks of my writing life. And perhaps there was never any change, except in that mysterious, extraneous thing which has nothing to do with the theories of art; a subtle change in the nature of the inspiration; a phenomenon for which I cannot in any way be held responsible. What, however, did cause me some concern was that after finishing the last story of the *Typhoon* volume it seemed somehow that there was nothing more in the world to write about.

This so strangely negative but disturbing mood lasted some little time; and then, as with many of my longer stories, the first hint for *Nostromo* came to me in the shape of a vagrant anecdote completely destitute of valuable details.

As a matter of fact in 1875 or '6, when very young, in the West Indies, or rather in the Gulf of Mexico, for my contacts with land were short, few, and fleeting, I heard the story of some man who was supposed to have stolen single-handed a whole lighter-full of silver, somewhere on the Tierra Firme seaboard during the troubles of a revolution.

On the face of it was something of a feat. But I heard no details, and having no particular interest in crime *qua* crime I was not likely to keep that one in my mind. And I forgot it till twenty-six or seven years afterwards I came upon the very thing in a shabby volume picked up outside a second-hand bookshop.

It was the life story of an American seaman written by himself with the assistance of a journalist.[1] In the course of his wanderings that American sailor worked for some months on board a schooner, the master and owner of which was the thief of whom I had heard in my very young days. I have no doubt of that because there could hardly have been two exploits of that peculiar kind in the same part of the world and both connected with a South American revolution.

The fellow had actually managed to steal a lighter with silver, and this, it seems only because he was implicitly trusted by his employers, who must have been singularly poor judges of character. In the sailor's story he is represented as an unmitigated rascal, a small cheat, stupidly ferocious, morose, of mean appearance, and altogether unworthy of the greatness this opportunity had thrust upon him. What was interesting was that he would boast of it openly.

He used to say: 'People think I make a lot of money in this schooner of mine. But that is nothing. I don't care for that. Now and then I go away quietly and lift a bar of silver. I must get rich slowly—you understand.'

There was also another curious point about the man. Once in the course of some quarrel the sailor threatened him: 'What's to prevent me reporting ashore what you have told me about that silver?'

The cynical ruffian was not alarmed in the least. He actually laughed. 'You fool, if you dare talk like that on shore about me you will get a knife stuck in your back. Every man, woman, and child in that port is my friend. And who's to prove the lighter wasn't sunk? I didn't show you where the silver is hidden. Did I? So you know nothing. And suppose I lied? Eh?'

Ultimately the sailor, disgusted with the sordid meanness of that impenitent thief, deserted from the schooner. The whole episode takes about three pages of his autobiography. Nothing to speak of; but as I looked them over, the curious confirmation of

1. The book has been identified as *On Many Seas: the Life of a Yankee Sailor*, by Herbert E. Hamblen. A number of lesser sources have also been identified. See Jocelyn Baines, *Joseph Conrad: A Critical Biography* (New York, 1960), pp. 293–297.

the few casual words heard in my early youth evoked the memories of that distant time when everything was so fresh, so surprising, so venturesome, so interesting; bits of strange coasts under the stars, shadows of hills in the sunshine, men's passions in the dusk, gossip half forgotten, faces grown dim . . . Perhaps, perhaps, there still was in the world something to write about. Yet I did not see anything at first in the mere story. A rascal steals a large parcel of a valuable commodity—so people say. It's either true or untrue; and in any case it has no value in itself. To invent a circumstantial account of the robbery did not appeal to me, because my talents not running that way I did not think that the game was worth the candle. It was only when it dawned upon me that the purloiner of the treasure need not necessarily be a confirmed rogue, that he could be even a man of character, an actor and possibly a victim in the changing scenes of a revolution, it was only then that I had the first vision of a twilight country which was to become the province of Sulaco, with its high shadowy Sierra and its misty Campo for mute witnesses of events flowing from the passions of men short-sighted in good and evil.

Such are in very truth the obscure origins of *Nostromo*—the book. From that moment, I suppose, it had to be. Yet even then I hesitated, as if warned by the instinct of self-preservation from venturing on a distant and toilsome journey into a land full of intrigues and revolutions. But it had to be done.

It took the best part of the years 1903–4 to do; with many intervals of renewed hesitation, lest I should lose myself in the ever-enlarging vistas opening before me as I progressed deeper in my knowledge of the country. Often, also, when I had thought myself to a standstill over the tangled-up affairs of the Republic, I would, figuratively speaking, pack my bag, rush away from Sulaco for a change of air, and write a few pages of *The Mirror of the Sea*. But generally, as I've said before, my sojourn on the continent of Latin America, famed for its hospitality, lasted for about two years. On my return I found (speaking somewhat in the style of Captain Gulliver) my family all well, my wife heartily glad to learn that the fuss was all over, and our small boy considerably grown during my absence.

My principal authority for the history of Costaguana is, of

course, my venerated friend, the late Don José Avellanos, Minister to the Courts of England and Spain, etc. etc., in his impartial and eloquent *History of Fifty Years of Misrule*. That work was never published—the reader will discover why—and I am in fact the only person in the world possessed of its contents. I have mastered them in not a few hours of earnest meditation, and I hope that my accuracy will be trusted. In justice to myself, and to allay the fears of prospective readers, I beg to point out that the few historical allusions are never dragged in for the sake of parading my unique erudition, but that each of them is closely related to actuality; either throwing a light on the nature of current events or affecting directly the fortunes of the people of whom I speak.

As to their own histories I have tried to set them down, Aristocracy and People, men and women, Latin and Anglo-Saxon, bandit and politician, with as cool a hand as was possible in the heat and clash of my own conflicting emotions. And after all this is also the story of their conflicts. It is for the reader to say how far they are deserving of interest in their actions and in the secret purposes of their hearts revealed in the bitter necessities of the time. I confess that, for me, that time is the time of firm friendships and unforgotten hospitalities. And in my gratitude I must mention here Mrs. Gould, 'the first lady of Sulaco,' whom we may safely leave to the secret devotion of Dr. Monygham, and Charles Gould, the Idealist-creator of Material Interests, whom we must leave to his mine—from which there is no escape in this world.

About Nostromo, the second of the two racially and socially contrasted men, both captured by the silver of the San Tomé Mine, I feel bound to say something more.

I did not hesitate to make that central figure an Italian. First of all the thing is perfectly credible: Italians were swarming into the Occidental Province at the time, as anybody who will read further can see; and secondly, there was no one who could stand so well by the side of Giorgio Viola the Garibaldino, the Idealist of the old, humanitarian revolutions. For myself I needed there a man of the People as free as possible from his class-conventions and all settled modes of thinking. This is not a side snarl at conventions. My reasons were not moral but artistic. Had he been an Anglo-Saxon he would have tried to get into local politics. But Nostromo does not aspire to be a leader in a personal game. He does not want to raise himself above the mass. He is content to feel himself a power—within the People.

But mainly Nostromo is what he is because I received the inspiration for him in my early days from a Mediterranean sailor. Those who have read certain pages of mine[2] will see at once what I mean when I say that Dominic, the *padrone* of the *Tremolino*, might under given circumstances have been a Nostromo. At any rate Dominic would have understood the younger man perfectly—if scornfully. He and I were engaged together in a rather absurd adventure, but the absurdity does not matter. It is a real satisfaction to think that in my very young days there must, after all, have been something in me worthy to command that man's half-bitter fidelity, his half-ironic devotion. Many of Nostromo's speeches I have heard first in Dominic's voice. His hand on the tiller and his fearless eyes roaming the horizon from within the monkish hood shadowing his face, he would utter the usual exordium of his remorseless wisdom: 'Vous autres gentilshommes!' in a caustic tone that hangs on my ear yet. Like Nostromo! 'You *hombres finos!*' Very much like Nostromo. But Dominic the Corsican nursed a certain pride of ancestry from which my Nostromo is free; for Nostromo's lineage had to be more ancient still. He is a man with the weight of countless generations behind him and no parentage to boast of...Like the People.

In his firm grip on the earth he inherits, in his improvidence and generosity, in his lavishness with his gifts, in his manly vanity, in the obscure sense of his greatness, and in his faithful devotion with something despairing as well as desperate in its impulses, he is a Man of the People, their very own unenvious force, disdaining to lead but ruling from within. Years afterwards, grown older as the famous Captain Fidanza, with a stake

2. *The Mirror of the Sea.*

in the country, going about his many affairs followed by respectful glances in the modernized streets of Sulaco, calling on the widow of the *cargador*, attending the Lodge, listening in unmoved silence to anarchist speeches at the meeting, the enigmatical patron of the new revolutionary agitation, the trusted, the wealthy comrade Fidanza with the knowledge of his moral ruin locked up in his breast, he remains essentialy a Man of the People. In his mingled love and scorn of life and in the bewildered conviction of having been betrayed, of dying betrayed he hardly knows by what or by whom, he is still of the People, their undoubted Great Man—with a private history of his own.

One more figure of those stirring times I would like to mention: and that is Antonia Avellanos—the 'beautiful Antonia.' Whether she is a possible variation of Latin-American girlhood I wouldn't dare to affirm. But, for me, she *is*. Always a little in the background by the side of her father (my venerated friend) I hope she has yet relief enough to make intelligible what I am going to say. Of all the people who had seen with me the birth of the Occidental Republic, she is the only one who has kept in my memory the aspect of continued life. Antonia the Aristocrat and Nostromo the Man of the People are the artisans of the New Era, the true creators of the New State; he by his legendary and daring feat, she, like a woman, simply by the force of what she is: the only being capable of inspiring a sincere passion in the heart of a trifler.

If anything could induce me to revisit Sulaco (I should hate to see all these changes) it would be Antonia. And the true reason for that—why not be frank about it?—the true reason is that I have modelled her on my first love. How we, a band of tallish schoolboys, the chums of her two brothers, how we used to look up to that girl just out of the schoolroom herself, as the standard-bearer of a faith to which we all were born but which she alone knew how to hold aloft with an unflinching hope! She had perhaps more glow and less serenity in her soul than Antonia, but she was an uncompromising Puritan of patriotism with no taint of the slightest worldliness in her thoughts. I was not the only one in love with her; but it was I who had to hear oftenest her scathing criticism of my levities—very much like poor Decoud—or stand the brunt of her austere, unanswerable invective. She did not quite understand—but never mind. That afternoon when I came in, a shrinking yet defiant sinner, to say the final good-bye I received a hand-squeeze that made my heart leap and saw a tear that took my breath away. She was softened at the last as though she had suddenly perceived (we were such children still!) that I was really going away for good, going very far away—even as far as Sulaco, lying unknown, hidden from our eyes in the darkness of the Placid Gulf.

That's why I long sometimes for another glimpse of the 'beautiful Antonia' (or can it be the Other?) moving in the dimness of the great cathedral, saying a short prayer at the tomb of the first and last Cardinal-Archbishop of Sulaco, standing absorbed in filial devotion before the monument of Don José Avellanos, and, with a lingering, tender, faithful glance at the medallion-memorial to Martin Decoud, going out serenely into the sunshine of the Plaza with her upright carriage and her white head; a relic of the past disregarded by men awaiting impatiently the Dawns of other New Eras, the coming of more Revolutions.

But this is the idlest of dreams; for I did understand perfectly well at the time that the moment the breath left the body of the Magnificent Capataz, the Man of the People, freed at last from the toils of love and wealth, there was nothing more for me to do in Sulaco.

An Outcast of the Islands (1919)

An Outcast of the Islands is my second novel in the absolute sense of the word; second in conception, second in execution, second as it were in its essence. There was no hesitation, half-formed plan, vague idea, or the vaguest reverie of anything else between it and *Almayer's Folly*. The only doubt I suffered from, after the publication of *Almayer's Folly*, was whether I should write another line for print. Those days, now grown so dim, had their poignant moments. Neither in my mind nor in my heart had I then given up the sea. In truth I was clinging to it desperately, all the more desperately because, against my will, I could

not help feeling that there was something changed in my relation to it. *Almayer's Folly* had been finished and done with.
The mood itself was gone. But it had left the memory of an
experience that, both in thought and emotion, was unconnected
with the sea, and I suppose that part of my moral being which
is rooted in consistency was badly shaken. I was a victim of contrary stresses which produced a state of immobility. I gave myself
up to indolence. Since it was impossible for me to face both ways
I had elected to face nothing. The discovery of new values in
life is a very chaotic experience; there is a tremendous amount of
jostling and confusion and a momentary feeling of darkness. I
let my spirit float supine over that chaos.

A phrase of Edward Garnett's is, as a matter of fact, responsible for this book. The first of the friends I made for myself by
my pen, it was but natural that he should be the recipient, at that
time, of my confidences. One evening when we had dined together
and he had listened to the account of my perplexities (I fear he
must have been growing a little tired of them) he pointed out
that there was no need to determine my future absolutely. Then
he added: 'You have the style, you have the temperament; why
not write another?' I believe that as far as one man may wish to
influence another man's life Edward Garnett had a great desire
that I should go on writing. At that time, and, I may say, ever
afterwards, he was always very patient and gentle with me.
What strikes me most, however, in the phrase quoted above which
was offered to me in a tone of detachment is not its gentleness but
its effective wisdom. Had he said, 'Why not go on writing?' it is
very probable he would have scared me away from pen and ink
for ever; but there was nothing either to frighten one or arouse
one's antagonism in the mere suggestion to 'write another.' And
thus a dead point in the revolution of my affairs was insidiously
got over. The word 'another' did it. At about eleven o'clock of a
nice London night, Edward and I walked along interminable
streets talking of many things, and I remember that on getting
home I sat down and wrote about half a page of *An Outcast of
the Islands* before I slept. This was committing myself definitely,
I won't say to another life, but to another book. There is appar-

ently something in my character which will not allow me to abandon for good any piece of work I have begun. I have laid aside many beginnings. I have laid them aside with sorrow, with disgust, with rage, with melancholy, and even with self-contempt; but even at the worst I had an uneasy consciousness that I would have to go back to them.

An Outcast of the Islands belongs to those novels of mine that were never laid aside; and though it brought me the qualification of 'exotic writer' I don't think the charge was at all justified. For the life of me I don't see that there is the slightest exotic spirit in the conception or style of that novel. It is certainly the most *tropical* of my eastern tales. The mere scenery got a great hold on me as I went on, perhaps because (I may just as well confess that) the story itself was never very near my heart. It engaged my imagination much more than my affection. As to my feeling for Willems it was but the regard one cannot help having for one's own creation. Obviously I could not be indifferent to a man on whose head I had brought so much evil simply by imagining him such as he appears in the novel—and that, too, on a very slight foundation.

The man who suggested Willems to me was not particularly interesting in himself. My interest was aroused by his dependent position, his strange, dubious status of a mistrusted, disliked, worn-out European living on the reluctant toleration of that settlement hidden in the heart of the forest-land, up that sombre stream which our ship was the only white men's ship to visit. With his hollow, clean-shaved cheeks, a heavy grey moustache and eyes without any expression whatever, clad always in a spotless sleeping suit much befrogged in front, which left his lean neck wholly uncovered, and with his bare feet in a pair of straw slippers, he wandered silently amongst the houses in daylight, almost as dumb as an animal and apparently much more homeless. I don't know what he did with himself at night. He must have had a place, a hut, a palm-leaf shed, some sort of hovel where he kept his razor and his change of sleeping suits. An air of futile mystery hung over him, something not exactly dark but obviously ugly. The only definite statement I could extract

from anybody was that it was he who had 'brought the Arabs
into the river.' That must have happened many years before. But
how did he bring them into the river? He could hardly have
done it in his arms like a lot of kittens. I knew that Almayer
founded the chronology of all his misfortunes on the date of
that fateful advent; and yet the very first time we dined with
Almayer there was Willems sitting at table with us in the manner
of the skeleton at the feast, obviously shunned by everybody,
never addressed by any one, and for all recognition of his existence getting now and then from Almayer a venomous glance
which I observed with great surprise. In the course of the whole
evening he ventured one single remark which I didn't catch
because his articulation was imperfect, as of a man who had
forgotten how to speak. I was the only person who seemed aware
of the sound. Willems subsided. Presently he retired, pointedly
unnoticed—into the forest maybe? Its immensity was there, within
three hundred yards of the veranda, ready to swallow up anything.
Almayer, conversing with my captain, did not stop talking while
he glared angrily at the retreating back. Didn't that fellow bring
the Arabs into the river! Nevertheless Willems turned up next
morning on Almayer's veranda. From the bridge of the steamer
I could see plainly these two, breakfasting together, *tête-à-tête*
and, I suppose, in dead silence, one with his air of being no
longer interested in this world and the other raising his eyes
now and then with intense dislike.

It was clear that in those days Willems lived on Almayer's
charity. Yet on returning two months later to Sambir I heard
that he had gone on an expedition up the river in charge of
a steam-launch belonging to the Arabs, to make some discovery
or other. On account of the strange reluctance that everyone
manifested to talk about Willems it was impossible for me to
get at the rights of that transaction. Morever, I was a new-
comer, the youngest of the company, and, I suspect, not judged
quite fit as yet for a full confidence. I was not much concerned
about that exclusion. The faint suggestion of plots and mysteries
pertaining to all matters touching Almayer's affairs amused me
vastly. Almayer was obviously very much affected. I believe he

missed Willems immensely. He wore an air of sinister preoccupation and talked confidentially with my captain. I could catch only snatches of mumbled sentences. Then one morning as I came along the deck to take my place at the breakfast table Almayer checked himself in his low-toned discourse. My captain's face was perfectly impenetrable. There was a moment of profound silence and then as if unable to contain himself Almayer burst out in a loud, vicious tone:

'One thing's certain; if he finds anything worth having up there they will poison him like a dog.'

Disconnected though it was, that phrase, as food for thought, was distinctly worth hearing. We left the river three days afterwards and I never returned to Sambir; but whatever happened to the protagonist of my Willems nobody can deny that I have recorded for him a less squalid fate.

Typhoon (1919)

The main characteristic of this volume consists in this, that all the stories composing it belong not only to the same period but have been written one after another in the order in which they appear in the book.

The period is that which follows on my connection with *Blackwood's Magazine*. I had just finished writing *The End of the Tether* and was casting about for some subject which could be developed in a shorter form than the tales in the volume of *Youth* when the instance of a steamship full of returning coolies from Singapore to some port in northern China occurred to my recollection. Years before I had heard it being talked about in the East as a recent occurrence. It was for us merely one subject of conversation amongst many others of the kind. Men earning their bread in any very specialized occupation will talk shop, not only because it is the most vital interest of their lives but also because they have not much knowledge of other subjects. They have never had the time to get acquainted with them. Life, for most of us, is not so much a hard as an exacting taskmaster.

I never met anybody personally concerned in this affair, the interest of which for us was, of course, not the bad weather but the extraordinary complication brought into the ship's life at a moment of exceptional stress by the human element below her deck. Neither was the story itself ever enlarged upon in my hearing. In that company each of us could imagine easily what the whole thing was like. The financial difficulty of it, presenting also a human problem, was solved by a mind much too simple to be perplexed by anything in the world except men's idle talk for which it was not adapted.

From the first the mere anecdote, the mere statement I might say, that such a thing had happened on the high seas, appeared to me a sufficient subject for meditation. Yet it was but a bit of a sea yarn after all. I felt that to bring out its deeper significance which was quite apparent to me, something other, something more was required; a leading motive that would harmonize all these violent noises, and a point of view that would put all that elemental fury into its proper place.

What was needed of course was Captain MacWhirr. Directly I perceived him I could see that he was the man for the situation. I don't mean to say that I ever saw Captain MacWhirr in the flesh, or had ever come in contact with his literal mind and his dauntless temperament. MacWhirr is not an acquaintance of a few hours, or a few weeks, or a few months. He is the product of twenty years of life. My own life. Conscious invention had little to do with him. If it is true that Captain MacWhirr never walked and breathed on this earth (which I find for my part extremely difficult to believe) I can also assure my readers that he is perfectly authentic. I may venture to assert the same of every aspect of the story, while I confess that the particular typhoon of the tale was not a typhoon of my actual experience.

At its first appearance *Typhoon,* the story, was classed by some critics as a deliberately intended storm-piece. Others picked out MacWhirr, in whom they perceived a definite symbolic intention. Neither was exclusively my intention. Both the typhoon and Captain MacWhirr presented themselves to me as the necessities of the deep conviction with which I approached the subject of the story. It was their opportunity. It was also my opportunity;

and it would be vain to discourse about what I made of it in a handful of pages, since the pages themselves are here, between the covers of this volume, to speak for themselves.

This is a belated reflection. If it had occurred to me before it would have perhaps done away with the existence of this Author's Note; for, indeed, the same remark applies to every story in this volume. None of them are stories of experience in the absolute sense of the word. Experience in them is but the canvas of the attempted picture. Each of them has its more than one intention. With each the question is what the writer has done with his opportunity; and each answers the question for itself in words which, if I may say so without undue solemnity, were written with a conscientious regard for the truth of my own sensations. And each of those stories, to mean something, must justify itself in its own way to the conscience of each successive reader.

Falk—the second story in the volume—offended the delicacy of one critic at least by certain peculiarities of its subject. But what is the subject of *Falk*? I personally do not feel so very certain about it. He who reads must find out for himself. My intention in writing *Falk* was not to shock anybody. As in most of my writings I insist not on the events but on their effect upon the persons in the tale. But in everything I have written there is always one invariable intention, and that is to capture the reader's attention, by securing his interest and enlisting his sympathies for the matter in hand, whatever it may be, within the limits of the visible world and within the boundaries of human emotions.

I may safely say that Falk is absolutely true to my experience of certain straightforward characters combining a perfectly natural ruthlessness with a certain amount of moral delicacy. Falk obeys the law of self-preservation without the slightest misgivings as to his right, but at a crucial turn of that ruthlessly preserved life he will not condescend to dodge the truth. As he is presented as sensitive enough to be affected permanently by a certain unusual experience, that experience had to be set by me before the reader vividly; but it is not the subject of the tale.

If we go by mere facts then the subject is Falk's attempt to get married; in which the narrator of the tale finds himself unexpectedly involved both on its ruthless and its delicate side.

Falk shares with one other of my stories (*The Return* in the *Tales of Unrest* volume) the distinction of never having been serialized. I think the copy was shown to the editor of some magazine who rejected it indignantly on the sole ground that 'the girl never says anything.' This is perfectly true. From first to last Hermann's niece utters no word in the tale—and it is not because she is dumb, but for the simple reason that whenever she happens to come under the observation of the narrator she has either no occasion or is too profoundly moved to speak. The editor, who obviously had read the story, might have perceived that for himself. Apparently he did not, and I refrained from pointing out the impossibility to him because, since he did not venture to say that 'the girl' did not live, I felt no concern at his indignation.

All the other stories were serialized. The *Typhoon* appeared in the early numbers of the *Pall Mall Magazine,* then under the direction of the late Mr. Halkett. It was on that occasion, too, that I saw for the first time my conceptions rendered by an artist in another medium. Mr. Maurice Greiffenhagen knew how to combine in his illustrations the effect of his own most distinguished personal vision with an aboslute fidelity to the inspiration of the writer. *Amy Foster* was published in the *Illustrated London News* with a fine drawing of Amy on her day out giving tea to the children at her home, in a hat with a big feather. *To-morrow* appeared first in the *Pall Mall Magazine.* Of that story I will only say that it struck many people by its adaptability to the stage and that I was induced to dramatize it under the title of *One Day More;* up to the present my only effort in that direction. I may also add that each of the four stories on their appearance in book form was picked out on various grounds as the 'best of the lot' by different critics, who reviewed the volume with a warmth of appreciation and understanding, a sympathetic insight, and a friendliness of expression for which I cannot be sufficiently grateful.

The Mirror of the Sea (1919)

Less perhaps than any other book written by me, or anybody else, does this volume require a preface. Yet since all the others, including even the *Personal Record,* which is but a fragment of biography, are to have their Author's Notes I cannot possibly leave this one without, lest a false impression of indifference or weariness should be created. I can see only too well that it is not going to be an easy task. Necessity—the mother of invention—being even unthinkable in this case, I do not know what to invent in the way of discourse; and necessity being also the greatest possible incentive to exertion I don't even know how to begin to exert myself. Here, too, the natural inclination comes in. I have been all my life averse from exertion.

Under these discouraging circumstances I am, however, bound to proceed from a sense of duty. This Note is a thing promised. In less than a minute's time, by a few incautious words I entered into a bond which has lain on my heart heavily ever since.

For, this book is a very intimate revelation; and what that is revealing can a few more pages add to some three hundred others of most sincere disclosures? I have attempted here to lay bare with the unreserve of a last hour's confession the terms of my relation with the sea, which beginning mysteriously, like any great passion the inscrutable Gods send to mortals, went on unreasoning and invincible, surviving the test of disillusion, defying the disenchantment that lurks in every day of a strenuous life; went on full of love's delight and love's anguish, facing them in open-eyed exultation, without bitterness and without repining, from the first hour to the last.

Subjugated but never unmanned I surrendered my being to that passion which, various and great like life itself, had also its periods of wonderful serenity which even a fickle mistress can give sometimes on her soothed breast, full of wiles, full of fury, and yet capable of an enchanting sweetness. And if anybody suggests that this must be the lyric illusion of an old, romantic heart, I can answer that for twenty years I had lived like a hermit with my passion! Beyond the line of the sea horizon the world for me did not exist as assuredly as it does not exist for the mystics who take refuge on the tops of high mountains. I am speaking now of that innermost life, containing the best and the worst that can happen to us in the temperamental depths of our being, where a man indeed must live alone but need not give up all hope of holding converse with his kind.

This perhaps is enough for me to say on this particular occasion about these, my parting words, about this, my last mood in my great passion for the sea. I call it great because it was great to me. Others may call it a foolish infatuation. Those words have been applied to every love story. But whatever it may be the fact remains that it was something too great for words.

This is what I always felt vaguely; and therefore the following pages rest like a true confession on matters of fact which to a friendly and charitable person may convey the inner truth of almost a lifetime. From sixteen to thirty-six cannot be called an age, yet it is a pretty long stretch of that sort of experience which teaches a man slowly to see and feel. It is for me a distinct period; and when I emerged from it into another air, as it were, and said to myself: 'Now I must speak of these things or remain unknown to the end of my days,' it was with the ineradicable hope, that accompanies one through solitude as well as through a crowd, of ultimately, some day, at some moment, making myself understood.

And I have been! I have been understood as completely as it is possible to be understood in this, our world, which seems to be mostly composed of riddles. There have been things said about this book which have moved me profoundly; the more profoundly because they were uttered by men whose occupation was avowedly to understand, and analyse, and expound—in a word, by literary critics. They spoke out according to their conscience, and some of them said things that made me feel both glad and sorry of ever having entered upon my confession. Dimly or clearly, they perceived the character of my intention and ended by judging me worthy to have made the attempt. They saw it was of a revealing character, but in some cases they thought that the revelation was not complete.

One of them said: 'In reading these chapters one is always

hoping for the revelation; but the personality is never quite revealed. We can only say that this thing happened to Mr. Conrad, that he knew such a man and that thus life passed him leaving those memories. They are the records of the events of his life, not in every instance striking or decisive events but rather those haphazard events which for no definite reason impress themselves upon the mind and recur in memory long afterward as symbols of one knows not what sacred ritual taking place behind the veil.'

To this I can only say that this book written in perfect sincerity holds back nothing—unless the mere bodily presence of the writer. Within these pages I make a full confession not of my sins but of my emotions. It is the best tribute my piety can offer to the ultimate shapers of my character, convictions, and, in a sense, destiny—to the imperishable sea, to the ships that are no more, and to the simple men who have had their day.

From *A Personal Record* (second Preface, 1919)

The reissue of this book in a new form does not, strictly speaking, require another Preface. But since this is distinctly a place for personnal remarks I take the opportunity to refer in this Author's Note to two points arising from certain statements about myself I have noticed of late in the press.

One of them bears upon the question of language. I have always felt myself looked upon somewhat in the light of a phenomenon, a position which outside the circus world cannot be regarded as desirable. It needs a special temperament for one to derive much gratification from the fact of being able to do freakish things intentionally, and as it were, from mere vanity.

The fact of my not writing in my native language has been of course commented upon frequently in reviews and notices of my various works and in the more extended critical articles. I suppose that was unavoidable; and indeed these comments were of the most flattering kind to one's vanity. But in that matter I have no vanity that could be flattered. I could not have it. The first object of this note is to disclaim any merit there might have been in an act of deliberate volition.

The impression of my having exercised a choice between the two languages, French and English, both foreign to me, has got abroad somehow. That impression is erroneous. It originated, I believe, in an article written by Sir Hugh Clifford and published in the year '98, I think of the last century.[3] Sometime before, Sir Hugh Clifford came to see me. He is, if not the first, then one of the first two friends I made for myself by my work, the other being Mr. Cunninghame Graham, who, characteristically enough, had been captivated by my story, *An Outpost of Progress.* These friendships which have endured to this day I count amongst my precious possessions.

Mr. Hugh Clifford (he was not decorated then) had just published his first volume of Malay sketches. I was naturally delighted to see him and infinitely gratified by the kind things he found to say about my first books and some of my early short stories, the action of which is placed in the Malay Archipelago. I remember that after saying many things which ought to have made me blush to the roots of my hair with outraged modesty, he ended by telling me with the uncompromising yet kindly firmness of a man accustomed to speak unpalatable truths even to Oriental potentates (for their own good of course) that as a matter of fact I didn't know anything about Malays. I was perfectly aware of this. I have never pretended to any such knowledge, and I was moved—I wonder to this day at my impertinence—to retort: 'Of course I don't know anything about Malays. If I knew only one hundredth part of what you and Frank Swettenham[4] know of Malays I would make everybody sit up.' He went on looking kindly (but firmly) at me and then we both burst out laughing. In the course of that most welcome visit twenty years ago, which I remember so well, we talked of many things; the characteristics of various languages was one of them, and it is on that day that my friend carried away with him the impression that I had exercised a deliberate choice between French and English. Later, when moved by his friendship (no empty word to him) to write a study

3. See the letter to William Blackwood, December 13, 1898.
4. Sir Frank Swettenham, author of *Malay Sketches* (1895), and *British Malaya* (1907).

in the *North American Review*[5] on Joseph Conrad, he conveyed that impression to the public.

This misapprehension, for it is nothing else, was no doubt my fault. I must have expressed myself badly in the course of a friendly and intimate talk when one doesn't watch one's phrases carefully. My recollection of what I meant to say is: that *had I been under the necessity* of making a choice between the two, and though I knew French fairly well and was familiar with it from infancy, I would have been afraid to attempt expression in a language so perfectly 'crystallized.' This, I believe, was the word I used. And then we passed to other matters. I had to tell him a little about myself; and what he told me of his work in the East, his own particular East of which I had but the mistiest, short glimpse, was of the most absorbing interest. The present Governor of Nigeria may not remember that conversation as well as I do, but I am sure that he will not mind this, what in diplomatic language is called 'rectification' of a statement made to him by an obscure writer his generous sympathy had prompted him to seek out and make his friend.

The truth of the matter is that my faculty to write in English is as natural as any other aptitude with which I might have been born. I have a strange and overpowering feeling that it had always been an inherent part of myself. English was for me neither a matter of choice nor adoption. The merest idea of choice had never entered my head. And as to adoption—well, yes, there was adoption; but it was I who was adopted by the genius of the language, which directly I came out of the stammering stage made me its own so completely that its very idioms I truly believe had a direct action on my temperament and fashioned my still plastic character.

It was a very intimate action and for that very reason it is too mysterious to explain. The task would be as impossible as trying to explain love at first sight. There was something in this conjunction of exulting, almost physical recognition, the same sort of emotional surrender and the same pride of possession, all

5. "The Genius of Mr. Joseph Conrad," *North American Review*, 178 (June, 1904), 842–852.

united in the wonder of a great discovery; but there was on it none of that shadow of dreadful doubt that falls on the very flame of our perishable passions. One knew very well that this was for ever.

A matter of discovery and not of inheritance, that very inferiority of the title makes the faculty still more precious, lays the possessor under a lifelong obligation to remain worthy of his great fortune. But it seems to me that all this sounds as if I were trying to explain—a task which I have just pronounced to be impossible. If in action we may admit with awe that the Impossible recedes before men's indomitable spirit, the Impossible in matters of analysis will always make a stand at some point or other. All I can claim after all those years of devoted practice, with the accumulated anguish of its doubts, imperfections and falterings in my heart, is the right to be believed when I say that if I had not written in English I would not have written at all.

The other remark which I wish to make here is also a rectification but of a less direct kind. It has nothing to do with the medium of expression. It bears on the matter of my authorship in another way. It is not for me to criticize my judges, the more so because I always felt that I was receiving more than justice at their hands. But it seems to me that their unfailingly interested sympathy has ascribed to racial and historical influences much of what, I believe, appertains simply to the individual. Nothing is more foreign than what in the literary world is called Sclavonism, to the Polish temperament with its tradition of self-government, its chivalrous view of moral restraints, and an exaggerated respect for individual rights: not to mention the important fact that the whole Polish mentality, Western in complexion, had received its training from Italy and France and, historically, had always remained, even in religious matters, in sympathy with the most liberal currents of European thought. An impartial view of humanity in all its degrees of splendour and misery together with a special regard for the rights of the unprivileged of this earth, not on any mystic ground but on the ground of simple fellowship and honourable reciprocity of services, was the dominant characteristic of the mental and moral atmosphere of the houses which sheltered my hazardous childhood: matters of calm and deep conviction both lasting and consistent, and removed as far as possible from that humanitarianism that seems to be merely a matter of crazy nerves or a morbid conscience.

Tales of Unrest (n.d.)

Of the five stories in this volume *The Lagoon,* the last in order, is the earliest in date. It is the first short story I ever wrote and marks, in a manner of speaking, the end of my first phase, the Malayan phase with its special subject and its verbal suggestions. Conceived in the same mood which produced *Almayer's Folly* and *An Outcast of the Islands,* it is told in the same breath (with what was left of it, that is, after the end of *An Outcast*), seen with the same vision, rendered in the same method—if such a thing as method did exist then in my conscious relation to this new adventure of writing for print. I doubt it very much. One does one's work first and theorizes about it afterwards. It is a very amusing and egotistical occupation of no use whatever to any one and just as likely as not to lead to false conclusions.

Anybody can see that between the last paragraph of *An Outcast* and the first of *The Lagoon* there has been no change of pen, figuratively speaking. It happens also to be literally true. It was the same pen: a common steel pen. Having been charged with a certain lack of emotional faculty I am glad to be able to say that on one occasion at least I did give way to a sentimental impulse. I thought the pen had been a good pen and that it had done enough for me, and so, with the idea of keeping it for a sort of memento on which I could look later with tender eyes, I put it into my waistcoat pocket. Afterwards it used to turn up in all sorts of places, at the bottom of small drawers, among my studs in cardboard boxes, till at last it found permanent rest in a large wooden bowl containing some loose keys, bits of sealing-wax, bits of string, small broken chains, a few buttons, and similar minute wreckage that washes out of a man's life into such receptacles. I would catch sight of it from time to time with a distinct feeling of satisfaction till, one day, I perceived with horror that there were two old pens in there. How the other pen found its way into the bowl instead of the fire-place or waste-paper basket I can't imagine, but there the two were, lying side by side, both encrusted with ink and completely undistinguishable from each other. It was very distressing, but being determined not to share my sentiment between two pens or run the risk of sentimentalizing over a mere stranger, I threw them both out of the window into a flower-bed—which strikes me now as a poetical grave for the remnants of one's past.

But the tale remained. It was first fixed in print in the *Cornhill Magazine*, being my first appearance in a serial of any kind; and I have lived long enough to see it most agreeably guyed by Mr. Max Beerbohm in a volume of parodies entitled *A Christmas Garland*, where I found myself in very good company. I was immensely gratified. I began to believe in my public existence. I have much to thank *The Lagoon* for.

My next effort in short story writing was a departure—I mean a departure from the Malay Archipelago. Without premeditation, without sorrow, without rejoicing, and almost without noticing it, I stepped into the very different atmosphere of *An Outpost of Progress*. I found there a different moral attitude. I seemed able to capture new reactions, new suggestions, and even new rhythms for my paragraphs. For a moment I fancied myself a new man— a most exciting illusion. It clung to me for some time, monstrous half conviction and half hope as to its body, with an iridescent tail of dreams and with a changeable head like a plastic mask. It was only later that I perceived that in common with the rest of men nothing could deliver me from my fatal consistency. We cannot escape from ourselves.

An Outpost of Progress is the lightest part of the loot I carried off from Central Africa, the main portion being of course the *Heart of Darkness*. Other men have found a lot of quite different things there and I have the comfortable conviction that what I took would not have been of much use to anybody else. And it must be said that it was but a very small amount of plunder. All of it could go into one's breast pocket when folded neatly. As for the story itself it is true enough in its essentials. The sustained invention of a really telling lie demands a talent which I do not possess.

'The Idiots' is such an obviously derivative piece of work that it is impossible for me to say anything about it here. The suggestion of it was not mental but visual: the actual idiots. It was after an interval of long groping amongst vague impulses and hesitations which ended in the production of *The Nigger* that I turned to my third short story in the order of time, the first in this volume: *Karain: A Memory*.

Reading it after many years *Karain* produced on me the effect of something seen through a pair of glasses from a rather advantageous position. In that story I had not gone back to the Archipelago, I had only turned for another look at it. I admit that I was absorbed by the distant view, so absorbed that I didn't notice then that the *motif* of the story is almost identical with the *motif* of *The Lagoon*. However, the idea at the back is very different; but the story is mainly made memorable to me by the fact that it was my first contribution to *Blackwood's Magazine* and that it led to my personal acquaintance with Mr. William Blackwood, whose guarded appreciation I felt nevertheless to be genuine, and prized accordingly. *Karain* was begun on a sudden impulse only three days after I wrote the last line of *The Nigger*, and the recollection of its difficulties is mixed up with the worries of the unfinished *Return*, the last pages of which I took up again at the time; the only instance in my life when I made an attempt to write with both hands at once as it were.

Indeed my innermost feeling, now, is that *The Return* is a left-handed production. Looking through that story lately I had the material impression of sitting under a large and expensive umbrella in the loud drumming of a furious rain-shower. It was very distracting. In the general uproar one could hear every individual drop strike on the stout and distended silk. Mentally, the reading rendered me dumb for the remainder of the day, not exactly with astonishment but with a sort of dismal wonder. I don't want to talk disrespectfully of any pages of mine. Psychologically there were no doubt good reasons for my attempt; and it was worth while, if only to see of what excesses I was capable in that sort of virtuosity. In this connection I should like to confess my surprise on finding that notwithstanding all its apparatus of analysis the story consists for the most part of physical impressions; impressions of sound and sight, railway station, streets, a trotting horse, reflections in mirrors, and so on, rendered as if for their own sake and combined with a sublimated description of a desirable middle class town-residence which somehow manages to produce a sinister effect. For the rest any kind word about *The Return* (and there have been such words said at different times) awakens in me the liveliest gratitude, for I know how much the writing of that fantasy has cost me in sheer toil, in temper, and in disillusion.

The Secret Agent (1920)

The origin of *The Secret Agent:* subject, treatment, artistic purpose, and every other motive that may induce an author to take up his pen, can, I believe, be traced to a period of mental and emotional reaction.

The actual facts are that I began this book impulsively and wrote it continuously. When in due course it was bound and delivered to the public gaze I found myself reproved for having produced it at all. Some of the admonitions were severe, others had a sorrowful note. I have not got them textually before me but I remember perfectly the general argument, which was very simple; and also my surprise at its nature. All this sounds a very old story now! And yet it is not such a long time ago. I must conclude that I had still preserved much of my pristine innocence in the year 1907. It seems to me now that even an artless person might have foreseen that some criticisms would be based on the ground of sordid surroundings and the moral squalor of the tale.

That of course is a serious objection. It was not universal. In fact it seems ungracious to remember so little reproof amongst so much intelligent and sympathetic appreciation; and I trust that the readers of this Preface will not hasten to put it down to wounded vanity or a natural disposition to ingratitude. I suggest that a charitable heart could very well ascribe my choice to natural modesty. Yet it isn't exactly modesty that makes me select reproof for the illustration of my case. No, it isn't exactly modesty. I am not at all certain that I am modest; but those who have read so far through my work will credit me with enough decency, tact, *savoir-faire*, what you will, to prevent me from making a song for my own glory out of the words of other people. No! The true motive of my selection lies in quite a different trait. I have always had a propensity to justify my action. Not to defend. To justify. Not to insist that I was right but simply to explain that there was no perverse intention, no secret scorn for the natural sensibilities of mankind at the bottom of my impulses.

That kind of weakness is dangerous only so far that it exposes one to the risk of becoming a bore; for the world generally is not interested in the motives of any overt act but in its consequences. Man may smile and smile but he is not an investigating animal. He loves the obvious. He shrinks from explanations. Yet I will go on with mine. It's obvious that I need not have written that book. I was under no necessity to deal with that subject; using the word subject both in the sense of the tale itself and in the larger one of a special manifestation in the life of mankind. This I fully admit. But the thought of elaborating mere ugliness in order to shock, or even simply to surprise my readers by a change of front, has never entered my head. In making this statement I expect to be believed, not only on the evidence of my general character but also for the reason, which anybody can see, that the whole treatment of the tale, its inspiring indignation and underlying pity and contempt, prove my detachment from the squalor and sordidness which lie simply in the outward circumstances of the setting.

The inception of *The Secret Agent* followed immediately on a two years' period of intense absorption in the task of writing that remote novel, *Nostromo*, with its far-off Latin-American atmosphere; and the profoundly personal *Mirror of the Sea*. The first an intense creative effort on what I suppose will always remain my largest canvas, the second an unreserved attempt to unveil for a moment the profounder intimacies of the sea and the formative influences of nearly half my lifetime. It was a period, too, in which my sense of the truth of things was attended by a very intense imaginative and emotional readiness which, all genuine and faithful to facts as it was, yet made me feel (the task once done) as if I were left behind, aimless amongst mere husks of sensations and lost in a world of other, of inferior, values.

I don't know whether I really felt that I wanted a change, change in my imagination, in my vision, and in my mental attitude. I rather think that a change in the fundamental mood had already stolen over me unawares. I don't remember anything definite happening. With *The Mirror of the Sea* finished in the full consciousness that I had dealt honestly with myself and my readers in every line of that book, I gave myself up to a not unhappy pause. Then, while I was yet standing still, as it were, and certainly not thinking of going out of my way to look for anything ugly, the subject of *The Secret Agent*—I mean the tale—came to me in the shape of a few words uttered by a friend in a casual conversation about anarchists or rather anarchist activities; how brought about I don't remember now.

I remember, however, remarking on the criminal futility of the whole thing, doctrine, action, mentality; and on the contemptible aspect of the half-crazy pose as of a brazen cheat exploiting the poignant miseries and passionate credulities of a mankind always so tragically eager for self-destruction. That was what made for me its philosophical pretences so unpardonable. Presently, passing to particular instances, we recalled the already old story of the attempt to blow up the Greenwich Observatory; a blood-stained inanity of so fatuous a kind that it was impossible to fathom its origin by any reasonable or even unreasonable process of thought. For perverse unreason has its own logical processes. But that outrage could not be laid hold of mentally in any sort of way, so that one remained faced by the fact of a man blown to bits for nothing even most remotely resembling an idea, anarchistic or other. As to the outer wall of the Observatory it did not show as much as the faintest crack.

I pointed all this out to my friend, who remained silent for a while and then remarked in his characteristically casual and omniscient manner: 'Oh, that fellow was half an idiot. His sister committed suicide afterwards.' These were absolutely the only

words that passed between us; for extreme surprise at this unexpected piece of information kept me dumb for a moment and
he began at once to talk of something else. It never occurred to
me later to ask how he arrived at his knowledge. I am sure that
if he had seen once in his life the back of an anarchist that must
have been the whole extent of his connection with the under-
world. He was, however, a man who liked to talk with all sorts
of people, and he may have gathered those illuminating facts at
second or third hand, from a crossing-sweeper, from a retired
police officer, from some vague man in his club, or even, perhaps,
from a Minister of State met at some public or private reception.

Of the illuminating quality there could be no doubt whatever. One felt like walking out of a forest on to a plain—there
was not much to see but one had plenty of light. No, there was
not much to see and, frankly, for a considerable time I didn't
even attempt to perceive anything. It was only the illuminating
impression that remained. It remained satisfactory but in a passive way. Then, about a week later, I came upon a book which
as far as I know had never attained any prominence, the rather
summary recollections of an Assistant Commissioner of Police,
an obviously able man with a strong religious strain in his character who was appointed to his post at the time of the dynamite
outrages in London, away back in the eighties. The book was
fairly interesting, very discreet of course; and I have by now forgotten the bulk of its contents. It contained no revelations, it
ran over the surface agreeably, and that was all. I won't even
try to explain why I should have been arrested by a little passage of about seven lines, in which the author (I believe his name
was Anderson) reproduced a short dialogue held in the lobby of
the House of Commons after some unexpected anarchist outrage,
with the Home Secretary. I think it was Sir William Harcourt
then. He was very much irritated and the official was very apologetic. The phrase, amongst the three which passed between them,
that struck me most was Sir W. Harcourt's angry sally: 'All
that's very well. But your idea of secrecy over there seems to consist of keeping the Home Secretary in the dark.' Characteristic
enough of Sir W. Harcourt's temper but not much in itself.

There must have been, however, some sort of atmosphere in the whole incident because all of a sudden I felt myself stimulated. And then ensued in my mind what a student of chemistry would best understand from the analogy of the addition of the tiniest little drop of the right kind, precipitating the process of crystallization in a test-tube containing some colourless solution.

It was at first for me a mental change, disturbing a quieted-down imagination, in which strange forms, sharp in outline but imperfectly apprehended, appeared and claimed attention as crystals will do by their bizarre and unexpected shapes. One fell to musing before the phenomenon—even of the past: of South America, a continent of crude sunshine and brutal revolutions, of the sea, the vast expanse of salt waters, the mirror of heaven's frowns and smiles, the reflector of the world's light. Then the vision of an enormous town presented itself, of a monstrous town more populous than some continents and in its man-made might as if indifferent to heaven's frowns and smiles; a cruel devourer of the world's light. There was room enough there to place any story, depth enough there for any passion, variety enough there for any setting, darkness enough to bury five millions of lives.

Irresistibly the town became the background for the ensuing period of deep and tentative meditations. Endless vistas opened before me in various directions. It would take years to find the right way! It seemed to take years! ... Slowly the dawning conviction of Mrs. Verloc's maternal passion grew up to a flame between me and that background, tingeing it with its secret ardour and receiving from it in exchange some of its own sombre colouring. At last the story of Winnie Verloc stood out complete from the days of her childhood to the end, unproportioned as yet, with everything still on the first plan, as it were; but ready now to be dealt with. It was a matter of about three days.

This book is *that* story, reduced to manageable proportions, its whole course suggested and centred round the absurd cruelty of the Greenwich Park explosion. I had there a task I will not say arduous but of the most absorbing difficulty. But it had to be done. It was a necessity. The figures grouped about Mrs. Verloc and related directly or indirectly to her tragic suspicion that 'life doesn't stand much looking into,' are the outcome of that very necessity. Personally I have never had any doubt of the reality of Mrs. Verloc's story; but it had to be disengaged from its obscurity in that immense town, it had to be made credible, I don't mean so much as to her soul but as to her surroundings, not so much as to her psychology but as to her humanity. For the surroundings hints were not lacking. I had to fight hard to keep at arm's length the memories of my solitary and nocturnal walks all over London in my early days, lest they should rush in and overwhelm each page of the story as these emerged one after another from a mood as serious in feeling and thought as any in which I ever wrote a line. In that respect I really think that *The Secret Agent* is a perfectly genuine piece of work. Even the purely artistic purpose, that of applying an ironic method to a subject of that kind, was formulated with deliberation and in the earnest belief that ironic treatment alone would enable me to say all I felt I would have to say in scorn as well as in pity. It is one of the minor satisfactions of my writing life that having taken that resolve I did manage, it seems to me, to carry it right through to the end. As to the personages whom the absolute necessity of the case—Mrs. Verloc's case—brings out in front of the London background, from them, too, I obtained those little satisfactions which really count for so much against the mass of oppressive doubts that haunt so persistently every attempt at creative work. For instance, of Mr. Vladimir himself (who was fair game for a caricatural presentation) I was gratified to hear that an experienced man of the world had said 'that Conrad must have been in touch with that sphere or else has an excellent intuition of things,' because Mr. Vladimir was 'not only possible in detail but quite right in essentials.' Then a visitor from America informed me that all sorts of revolutionary refugees in New York would have it that the book was written by somebody who knew a lot about them. This seemed to me a very high compliment, considering that, as a matter of hard fact, I had seen even less of their kind than the omniscient friend who gave me the first suggestion for the novel. I have no doubt, however, that there had been moments during the writing of the book when I was an extreme revolutionist, I won't say more convinced than they but certainly cherishing a more concentrated purpose than any of them had ever done in the whole course of his life. I don't say this to boast. I was simply attending to my business. In the matter of all my books I have always attended to my business. I have attended to it with complete self-surrender. And this statement, too, is not a boast. I could not have done otherwise. It would have bored me too much to make believe.

The suggestions for certain personages of the tale, both law-abiding and lawless, came from various sources which, perhaps, here and there, some reader may have recognized. They are not very recondite. But I am not concerned here to legitimize any of those people, and even as to my general view of the moral reactions as between the criminal and the police all I will venture to say is that it seems to me to be at least arguable.

The twelve years that have elapsed since the publication of the book have not changed my attitude. I do not regret having written it. Lately, circumstances, which have nothing to do with the general tenor of this preface, have compelled me to strip this tale of the literary robe of indignant scorn it had cost me so much to fit on it decently, years ago. I have been forced, so to speak, to look upon its bare bones. I confess that it makes a grisly skeleton. But still I will submit that telling Winnie Verloc's story to its anarchistic end of utter desolation, madness, and despair, and telling it as I have told it here, I have not intended to commit a gratuitous outrage on the feelings of mankind.

A Set of Six (1920)

The six stories in this volume are the result of some three or four years of occasional work. The dates of their writing are far apart, their origins are various. None of them are connected directly with personal experiences. In all of them the facts are inherently true, by which I mean that they are not only possible but that they have actually happened. For instance, the last story in the volume, the one I call *Pathetic*, whose first title is *Il Conde* (mis-spelt by the by), is an almost verbatim transcript of the tale told me by a very charming old gentleman whom I met in Italy.

I don't mean to say it is only that. Anybody can see that it is something more than a verbatim report, but where he left off and where I began must be left to the acute discrimination of the reader who may be interested in the problem. I don't mean to say that the problem is worth the trouble. What I am certain of, however, is that it is not to be solved, for I am not at all clear about it myself by this time. All I can say is that the personality of the narrator was extremely suggestive quite apart from the story he was telling me. I heard a few years ago that he had died far away from his beloved Naples where that 'abominable adventure' did really happen to him.

Thus the genealogy of *Il Conde* is simple. It is not the case with the other stories. Various strains contributed to their composition, and the nature of many of those I have forgotten, not having the habit of making notes either before or after the fact. I mean the fact of writing a story. What I remember best about *Gaspar Ruiz* is that it was written, or at any rate begun, within a month of finishing *Nostromo*; but apart from the locality, and that a pretty wide one (all the South American continent), the novel and the story have nothing in common, neither mood nor intention, and, certainly, not the style. The manner for the most part is that of General Santierra, and that old warrior, I note with satisfaction, is very true to himself all through. Looking now dispassionately at the various ways in which this story could have been presented I can't honestly think the General superfluous. It is he, an old man talking of the days of his youth, who characterizes the whole narrative and gives it an air of actuality which I doubt whether I could have achieved without his help. In the mere writing his existence of course was of no help at all, because the whole thing had to be carefully kept within the frame of his simple mind. But all this is but a laborious searching of memories. My present feeling is that the story could not have been told otherwise. The hint for Gaspar Ruiz the man I found in a book[6] by Captain Basil Hall, R.N., who was for some time,

6. *Extracts from a Journal Written on the Coasts of Chili, Peru, and Mexico.*

between the years 1824 and 1828, senior officer of a small British squadron on the west coast of South America. His book, published in the thirties, obtained a certain celebrity and I suppose is to be found still in some libraries. The curious who may be mistrusting my imagination are referred to that printed document, volume two, I forget the page, but it is somewhere not far from the end. Another document connected with this story is a letter of a biting and ironic kind from a friend then in Burma, passing certain strictures upon 'the gentleman with the gun on his back' which I do not intend to make accessible to the public. Yet the gun episode did really happen, or at least I am bound to believe it because I remember it, described in an extremely matter-of-fact tone, in some book I read in my boyhood; and I am not going to discard the beliefs of my boyhood for anybody on earth.

The Brute, which is the only sea-story in the volume, is, like Il Conde, associated with a direct narrative and based on a suggestion gathered on warm human lips. I will not disclose the real name of the criminal ship but the first I heard of her homicidal habits was from the late Captain Blake, commanding a London ship in which I served in 1884 as second officer. Captain Blake was, of all my commanders, the one I remember with the greatest affection. I have sketched in his personality, without, however, mentioning his name, in the first paper of The Mirror of the Sea. In his young days he had had a personal experience of the brute, and it is perhaps for that reason that I have put the story into the mouth of a young man and made of it what the reader will see. The existence of the brute was a fact. The end of the brute as related in the story is also a fact, well known at the time though it really happened to another ship, of great beauty of form and of blameless character, which certainly deserved a better fate. I have unscrupulously adapted it to the needs of my story, thinking that I had there something in the nature of poetical justice. I hope that little villainy will not cast a shadow upon the general honesty of my proceedings as a writer of tales.

Of The Informer and The Anarchist I will say next to nothing. The pedigree of these tales is hopelessly complicated and not worth disentangling at this distance of time. I found them and here they are. The discriminating reader will guess that I have found them within my mind; but how they or their elements came in there I have forgotten for the most part; and for the rest I really don't see why I should give myself away more than I have done already.

It remains for me only now to mention *The Duel*, the longest story in the book. That story attained the dignity of publication all by itself in a small illustrated volume, under the title, *The Point of Honour*. That was many years ago. It has been since reinstated in its proper place, which is the place it occupies in this volume, in all the subsequent editions of my work. Its pedigree is extremely simple. It springs from a ten-line paragraph in a small provincial paper published in the south of France. That paragraph, occasioned by a duel with a fatal ending between two well-known Parisian personalities, referred for some reason or other to the 'well-known fact' of two officers in Napoleon's Grand Army having fought a series of duels in the midst of great wars and on some futile pretext. The pretext was never disclosed. I had therefore to invent it; and I think that, given the character of the two officers, which I had to invent, too, I have made it sufficiently convincing by the mere force of its absurdity. The truth is that in my mind the story is nothing but a serious and even earnest attempt at a bit of historical fiction. I had heard in my boyhood a good deal of the great Napoleonic legend. I had a genuine feeling that I would find myself at home in it, and *The Duel* is the result of that feeling, or, if the reader prefers, of that presumption. Personally I have no qualms of conscience about this piece of work. The story might have been better told, of course. All one's work might have been better done; but this is the sort of reflection a worker must put aside courageously if he doesn't mean every one of his conceptions to remain for ever a private vision, an evanescent reverie. How many of those visions have I seen vanish in my time! This one, however, has remained, a testimony, if you like, to my courage or a proof of my rashness. What I care to remember best is the testimony of some French readers who volunteered the opinion that in those hundred pages or so I had managed to render 'wonderfully' the spirit of the whole epoch. Exaggeration of kindness no doubt; but even so I hug it still to my breast, because in truth that is exactly what I was trying to capture in my small net: The Spirit of the Epoch— never purely militarist in the long clash of arms, youthful, almost childlike in its exaltation of sentiment—naïvely heroic in its faith.

Under Western Eyes (1920)

It must be admitted that by the mere force of circumstances *Under Western Eyes* has become already a sort of historical novel dealing with the past.

This reflection bears entirely upon the events of the tale; but being as a whole an attempt to render not so much the political state as the psychology of Russia itself, I venture to hope that it has not lost all its interest. I am encouraged in this flattering belief by noticing that in many articles on Russian affairs of the present day reference is made to certain sayings and opinions uttered in the pages that follow, in a manner testifying to the clearness of my vision and the correctness of my judgment. I need not say that in writing this novel I had no other object in view than to express imaginatively the general truth which underlies its action, together with my honest convictions as to the moral complexion of certain facts more or less known to the whole world.

As to the actual creation I may say that when I began to write I had a distinct conception of the first part only, with the three figures of Haldin, Razumov, and Councillor Mikulin, de- fined exactly in my mind. It was only after I had finished writing the first part that the whole story revealed itself to me in its tragic character and in the march of its events as unavoidable and suffi- ciently ample in its outline to give free play to my creative instinct and to the dramatic possibilities of the subject.

The course of action need not be explained. It has suggested itself more as a matter of feeling than a matter of thinking. It is the result not of a special experience but of general knowledge, fortified by earnest meditation. My greatest anxiety was in being able to strike and sustain the note of scrupulous impartiality. The obligation of absolute fairness was imposed on me historically and hereditarily, by the peculiar experience of race and family, in addition to my primary conviction that truth alone is the justification of any fiction which makes the least claim to the quality of art or may hope to take its place in the culture of men and women of its time. I had never been called before to a greater effort of detachment: detachment from all passions, prejudices, and even from personal memories. *Under Western Eyes* on its first appearance in England was a failure with the public, perhaps because of that very detachment. I obtained my reward some six years later when I first heard that the book had found universal recognition in Russia and had been republished there in many editions.

The various figures playing their part in the story also owe their existence to no special experience but to the general knowledge of the condition of Russia and of the moral and emotional reactions of the Russian temperament to the pressure of tyrannical lawlessness, which, in general human terms, could be reduced to the formula of senseless desperation provoked by senseless tyranny. What I was concerned with mainly was the aspect, the character, and the fate of the individuals as they appeared to the Western Eyes of the old teacher of languages. He himself has been much criticized; but I will not at this late hour undertake to justify his existence. He was useful to me and therefore I think that he must be useful to the reader both in the way of comment and by the part he plays in the development of the story. In my desire to produce the effect of actuality it seemed to me indispensible to have an eye-witness of the transactions in Geneva. I needed also a sympathetic friend for Miss Haldin, who otherwise would have been too much alone and unsupported to be perfectly credible. She would have had no one to whom she could give a glimpse of her idealistic faith, of her great heart, and of her simple emotions.

Razumov is treated sympathetically. Why should he not be? He is an ordinary young man, with a healthy capacity for work and sane ambitions. He has an average conscience. If he is slightly abnormal it is only in his sensitiveness to his position. Being nobody's child he feels rather more keenly than another would that he is a Russian—or he is nothing. He is perfectly right in looking on all Russia as his heritage. The sanguinary futility of the crimes and the sacrifices seething in that amorphous mass envelops and crushes him. But I don't think that in his distraction he is ever monstrous. Nobody is exhibited as a monster here —neither the simple-minded Tekla nor the wrong-headed Sophia Antonovna. Peter Ivanovitch and Madame de S. are fair game. They are the apes of a sinister jungle and are treated as their grimaces deserve. As to Nikita—nicknamed Necator—he is the perfect flower of the terroristic wilderness. What troubled me most in dealing with him was not his monstrosity but his banality. He has been exhibited to the public eye for years in so-called 'disclosures' in newspaper articles, in secret histories, in sensational novels.

The most terrifying reflection (I am speaking now for myself) is that all these people are not the product of the exceptional but of the general—of the normality of their place, and time, and race. The ferocity and imbecility of an autocratic rule rejecting all legality and in fact basing itself upon complete moral anarchism provokes the no less imbecile and atrocious answer of a purely Utopian revolutionism encompassing destruction by the first means to hand, in the strange conviction that a fundamental change of hearts must follow the downfall of any given human institutions. These people are unable to see that all they can effect is merely a change of names. The oppressors and the oppressed are all Russians together; and the world is brought once more face to face with the truth of the saying that the tiger cannot change his stripes nor the leopard his spots.

'Twixt Land and Sea Tales (1920)

The only bond between these three stories is, so to speak, geographical, for their scene, be it land, be it sea, is situated in the same region, which may be called the region of the Indian Ocean with its offshoots and prolongations north of the equator even as far as the Gulf of Siam. In point of time they belong to the period immediately after the publication of that novel with the awkward title *Under Western Eyes* and, as far as the life of the writer is concerned, their appearance in a volume marks a definite change in the fortunes of his fiction. For there is no denying the fact that *Under Western Eyes* found no favour in the public eye, whereas the novel called *Chance* which followed *'Twixt Land and Sea* was received on its first appearance by many more readers than any other of my books.

This volume of three tales was also well received, publicly and privately and from a publisher's point of view. This little success was a most timely tonic for my enfeebled bodily frame. For this may indeed be called the book of a man's convalescence, at least as to three-fourths of it; because *The Secret Sharer*, the middle story, was written much earlier than the other two.

For in truth the memories of *Under Western Eyes* are associated with the memory of a severe illness which seemed to wait like a tiger in the jungle on the turn of a path to jump on me the moment the last words of that novel were written. The memory of an illness is very much like the memory of a nightmare. On emerging from it in a much enfeebled state I was inspired to direct my tottering steps toward the Indian Ocean, a complete change of surroundings and atmosphere from the Lake of Geneva, as nobody would deny. Begun so languidly and with such a fumbling hand that the first twenty pages or more had to be thrown into the waste-paper basket, *A Smile of Fortune*, the most purely Indian Ocean story of the three, has ended by becoming what the reader will see. I will only say for myself that I have been patted on the back for it by most unexpected people, personally unknown to me, the chief of them of course being the editor of a popular illustrated magazine who published it serially in one mighty instalment. Who will dare say after this that the change of air had not been an immense success?

The origins of the middle story, *The Secret Sharer*, are quite other. It was written much earlier and was published first in *Harper's Magazine*, during the early part, I think, of 1911.[7] Or perhaps the latter part? My memory on that point is hazy. The

7. The story appeared in the August–September, 1910, number.

basic fact of the tale I had in my possession for a good many years. It was in truth the common possession of the whole fleet of merchant ships trading to India, China, and Australia: a great company the last years of which coincided with my first years on the wider seas. The fact itself happened on board a very distinguished member of it, *Cutty Sark* by name and belonging to Mr. Willis, a notable shipowner in his day, one of the kind (they are all underground now) who used personally to see his ships start on their voyages to those distant shores where they showed worthily the honoured house-flag of their owner. I am glad I was not too late to get at least one glimpse of Mr. Willis on a very wet and gloomy morning watching from the pier head of the New South Dock one of his clippers starting on a China voyage—an imposing figure of a man under the invariable white hat so well known in the Port of London, waiting till the head of his ship had swung downstream before giving her a dignified wave of a big gloved hand. For all I know it may have been the *Cutty Sark* herself, though certainly not on that fatal voyage. I do not know the date of the occurrence on which the scheme of *The Secret Sharer* is founded; it came to light and even got into newspapers about the middle eighties, though I had heard of it before, as it were privately, among the officers of the great wool fleet in which my first years in deep water were served. It came to light under circumstances dramatic enough, I think, but which have nothing to do with my story. In the more specially maritime part of my writings this bit of presentation may take its place as one of my two Calm-pieces. For, if there is to be any classification by subjects, I have done two Storm-pieces in *The Nigger of the 'Narcissus'* and in *Typhoon*; and two Calm-pieces: this one and *The Shadow-Line,* a book which belongs to a later period.

Notwithstanding their autobiographical form the above two stories are not the record of personal experience. Their quality, such as it is, depends on something larger if less precise: on the character, vision, and sentiment of the first twenty independent years of my life. And the same may be said of the *Freya of the Seven Isles.* I was considerably abused for writing that story on the ground of its cruelty, both in public prints and in private letters. I remember one from a man in America who was quite furiously angry. He told me with curses and imprecations that I had no right to write such an abominable thing which, he said, had gratuitously and intolerably harrowed his feelings. It was a very interesting letter to read. Impressive too. I carried it for some days in my pocket. Had I the right? The sincerity of the anger impressed me. Had I the right? Had I really sinned as he said or was it only that man's madness? Yet there was a method in his fury . . . I composed in my mind a violent reply, a reply of mild argument, a reply of lofty detachment; but they never got on paper in the end and I have forgotten their phrasing. The very letter of the angry man has got lost somehow; and nothing remains now but the pages of the story which I cannot recall and would not recall if I could.

But I am glad to think that the two women in this book: Alice, the sullen, passive victim of her fate, and the actively individual Freya, so determined to be the mistress of her own destiny, must have evoked some sympathies because of all my volumes of short stories this was the one for which there was the greatest immediate demand.

Chance (1920)

Chance is one of my novels that shortly after having been begun were laid aside for a few months. Starting impetuously like a sanguine oarsman setting forth in the early morning I came very soon to a fork in the stream and found it necessary to pause and reflect seriously upon the direction I would take. Either presented to me equal fascinations, at least on the surface, and for that very reason my hesitation extended over many days. I floated in the calm water of pleasant speculation, between the diverging currents of conflicting impulses, with an agreeable but perfectly irrational conviction that neither of those currents would take me to destruction. My sympathies being equally divided and the two forces being equal it is perfectly obvious that nothing but mere chance influenced my decision in the end. It is a mighty force, that of mere chance; absolutely irresistible yet manifesting itself often in delicate forms, such for instance as the charm, true or illusory, of a human being. It is very difficult to put one's finger on the imponderable, but I may venture to say that it is Flora de Barral who is really responsible for this novel which relates, in fact, the story of her life.

At the crucial moment of my indecision Flora de Barral passed before me, but so swiftly that I failed at first to get hold of her. Though loth to give her up I didn't see the way of pursuit clearly and was on the point of becoming discouraged when my natural liking for Captain Anthony came to my assistance. I said to myself that if that man was so determined to embrace a 'wisp of mist' the best thing for me was to join him in that eminently practical and praiseworthy adventure. I simply followed Captain Anthony. Each of us was bent on capturing his own dream. The reader will be able to judge of our success.

Captain Anthony's determination led him a long and roundabout course and that is why this book is a long book. That the course was of my own choosing I will not deny. A critic had remarked that if I had selected another method of composition and taken a little more trouble the tale could have been told in about two hundred pages. I confess I do not perceive exactly the bearings of such criticism or even the use of such a remark. No doubt that by selecting a certain method and taking great pains the whole story might have been written out on a cigarette paper. For that matter, the whole history of mankind could be written thus if only approached with sufficient detachment. The history of men on this earth since the beginning of ages may be resumed in one phrase of infinite poignancy: They were born, they suffered, they died...Yet it is a great tale! But in the infinitely minute stories about men and women it is my lot on earth to narrate I am not capable of such detachment.

What makes this book memorable to me apart from the natural sentiment one has for one's creation is the response it provoked. The general public responded largely, more largely perhaps than to any other book of mine, in the only way the general public can respond, that is by buying a certain number of copies. This gave me a considerable amount of pleasure, because what I always feared most was drifting unconsciously into the position of a writer for a limited coterie; a position which would have been odious to me as throwing a doubt on the soundness of my belief in the solidarity of all mankind in simple ideas and in sincere emotions. Regarded as a manifestation of criticism (for it would be outrageous to deny to the general public the possession of a critical mind) the reception was very satisfactory. I saw that I had managed to please a certain number of minds busy attending to their own very real affairs. It is agreeable to think one is able to please. From the minds whose business it is precisely to criticize such attempts to please, this book received an amount of discussion and of a rather searching analysis which not only satisfied that personal vanity I share with the rest of mankind but reached my deeper feelings and aroused my gratified interest. The undoubted sympathy informing the varied appreciations of that book was, I love to think, a recognition of my good faith in the pursuit of my art—the art of the novelist which a distinguished French writer at the end of a successful career complained of as being 'trop difficile'! It is indeed *too* arduous in the sense that the effort must be invariably so much greater than the possible achievement. In that sort of foredoomed task which is in its nature very lonely also, sympathy is a precious thing. It can make the most severe criticism welcome. To be told that better things have been expected of one may be soothing in view of how much better things one had expected from oneself in this art which, in these days, is no longer justified by the assumption, somewhere and somehow, of a didactic purpose.

I do not mean to hint that anybody had ever done me the injury (I don't mean insult, I mean injury) of charging a single one of my pages with didactic purpose. But every subject in the region of intellect and emotion must have a morality of its own if it is treated at all sincerely; and even the most artful of writers will give himself (and his morality) away in about every third sentence. The varied shades of moral significance which have been discovered in my writings are very numerous. None of them, however, have provoked a hostile manifestation. It may have happened to me to sin against taste now and then, but apparently I have never sinned against the basic feelings and elementary convictions which make life possible to the mass of mankind and, by establishing a standard of judgment, set their idealism free to look for plainer ways, for higher feelings, for deeper purposes.

I cannot say that any particular moral complexion has been put on this novel but I do not think that anybody had detected in it an evil intention. And it is only for their intentions that men can be held responsible. The ultimate effects of whatever they do are far beyond their control. In doing this book my intention was to interest people in my vision of things, which is indissolubly allied to the style in which it is expressed. In other words I wanted to write a certain amount of pages in prose, which, strictly speaking, is my proper business. I have attended to it conscientiously with the hope of being entertaining or at least not insufferably boring to my readers. I cannot sufficiently insist upon the truth that when I sit down to write my intentions are always blameless however deplorable the ultimate effect of the act may turn out to be.

Within the Tides (1920)

The tales collected in this book have elicited on their appearance two utterances in the shape of comment and one distinctly critical charge. A reviewer observed that I liked to write of men who go to sea or live on lonely islands untrammelled by the pressure of worldly circumstances, because such characters allowed freer play to my imagination which in their case was only bounded by natural laws and the universal human conventions. There is a certain truth in this remark no doubt. It is only the suggestion of deliberate choice that misses its mark. I have not sought for special imaginative freedom or a larger play of fancy in my choice of characters and subjects. The nature of the knowledge, suggestions or hints used in my imaginative work has depended directly on the conditions of my active life. It depended more on contacts, and very slight contacts at that, than on actual experience; because my life as a matter of fact was far from being adventurous in itself. Even now when I look back on it with a certain regret (who would not regret his youth?) and positive affection, its coloring wears the sober hue of hard work and exacting calls of duty, things which in themselves are not much charged with a feeling of romance. If these things appeal strongly to me even in retrospect it is, I suppose, because the romantic feeling of reality was in me an inborn faculty. This in itself may be a curse but when disciplined by a sense of personal responsibility and a recognition of the hard facts of existence shared with the rest of mankind becomes but a point of view from which the very shadows of life appear endowed with an internal glow. And such romanticism is not a sin. It is none the worse for the knowledge of truth. It only tries to make the best of it, hard as it may be; and in this hardness discovers a certain aspect of beauty.

I am speaking here of romanticism in relation to life, not of romanticism in relation to imaginative literature, which, in its early days, was associated simply with medieval subjects, or, at any rate, with subjects sought for in a remote past. My subjects are not medieval and I have a natural right to them because my past is very much my own. If their course lie out of the beaten path of organized social life, it is, perhaps, because I myself did in a sort break away from it early in obedience to an impulse which must have been very genuine since it has sustained me through all the dangers of disillusion. But that origin of my literary work was very far from giving a larger scope to my imagination. On the contrary, the mere fact of dealing with matters outside the general run of everyday experience laid me under the obligation of a more scrupulous fidelity to the truth of my own sensations. The problem was to make unfamiliar things credible. To do that I had to create for them, to reproduce for them, to envelop them in their proper atmosphere of actuality. This was the hardest task of all and the most important, in view of that conscientious rendering of truth in thought and fact which has been always my aim.

The other utterance of the two I have alluded to above consisted in the observation that in this volume of mine the whole was greater than its parts. I pass it on to my readers, merely remarking that if this is really so then I must take it as a tribute to my personality, since those stories which by implication seem to hold so well together as to be surveyed *en bloc* and judged as the product of a single mood, were written at different times, under various influences, and with the deliberate intention of trying several ways of telling a tale. The hints and suggestions for all of them had been received at various times and in distant parts of the globe. The book received a good deal of varied criticism, mainly quite justifiable, but in a couple of instances quite surprising in its objections. Amongst them was the critical charge of false realism brought against the opening story, *The Planter of Malata*. I would have regarded it as serious enough if I had not discovered on reading further that the distinguished critic was accusing me simply of having sought to evade a happy ending out of a sort of moral cowardice, lest I should be condemned as a superficially sentimental person. Where (and of what sort) there are to be found in *The Planter of Malata* any germs of happiness that could have fructified at the end I am at a loss to see. Such criticism seems to miss the whole purpose and significance of a piece of writing the primary intention of which was mainly aesthetic; an essay in description and narrative around a given psychological situation. Of more seriousness was the spoken criticism of an old and valued friend who thought that in the scene near the rock, which from the point of view of psychology is crucial, neither Felicia Moorsom nor Geoffrey Renouard find the right things to say to each other. I didn't argue the point at the time, for, to be candid, I didn't feel quite satisfied with the scene myself. On re-reading it lately for the purpose of this edition, I have come to the conclusion that there is that much truth in my friend's criticism that I have made those people a little too explicit in their emotion and thus have destroyed to a certain extent the characteristic illusory glamour of their personalities. I regret this defect very much, for I regard *The Planter of Malata* as a nearly successful attempt at doing a very difficult thing which I would have liked to have made as perfect as it lay in my power. Yet considering the pitch and the tonality of the whole tale it is very difficult to imagine what else those two people could have found to say at that time and on that particular spot of the earth's surface. In the mood in which they both were, and given the exceptional state of their feelings, anything might have been said.

The eminent critic who charged me with false realism, the outcome of timidity, was quite wrong. I should like to ask him what he imagines the, so to speak, lifelong embrace of Felicia Moorsom and Geoffrey Renouard could have been like? Could it have been at all? Would it have been credible? No! I did not shirk anything, either from timidity or laziness. Perhaps a little mistrust of my own powers would not have been altogether out of place in this connection. But it failed me; and I resemble Geoffrey Renouard in so far that when once engaged in an adventure I cannot bear the idea of turning back. The moment had arrived for these people to disclose themselves. They had to do it. To render a crucial point of feelings in terms of human speech is really an impossible task. Written words can only form a sort of translation. And if that translation happens from want of skill or from over-anxiety, to be too literal, the people caught in the toils of passion, instead of disclosing themselves, which would be art, are made to give themselves away, which is neither art nor life. Nor yet truth! At any rate, not the whole truth; for it is truth robbed of all its necessary and sympathetic reservations and quali-fications which give it its fair form, its just proportions, its sem-blance of human fellowship.

Indeed the task of the translator of passions into speech may be pronounced 'too difficult.' However, with my customary im-penitence I am glad I have attempted the story with all its impli-cations and difficulties, including the scene by the side of the grey rock crowning the height of Malata. But I am not so inordinately pleased with the result as not to be able to forgive a patient reader who may find it somewhat disappointing.

I have left myself no space to talk about the other three stories because I do not think that they call for detailed comment. Each of them has its special mood and I have tried purposely to give each its special tone and a different construction of phrase. A reviewer asked in reference to *The Inn of the Two Witches* whether I ever came across a tale called 'A Very Strange Bed' published in *Household Words* in 1852 or '54. I never saw a num-ber of *Household Words* of that decade. A bed of the sort was discovered in an inn on the road between Rome and Naples at the end of the eighteenth century. Where I picked up the information I cannot say now, but I am certain it was not in a tale. This bed is the only 'fact' of *The Witches' Inn*. The other two stories have considerably more 'fact' in them, derived from my own personal knowledge.

Victory (first Author's Note, 1915)

The last word of this novel was written on the 29th of May 1914. And that last word was the single word of the title.

Those were the times of peace. Now that the moment of publication approaches I have been considering the discretion of altering the title-page. The word *Victory*, the shining and tragic goal of noble effort, appeared too great, too august, to stand at the head of a mere novel. There was also the possibility of falling under the suspicion of commercial astuteness deceiving the public into the belief that the book had something to do with war.

Of that, however, I was not afraid very much. What influenced my decision most were the obscure promptings of that pagan residuum of awe and wonder which lurks still at the bottom of our old humanity. *Victory* was the last word I had written in peace time. It was the last literary thought which had occurred to me before the doors of the Temple of Janus flying open with a crash shook the minds, the hearts, the consciences of men all over the world. Such coincidence could not be treated lightly. And I made up my mind to let the word stand, in the same hopeful spirit in which some simple citizen of Old Rome would have 'accepted the omen.'

The second point on which I wish to offer a remark is the existence (in the novel) of a person named Schomberg.

That I believe him to be true goes without saying. I am not likely to offer pinchbeck wares to my public consciously. Schomberg is an old member of my company. A very subordinate personage in *Lord Jim* as far back as the year 1899, he became notably active in a certain short story of mine published in 1902.[8] Here he appears in a still larger part, true to life (I hope), but

8. "Falk," published in 1901.

also true to himself. Only, in this instance, his deeper passions come into play, and thus his grotesque psychology is completed at last.

I don't pretend to say that this is the entire Teutonic psychology; but it is indubitably the psychology of a Teuton. My object in mentioning him here is to bring out the fact that, far from being the incarnation of recent animosities, he is the creature of my old, deep-seated and, as it were, impartial conviction.

Victory (second Author's Note, 1920)

On approaching the task of writing this Note for *Victory* the first thing I am conscious of is the actual nearness of the book, its nearness to me personally, to the vanished mood in which it was written and to the mixed feelings aroused by the critical notices the book obtained when first published almost exactly a year after the beginning of the Great War. The writing of it was finished in 1914 long before the murder of an Austrian archduke sounded the first note of warning for a world already full of doubts and fears.

The contemporaneous very short Author's Note which is preserved in this edition bears sufficient witness to the feelings with which I consented to the publication of the book. The fact of the book having been published in the United States early in the year made it difficult to delay its appearance in England any longer. It came out in the thirteenth month of the War, and my conscience was troubled by the awful incongruity of throwing this bit of imagined drama into the welter of reality, tragic enough in all conscience but even more cruel than tragic and more inspiring than cruel. It seemed awfully presumptuous to think there would be eyes to spare for those pages in a community which in the crash of the big guns and in the din of brave words expressing the truth of an indomitable faith could not but feel the edge of a sharp knife at its throat.

The unchanging Man of history is wonderfully adaptable both by his power of endurance and in his capacity for detachment. The fact seems to be that the play of his destiny is too great for his fears and too mysterious for his understanding. Were the trump of the Last Judgment to sound suddenly on a working day the musician at his piano would go on with his performance of Beethoven's sonata and the cobbler at his stall stick to his last in undisturbed confidence in the virtues of the leather. And with perfect propriety. For what are we to let ourselves be disturbed by an angel's vengeful music too mighty for our ears and too awful for our terrors? Thus it happens to us to be struck suddenly by the lightning of wrath. The reader will go on reading if the book pleases him and the critic will go on criticizing with that faculty of detachment born perhaps from a sense of infinite littleness and which is yet the only faculty that seems to assimilate man to the immortal gods.

It is only when the catastrophe matches the natural obscurity of our fate that even the best representative of the race is liable to lose his detachment. It is very obvious that on the arrival of the gentlemanly Mr. Jones, the single-minded Ricardo and the faithful Pedro, Heyst, the man of universal detachment, loses his mental self-possession, that fine attitude before the universally irremediable which wears the name of stoicism. It is all a matter of proportion. There should have been a remedy for that sort of thing. And yet there is no remedy. Behind this minute instance of life's hazards Heyst sees the power of blind destiny. Besides, Heyst in his fine detachment had lost the habit of asserting himself. I don't mean the courage of self-assertion, either moral or physical, but the mere way of it, the trick of the thing, the readiness of mind and the turn of the hand that come without reflection and lead the man to excellence in life, in art, in crime, in virtue, and for the matter of that, even in love. Thinking is the great enemy of perfection. The habit of profound reflection, I am compelled to say, is the most pernicious of all the habits formed by the civilized man.

But I wouldn't be suspected even remotely of making fun of Axel Heyst. I have always liked him. The flesh and blood individual who stands behind the infinitely more familiar figure of the book I remember as a mysterious Swede right enough. Whether he was a baron, too, I am not so certain. He himself never laid a claim to that distinction. His detachment was too great to make any claims, big or small, on one's credulity. I will not say where I met him because I fear to give my readers a wrong impression, since a marked incongruity between a man and his surroundings is often a very misleading circumstance. We became very friendly for a time and I would not like to expose him to unpleasant suspicions though, personally, I am sure he would have been indifferent to suspicions as he was indifferent to all the other disadvantages of life. He was not the whole Heyst of course; he is only the physical and moral foundation of my Heyst laid on the ground of a short acquaintance. That it was short was certainly not my fault for he had charmed me by the mere amenity of his detachment which, in this case, I cannot help thinking he had carried to excess. He went away from his rooms without leaving a trace. I wondered where he had gone to—but now I know. He vanished from my ken only to drift into this adventure that, unavoidable, waited for him in a world which he persisted in looking upon as a malevolent shadow spinning in the sunlight. Often in the course of years an expressed sentiment, the particular sense of a phrase heard casually, would recall him to my mind so that I have fastened on to him many words heard on other men's lips and belonging to other men's less perfect, less pathetic moods.

The same observation will apply *mutatis mutandis* to Mr. Jones, who is built on a much slenderer connection. Mr. Jones (or whatever his name was) did not drift away from me. He turned his back on me and walked out of the room. It was in a little hotel in the island of St. Thomas in the West Indies (in the year '75) where we found him one hot afternoon extended on three chairs, all alone in the loud buzzing of flies to which his immobility and his cadaverous aspect gave a most gruesome significance. Our invasion must have displeased him because he got off the chairs brusquely and walked out, leaving with me an indelibly weird impression of his thin shanks. One of the men with me said that the fellow was the most desperate gambler he had ever come across. I said: 'A professional sharper?' and got for answer: 'He's a terror; but I must say that up to a certain point he will play fair...' I wonder what the point was. I never saw

him again because I believe he went straight on board a mail-
boat which left within the hour for other ports of call in the
direction of Aspinall. Mr. Jones's characteristic insolence belongs
to another man of a quite different type. I will say nothing as to
the origins of his mentality because I don't intend to make any
damaging admissions.

It so happened that the very same year Ricardo—the physical
Ricardo—was a fellow-passenger of mine on board an extremely
small and extremely dirty little schooner, during a four days' passage between two places in the Gulf of Mexico whose names don't
matter. For the most part he lay on deck aft as it were at my feet,
and raising himself from time to time on his elbow would talk
about himself and go on talking, not exactly to me or even at me
(he would not even look up but kept his eyes fixed on the deck)
but more as if communing in a low voice with his familiar devil.
Now and then he would give me a glance and make the hairs of
his stiff little moustache stir quaintly. His eyes were green and
every cat I see to this day reminds me of the exact contour of his
face. What he was travelling for or what was his business in life
he never confided to me. Truth to say, the only passenger on
board that schooner who could have talked openly about his
activities and purposes was a very snuffy and conversationally
delightful friar, the Superior of a convent, attended by a very
young lay brother, of a particularly ferocious countenance. We
had with us also, lying prostrate in the dark and unspeakable
cuddy of that schooner, an old Spanish gentleman, owner of much
luggage and, as Ricardo assured me, very ill indeed. Ricardo
seemed to be either a servant or the confidant of that aged and
distinguished-looking invalid, who early on the passage held a
long murmured conversation with the friar, and after that did
nothing but groan feebly, smoke cigarettes, and now and then
call for Martin in a voice full of pain. Then he who has become
Ricardo in the book would go below into that beastly and noi-
some hole, remain there mysteriously, and coming up on deck
again with a face on which nothing could be read, would as likely
as not resume for my edification the exposition of his moral attitude toward life illustrated by striking particular instances of the

most atrocious complexion. Did he mean to frighten me? Or seduce me? Or astonish me? Or arouse my admiration? All he did was to arouse my amused incredulity. As scoundrels go he was far from being a bore. For the rest my innocence was so great then that I could not take his philosophy seriously. All the time he kept one ear turned to the cuddy in the manner of a devoted servant, but I had the idea that in some way or other he had imposed the connection on the invalid for some end of his own. The reader, therefore, won't be surprised to hear that one morning I was told without any particular emotion by the *padrone* of the schooner that the 'rich man' down there was dead: he had died in the night. I don't remember ever being so moved by the desolate end of a complete stranger. I looked down the skylight and there was the devoted Martin busy cording cowhide trunks belonging to the deceased, whose white beard and hooked nose were the only parts I could make out in the dark depths of a horrible, stuffy bunk.

As it fell calm in the course of the afternoon and continued calm during all that night and the terrible, flaming day, the late 'rich man' had to be thrown overboard at sunset, though as a matter of fact we were in sight of the low, pestilential, mangrove-lined coast of our destination. The excellent Father Superior mentioned to me with an air of immense commiseration: 'The poor man has left a young daughter.' Who was to look after her I don't know, but I saw the devoted Martin taking the trunks ashore with great care just before I landed myself. I would perhaps have tracked the ways of that man of immense sincerity for a little while, but I had some of my own very pressing business to attend to, which in the end got mixed up with an earthquake, and so I had no time to give to Ricardo. The reader need not be told that I have not forgotten him, though.

My contact with the faithful Pedro was much shorter and my observation of him was less complete but incomparably more anxious. It ended in a sudden inspiration to get out of his way. It was in a hovel of sticks and mats by the side of a path. As I went in there only to ask for a bottle of lemonade I have not to this day the slightest idea what in my appearance or actions could have roused his terrible ire. It became manifest to me less than two minutes after I had set eyes on him for the first time, and though immensely surprised of course I didn't stop to think it out. I took the nearest short cut—through the wall. This bestial apparition, and a certain enormous buck nigger encountered in Haiti only a couple of months afterwards, have fixed my conception of blind, furious, unreasoning rage, as manifested in the human animal, to the end of my days. Of the nigger I used to dream for years afterwards. Of Pedro never. The impression was less vivid. I got away from him too quickly.

It seems to me but natural that those three buried in a corner of my memory should suddenly get out into the light of the world —so natural that I offer no excuse for their existence. They were there, they had to come out; and this is a sufficient excuse for a writer of tales who had taken to his trade without preparation, or premeditation, and without any moral intention but that which pervades the whole scheme of this world of senses.

Since this Note is mostly concerned with personal contacts and the origins of the persons in the tale, I am bound also to speak of Lena, because if I were to leave her out it would look like a slight; and nothing would be further from my thoughts than putting a slight on Lena. If of all the personages involved in the 'mystery of Samburan' I have lived longest with Heyst (or with him I call Heyst) it was at her, whom I call Lena, that I have looked the longest and with a most sustained attention. This attention originated in idleness, for which I have a natural talent. One evening I wandered into a café, in a town not of the tropics but of the south of France. It was filled with tobacco smoke, the hum of voices, the rattling of dominoes, and the sounds of strident music. The orchestra was rather smaller than the one that performed at Schomberg's hotel, had the air more of a family party than of an enlisted band, and, I must confess, seemed rather more respectable than the Zangiacomo musical enterprise. It was less pretentious also, more homely and familiar, so to speak, insomuch that in the intervals when all the performers left the platform one of them went amongst the marble tables collecting offerings of sous and francs in a battered tin receptacle recalling the shape of a sauceboat. It was a girl. Her detachment from her task seems to me now to have equalled or even surpassed Heyst's aloofness from all the mental degradations to which a man's intelligence is exposed in its way through life. Silent and wide-eyed she went from table to table with the air of a sleep-walker and with no other sound but the slight rattle of the coins to attract attention. It was long after the sea-chapter of my life had been closed but it is difficult to discard completely the characteristics of half a lifetime, and it was in something of the Jack-ashore spirit that I dropped a five-franc piece into the sauceboat; whereupon the sleep-walker turned her head to gaze at me and said 'Merci, monsieur,' in a tone in which there was no gratitude but only surprise. I must have been idle indeed to take the trouble to remark on such slight evidence that the voice was very charming and when the performers resumed their seats I shifted my position slightly in order not to have that particular performer hidden from me by the little man with the beard who conducted, and who might for all I know have been her father, but whose real mission in life was to be a model for the Zangiacomo of Victory. Having got a clear line of sight I naturally (being idle) continued to look at the girl through all the second part of the programme. The shape of her dark head inclined over the violin was fascinating, and, while resting between the pieces of that interminable programme, she was, in her white dress and with her brown hands reposing in her lap, the very image of dreamy innocence. The mature, bad-tempered woman at the piano might have been her mother, though there was not the slightest resemblance between them. All I am certain of in their personal relation to each other is that cruel pinch on the upper part of the arm. That I am sure I have seen! There could be no mistake. I was in a too idle mood to imagine such a gratuitous barbarity. It may have been playfulness, yet the girl jumped up as if she had been stung by a wasp. It may have been playfulness. Yet I saw plainly poor 'dreamy innocence' rub gently the affected place as she filed off with the other performers down the middle aisle between the marble tables in the uproar of voices, the rattling of dominoes, through a blue atmosphere of tobacco smoke. I believe that those people left the town next day.

Or perhaps they had only migrated to the other big café, on the other side of the Place de la Comédie. It is very possible. I did not go across to find out. It was my perfect idleness that had invested the girl with a peculiar charm, and I did not want to destroy it by any superfluous exertion. The receptivity of my indolence made the impression so permanent that when the moment came for her meeting with Heyst I felt that she would be heroically equal to every demand of the risky and uncertain future. I was so convinced of it that I let her go with Heyst, I won't say without a pang but certainly without misgivings. And in view of her triumphant end what more could I have done for her rehabilitation and her happiness?

The Shadow Line (1920)

This story, which I admit to be in its brevity a fairly complex piece of work, was not intended to touch on the supernatural. Yet more than one critic has been inclined to take it in that way, seeing in it an attempt on my part to give the fullest scope to my imagination by taking it beyond the confines of the world of the living, suffering humanity. But as a matter of fact my imagination is not made of stuff so elastic as all that. I believe that if I attempted to put the strain of the supernatural on it it would fail deplorably and exhibit an unlovely gap. But I could never have attempted such a thing, because all my moral and intellectual being is penetrated by an invincible conviction that whatever falls under the dominion of our senses must be in nature and, however exceptional, cannot differ in its essence from all the other effects of the visible and tangible world of which we are a self-conscious part. The world of the living contains enough marvels and mysteries as it is; marvels and mysteries acting upon our emotions and intelligence in ways so inexplicable that it would almost justify the conception of life as an enchanted state. No, I am too firm in my consciousness of the marvellous to be ever fascinated by the mere supernatural, which (take it any way you like) is but a manufactured article, the fabrication of minds insensitive to the intimate delicacies of our relation to the dead and to the living, in their countless multitudes; a desecration of our tenderest memories; an outrage on our dignity.

Whatever my native modesty may be it will never condescend so low as to seek help for my imagination within those vain imaginings common to all ages and that in themselves are enough to fill all lovers of mankind with unutterable sadness. As to the effect of a mental or moral shock on a common mind, that is quite a legitimate subject for study and description. Mr. Burns's moral being receives a severe shock in his relations with his late captain, and this in his diseased state turns into a mere superstitious fancy compounded of fear and animosity. This fact is one of the elements of the story, but there is nothing supernatural in it, nothing so to speak from beyond the confines of this world, which in all conscience holds enough mystery and terror in itself.

Perhaps if I had published this tale, which I have had for a long time in my mind, under the title of 'First Command' no suggestion of the supernatural would have been found in it by any impartial reader, critical or otherwise. I will not consider here the origins of the feeling in which its actual title, *The Shadow-Line*, occurred to my mind. Primarily the aim of this piece of writing was the presentation of certain facts which certainly were associated with the change from youth, care-free and fervent, to the more self-conscious and more poignant period of maturer life. Nobody can doubt that before the supreme trial of a whole generation I had an acute consciousness of the minute and insignificant character of my own obscure experience. There could be no question here of any parallelism. That notion never entered my head. But there was a feeling of identity, though with an enormous difference of scale—as of one single drop measured against the bitter and stormy immensity of an ocean. And this was very natural too. For when we begin to meditate on the meaning of our own past it seems to fill all the world in its profundity and its magnitude. This book was written in the last three months of the year 1916. Of all the subjects of which a writer of tales is more or less conscious within himself this is the only one I found it possible to attempt at the time. The depth and the nature of the mood with which I approached it is best expressed perhaps in the dedication, which strikes me now as a most disproportionate thing—as another instance of the overwhelming greatness of our own emotion to ourselves.

This much having been said I may pass on now to a few remarks about the mere material of the story. As to locality it belongs to that part of the Eastern Seas from which I have carried away into my writing life the greatest number of suggestions. From my statement that I thought of this story for a long time under the title of 'First Command' the reader may guess that it it is concerned with my personal experience. And as a matter of fact it *is* personal experience seen in perspective with the eye of the mind and coloured by that affection one can't help feeling for such events of one's life as one has no reason to be ashamed of. And that affection is as intense (I appeal here to universal experience) as the shame, and almost the anguish with which one remembers some unfortunate occurrences, down to mere mistakes in speech, that have been perpetrated by one in the past. The effect of perspective in memory is to make things loom large because the essentials stand out isolated from their surroundings of insignificant daily facts which have naturally faded out of one's mind. I remember that period of my sea-life with pleasure because, begun inauspiciously, it turned out in the end a success from a personal point of view, leaving a tangible proof in the terms of the letter the owners of the ship wrote to me two years afterwards when I resigned my command in order to come home. This resignation marked the beginning of another phase of my seaman's life, its terminal phase, if I may say so, which in its own way has coloured another portion of my writings. I didn't know then how near its end my sea-life was, and therefore I felt no sorrow except at parting with the ship. I was sorry also to break my connection with the firm which owned her and who were pleased to receive with friendly kindness and give their confidence to a man who had entered their service in an accidental manner and in very adverse circumstances. Without disparaging the earnestness of my purpose I suspect now that luck had no small part in the success of the trust reposed in me. And one cannot help remembering with pleasure the time when one's best efforts were seconded by a run of luck.

The words 'Worthy of my undying regard' selected by me for the motto on the title-page are quoted from the text of the book itself; and, though one of my critics surmised that they applied to the ship, it is evident from the place where they stand that they refer to the men of that ship's company: complete strangers to their new captain and yet who stood by him so well during those twenty days that seemed to have been passed on the brink of a slow and agonizing destruction. And *that* is the greatest memory of all! For surely it is a great thing to have commanded a handful of men worthy of one's undying regard.

The Arrow of Gold (1920)

Having named all the short prefaces written for my books, Author's Notes, this one too must have the same heading for the sake of uniformity if at the risk of some confusion. *The Arrow of Gold,* as its sub-title states, is a story between two Notes. But these Notes are embodied in its very frame, belong to its texture, and their mission is to prepare and close the story. They are material to the comprehension of the experience related in the narrative and are meant to determine the time and place together with certain historical circumstances conditioning the existence of the people concerned in the transactions of the twelve months covered by the narrative. It was the shortest way of getting over the preliminaries of a piece of work which could not have been of the nature of a chronicle.

The Arrow of Gold is my first after-the-War publication. The writing of it was begun in the autumn of 1917 and finished in the summer of 1918. Its memory is associated with that of the darkest hour of the War, which, in accordance with the well-known proverb—preceded the dawn—the dawn of peace.

As I look at them now, these pages, written in the days of stress and dread, wear a look of strange serenity. They were written calmly, yet not in cold blood, and are perhaps the only kind of pages I could have written at that time full of menace, but also full of faith.

The subject of this book I had been carrying about with me for many years, not so much a possession of my memory as an inherent part of myself. It was ever present to my mind and ready to my hand, but I was loth to touch it, from a feeling of what I imagined to be mere shyness but which in reality was a very comprehensible mistrust of myself.

In plucking the fruit of memory one runs the risk of spoiling its bloom, especially if it has got to be carried into the marketplace. This being the product of my private garden my reluctance can be easily understood; and though some critics have expressed their regret that I had not written this book fifteen years earlier I do not share that opinion. If I took it up so late in life it is because the right moment had not arrived till then. I mean the positive feeling of it, which is a thing that cannot be discussed. Neither will I discuss here the regrets of those critics, which seem to me the most irrelevant thing that could have been said in connection with literary criticism.

I never tried to conceal the origins of the subject-matter of this book which I have hesitated so long to write; but some reviewers indulged themselves with a sense of triumph in discovering in it my Dominic of *The Mirror of the Sea* under his own name (a truly wonderful discovery) and in recognizing the *balancelle Tremolino* in the unnamed little craft in which Mr. George plied his fantastic trade and sought to allay the pain of his incurable wound. I am not in the least disconcerted by this display of perspicacity. It is the same man and the same balancelle. But for the purposes of a book like *The Mirror of the Sea* all I could make use of was the personal history of the little *Tremolino*. The present work is not in any sense an attempt to develop a subject lightly touched upon in former years and in connection with quite another kind of love. What the story of the *Tremolino* in its anecdotic character has in common with the story of *The Arrow of Gold* is the quality of initiation (through an ordeal which required some resolution to face) into the life of passion.

In the few pages at the end of *The Mirror of the Sea* and in the whole volume of *The Arrow of Gold, that* and no other is the subject offered to the public. The pages and the book form together a complete record; and the only assurance I can give my readers is, that as it stands here with all its imperfections it is given to them complete.

I venture this explicit statement because, amidst much sympathetic appreciation, I have detected here and there a note, as it were, of suspicion. Suspicion of facts concealed, of explanations held back, of inadequate motives. But what is lacking in the facts is simply what I did not know, and what is not explained is what I did not understand myself, and what seems inadequate is the fault of my imperfect insight. And all that I could not help. In the case of this book I was unable to supplement these deficiencies by the exercise of my inventive faculty. It was never very strong; and on this occasion its use would have seemed exceptionally dishonest. It is from that ethical motive and not from timidity that I elected to keep strictly within the limits of unadorned sincerity and to try to enlist the sympathies of my readers without assuming lofty omniscience or descending to the subterfuge of exaggerated emotions.

From *The Rescue* (1920)

Of the three long novels of mine which suffered an interruption, *The Rescue* was the one that had to wait the longest for the good pleasure of the Fates. I am betraying no secret when I state here that it had to wait precisely for twenty years. I laid it aside at the end of the summer of 1898 and it was about the end of the summer of 1918 that I took it up again with the firm determination to see the end of it and helped by the sudden feeling that I might be equal to the task. * * *

The truth is that when *The Rescue* was laid aside it was not laid aside in despair. Several reasons contributed to this abandonment and, no doubt, the first of them was the growing sense of general difficulty in the handling of the subject. The contents and the course of the story I had clearly in my mind. But as to the way of presenting the facts, and perhaps in a certain measure as to the nature of the facts themselves, I had many doubts. I mean the telling, representative facts, helpful to carry on the idea, and, at the same time, of such a nature as not to demand an elaborate creation of the atmosphere to the detriment of the action. I did not see how I could avoid becoming wearisome in the presentation of detail and in the pursuit of clearness. I saw the action plainly enough. What I had lost for the moment was the sense of the proper formula of expression, the only formula that would suit. This, of course, weakened my confidence in the intrinsic worth and in the possible interest of the story—that is, in my invention. But I suspect that all the trouble was, in reality, the doubt of my prose, the doubt of its adequacy, of its power to master both the colours and the shades.

It is difficult to describe, exactly as I remember it, the complex state of my feelings; but those of my readers who take an interest in artistic perplexities will understand me best when I point out that I dropped *The Rescue* not to give myself up to idleness, regrets, or dreaming, but to begin *The Nigger of the 'Narcissus'* and to go on with it without hesitation and without a pause. A comparison of any page of *The Rescue* with any page of *The Nigger* will furnish an ocular demonstration of the nature and the inward meaning of this first crisis of my writing life. For it was a crisis undoubtedly. The laying aside of a work so far advanced was a very awful decision to take. It was wrung from me by a sudden conviction that *there* only was the road of salvation, the clear way out for an uneasy conscience. The finishing of *The Nigger* brought to my troubled mind the comforting sense of an accomplished task, and the first consciousness of a certain sort of mastery which could accomplish something with the aid of propitious stars. Why I did not return to *The Rescue* at once then, was not for the reason that I had grown afraid of it. Being able now to assume a firm attitude I said to myself deliberately: 'That thing can wait. At the same time I was just as certain in my mind that *Youth,* a story which I had then, so to speak, on the tip of my pen, could *not* wait. Neither could *Heart of Darkness* be put off; for the practical reason that Mr. Wm. Blackwood hav-

ing requested me to write something for the No. M of his magazine I had to stir up at once the subject of that tale which had
been long lying quiescent in my mind; because, obviously, the
venerable *Maga*[9] at her patriarchal age of 1,000 numbers could
not be kept waiting. Then *Lord Jim*, with about seventeen pages
already written at odd times, put in his claim which was irresistible. Thus every stroke of the pen was taking me further away
from the abandoned *Rescue*, not without some compunction on
my part but with a gradually diminishing resistance; till at last I
let myself go, as if recognizing a superior influence against which
it was useless to contend.

The years passed and the pages grew in number, and the long
reveries of which they were the outcome stretched wide between
me and the deserted *Rescue* like the smooth hazy spaces of a
dreamy sea. Yet I never actually lost sight of that dark speck in
the misty distance. It had grown very small but it asserted itself
with the appeal of old associations. It seemed to me that it would
be a base thing for me to slip out of the world leaving it out there
all alone, waiting for its fate—that would never come!

Sentiment, pure sentiment as you see, prompted me in the last
instance to face the pains and hazards of that return. As I moved
slowly towards the abandoned body of the tale it loomed up big
amongst the glittering shallows of the coast, lonely but not for-
bidding. There was nothing about it of a grim derelict. It had an
air of expectant life. One after another I made out the familiar
faces watching my approach with faint smiles of amused recognition. They had known well enough that I was bound to come
back to them. But their eyes met mine seriously, as was only to be
expected since I, myself, felt very serious as I stood amongst them
again after years of absence. At once, without wasting words, we
went to work together on our renewed life; and every moment I
felt more strongly that They Who had Waited bore no grudge
to the man who, however widely he may have wandered at times,
had played truant only once in his life.

9. *Blackwood's Magazine.*

From *Notes on Life and Letters* (1920)

The section within this volume called Letters explains itself, though I do not pretend to say that it justifies its own existence. It claims nothing in its defence except the right of speech which I believe belongs to everybody outside a Trappist monastery. The part I have ventured, for shortness's sake, to call Life, may perhaps justify itself by the emotional sincerity of the feelings to which the various papers included under that head owe their origin. And as they relate to events of which every one has a date, they are in the nature of signposts pointing out the direction my thoughts were compelled to take at the various cross-roads. If anybody detects any sort of consistency in the choice this will be only proof positive that wisdom had nothing to do with it. Whether right or wrong, instinct alone is invariable; a fact which only adds a deeper shade to its inherent mystery. The appearance of intellectuality these pieces may present at first sight is merely the result of the arrangement of words. The logic that may be found there is only the logic of the language. But I need not labour the point. There will be plenty of people sagacious enough to perceive the absence of all wisdom from these pages. But I believe sufficiently in human sympathies to imagine that very few will question their sincerity. Whatever delusions I may have suffered from I have had no delusions as to the nature of the facts commented on here. I may have misjudged their import: but that is the sort of error for which one may expect a certain amount of toleration.

The Shorter Tales of Joseph Conrad (1924)

The idea of publishing a volume of selected stories has not been received without a good deal of hesitation on my part. So much in fact as to drive me into the dangerous attempt to disclose the state of the feelings with which I approach this explanatory preface. My hesitation was, I may say, of a private character; private in the sense of being rooted deep in my personality, and not easily explainable even to such good friends as it has been my fortune to find in the American public. The deep, complex (and at times even contradictory) feelings which make up the very essence of an author's attitude to his own creation are real enough, yet they may be, often are, but shapes of cherished illusions. Frail plants, you will admit, and fit only for the shade of solitary thought. Precious—perhaps? Yes. But by their very nature precious to only one man, to him in whose mind—or is it the heart?—they are rooted.

That consideration would seem to me conclusive against anyone writing any preface whatever, if it were not for my ineradicable suspicion that in this world, which some philosophers have defined merely as a series of "vain appearances," our very illusions must have a practical meaning. Are they not as characteristic of an individual as his opinions, for instance, or the features of his face? In fact, being less controllable they must be even more dangerously revelatory. This is an alarming consideration. But whether because of a strain of native impudence, acquired callousness, or inborn trust in the goodness of human nature, it has not prevented me during the last few years from writing a good many revelatory prefaces, for which I have not been, so far, called to account. At any rate, no incensed man with a shot-gun has yet called here to invite me to desist. Thus encouraged, here I am again volunteering yet one more of these sincere confessions.

To begin with, I may venture to affirm that, however spontaneous the initial impulse, not one of the stories from which those included in this volume have been selected was achieved without much conscious thought bearing not only on the problems of their style but upon their relation to life as I have known it, and on the nature of my reactions to the particular instances as well as to the general tenor of my personal experience. This gave to each of the successive tales, composed at various times and in varied mental conditions, a characteristic tone of its own. At least I thought so. Later, when I had to consider my past work in detail, in order to write the Author's Notes for my first collected edition, I was confirmed in my impression that each of my short-story volumes had a consistent unity of outlook covering the mingled subjects of civilisation and wilderness, of land life and life on the sea.

It would not be too much to say that this trait would be apparent to the least critical of readers, in, for instance, the *Tales of Unrest*. No story from that volume is included in this collection for a reason which will become apparent later to the patient reader of this preface. It is the very first collection of short stories I ever published, with a range of scene including the Malay Archipelago, rustic Brittany, Central Africa, and the interior of an upper middle-class house in a residential street of London. It also seems to me perfectly clear on the face of it, that the volume called *A Set of Six*—from which one story has been selected for this book—is very different in its consistent mood of clear and detached presentation from any other volume of short stories which I have published before or after. Yet, in time, it covers almost the whole of the nineteenth century; and in space it moves from South America, through England and Russia, to end in the south of Italy. A benevolent critic has remarked to me privately that it was the least atmospheric of all my works; and from my point of view I accepted this as a tribute to that inner consistency which I would claim for every set of my shorter tales. In the same way in the case of the volume *Within the Tides* I take the opinion expressed by one of the reviewers: "that the whole of the book seemed to produce the impression of being greater than its component parts" as a confirmation of my sentiment of having welded the diversities of subject and treatment into a consistency characteristic, in its nature, of a certain period of my literary production.

The friendly reader will understand how, holding that belief on the subject of my shorter productions, I would recoil at first from taking any of my stories out of their appointed places in the group to which they originally belonged. And this the more because their grouping was never the result of a preconceived plan. It "just happened." And things that "just happen" in one's work seem impressive and valuable because they spring from sources profounder than the logic of a deliberate theory suggested by acquiring learning, let us say, or by lessons drawn from analysed practice. And no one need quarrel for such a view with an artist for whom self-expression must, by definition, be the principal object, if not the only *raison d'être*, of his existence. He will naturally take for his own, for better or worse, all the characteristics of his work; since all of them, intended or not intended, make up the individuality of his self-expression.

I suspect there are moments when what a man most values in his work—I mean even a man of action—is precisely the part the general mystery of things plays in its shaping: the discovery of those qualities that have "just happened" in that obscure region where honest success or honourable failure is unconsciously elaborated. But there are moments, too, when one's idealism (for idealism is practical and sane and the enemy of things that "just happen" and suchlike mysteries) prompts one to take up a different, more precise view of one's achievement—whatever it may be.

It must have been in one of those moments that the suggestion of a selected volume of my shorter stories came before me from my old friend and publisher, Mr. F. N. Doubleday, who is an idealist and who would simply hate to let anything "just happen" in his business. His business, to my mind, consists, mainly, in being the intermediary between certain men's reveries and the wide-awake brain of the rest of the world. Stated like this it seems a strangely fantastic occupation; yet his ways of carrying it on are always of a practical sort. I have learned to trust his conclusions implicitly on that ground. Also, for reasons of a deeper personal kind, having nothing to do with business, his words have great weight with me. But in order to reconcile my own idealism to the notion of taking the stories out of their natural surroundings, out of their native atmosphere as it were, some principle of selection had to be found. The only one that offered itself with any chance of being acceptable was the principle of classification by subject; one that, whatever its disadvantages, has at least the advantage of being immune from the infection of illusions.

But I soon found that for a writer whose simple purpose has ever been the sincere rendering of his own deeper and more sympathetic emotions in the face of his belief in men and things—the philosopher's "vain appearances" which yet have endured, poignant or amusing, for so many ages, moving processionally towards the End of the World, which when it comes will be the vainest thing of all—the principle was not so easy in its application as it seemed to be at first sight. Though I have been often classed as a writer of the sea I have always felt that I had no speciality in that or any other specific subject. It is true that I have found a full text of life on the sea, long before I thought of writing a line, or even felt the faintest stirring towards self-expression by means of the printed word. Sea life had been my life. It had been my own self-sufficient, self-satisfying possession. When the change came over the spirit of my dream (Calderon said that "Life is a Dream") my past had, by the very force of my work, become one of the sources of what I may call, for want of a better word, my inspiration—of the inner force which sets the pen in motion. I would add here "for better or worse," if those words did not sound horribly ungrateful after so many proofs of sympathy from the public for which this particular Preface is destined.

As a matter of fact I have written of the sea very little, if the pages were counted. It has been the scene, but very seldom the aim, of my endeavour. It is too late after all those years to try to keep back the truth; so I will confess here that when I launched my first paper boats in the days of my literary childhood, I aimed at an element as restless, as dangerous, as changeable as the sea, and even more vast—the unappeasable ocean of human life. I trust this grandiloquent image will be accepted with an indulgent smile of the kind that is accorded to the lofty ambitions of well-meaning beginners. Much time has passed since, and I can assure my readers that I have never felt more humble than I do to-day while I sit tracing these words, and that I see now, more clearly than ever before, that indeed those were but paper boats, freighted with a grown-up child's dreams and launched innocently upon that terrible sea that, unlike the honest salt-water of my early life, knows no hope of changing horizons, but lies within the circle of an Eternal Shadow.

Approaching the problem of selection for this book in the full consciousness of my feelings, my concern was to give it some sort of unity, or in other words, its own character. Looking over the directive impulses of my writing life I discovered my guide in the one that had prompted me so often to deal with men whose existence was, so to speak, cast early upon the waters. Thus the characteristic trait of the stories included in this volume consists in the central figure of each being a seaman presented either in the relations of his professional life with his own kind, or in contact with landsmen and women, and embroiled in the affairs of that larger part of mankind which dwells on solid earth.

It would have been misleading to label those productions as sea tales. They deal with feelings of universal import, such, for instance, as the sustaining and inspiring sense of youth, or the support given by a stolid courage which confronts the unmeasurable force of an elemental fury simply as a thing that has got to be met and lived through with professional constancy. Of course, there is something more than mere ideas in those stories. I modestly hope that there are human beings in them, and also the articulate appeal of their humanity so strangely constructed from inertia and restlessness, from weakness and from strength and many other interesting contradictions which affect their conduct, and in a certain sense are meant to give a colouring to the actual events of the tale, and even to the response which is expected from the reader. To call them "studies of seamen" would have been pretentious and even misleading, in view of the obscurity of the individuals and the private character of the incidents. *Shorter Tales* is yet the best title I can think of for this collection. It commends itself to me by its non-committal character, which will neither raise false hopes nor awaken blind antagonisms.

Why a volume aiming at unity should be wilfully divided into two parts is explained by my desire to give prominence to the stories which begin them: *Youth,* which is certainly a piece of autobiography ("emotions remembered in tranquility"), and *Typhoon,* which, defined from a purely descriptive point of view, is the shorter of the two storm-pieces which I have written at different times.

From another point of view, the "guiding" point of view (that is of each story being concerned with a man who is also a seaman), the first part deals with younger and the second with older men. I hardly need say that in the arrangement of those two parts there has been no attempt at chronological order.

Therefore let neither friend nor enemy look for the development of the writer's literary faculty in this collection. As far as that is concerned the book is a jumble. The unity of purpose lies elsewhere. In Part First, *Youth* speaks for itself, both in its triumphant feeling and in its wistful regrets. The second story deals with what may be called the *esprit de corps*, the deep fellowship of two young seamen meeting for the first time. Those two tales may be regarded as purely professional. Of the other two in Part First, one, it must be confessed, is written round a ship rather than round a seaman. The last, trying to render the effect of the fascination of a roving life, has the hard lot of a woman for its principal interest.[10]

Part Two deals with men of a more mature age. There is no denying that in the typhoon which is being wrestled with by Captain McWhirr, it is the typhoon that takes on almost a symbolic figure. The next story is the story of a married seaman, badly married I admit, whose humanity to a pathetic waif spoils his life for him. The third is the story of a swindle, to be frank, planned on shore, but the sympathetic person is a seaman all right. The last may be looked upon as a story of a seaman's love for a very silent girl; but what I tried partly to suggest there was the existence of certain straightforward characters combining a natural ruthlessness with an unexpected depth of moral delicacy. Falk obeys the law of self-preservation pitilessly; but at the crucial moment of his bizarre love-story he will not condescend to dodge the truth—the horrid truth! Finally, let me say that with the exception of *Youth* none of these stories is a record of experience in the absolute sense of the word. As I have said before in another preface, they are all authentic because they are the product of twenty years of life—my own life. Deliberate invention had little to do with their existence—if they do exist. In each there lurks more than one intention. The facts gleaned from hearsay or experience in the various parts of the globe were but opportunities offered to the writer. What he has done with them is matter for a verdict which must be left to the individual consciences of the readers.

10. The tales in Part I are "Youth," "The Secret Sharer," "The Brute," "Tomorrow"; in Part II, "Typhoon," "Because of the Dollars," "The Partner," "Falk."